EUROPE'S ALLIANCE WITH ISRAEL

To Sue

With thanks and
best wishes

David Cronin

Europe's Alliance with Israel

Aiding the Occupation

David Cronin

First published 2011 by Pluto Press
345 Archway Road, London N6 5AA and
175 Fifth Avenue, New York, NY 10010

Distributed in the United States of America exclusively by
Palgrave Macmillan, a division of St. Martin's Press LLC,
175 Fifth Avenue, New York, NY 10010

www.plutobooks.com

British Library Cataloguing in Publication Data
A catalogue record for this book is available from the British Library

ISBN 978 0 7453 3066 2 Hardback
ISBN 978 0 7453 3065 5 Paperback

Library of Congress Cataloging in Publication Data applied for

This book is printed on paper suitable for recycling and made from fully managed and sustained forest sources. Logging, pulping and manufacturing processes are expected to conform to the environmental standards of the country of origin.

10 9 8 7 6 5 4 3 2 1

Designed and produced for Pluto Press by
Curran Publishing Services, Norwich

Printed and bound in the European Union by
CPI Antony Rowe, Chippenham and Eastbourne

CONTENTS

Acknowledgements *vii*

Introduction **1**
Bad conscience no excuse for bad policy 4
Israel's charm offensive 6
Tainted by torture 9

1 **Building the unholy alliance** **14**
Gaza City, May 2009 14
Brussels, January 2009 16
More defensive than offensive? 16
After the bombs, a banquet 18
Spin triumphs over substance 19
Falling in love with Livni 21
Rewarding a rogue 28

2 **Bowing to the United States** **34**
Sarkozy swallows, Merkel marvels 36
Berlusconi: A cheerleader for the occupation 38
Dutch courage? 40
From Blair to Brown: things can only get better? 42
Eastern Europe: in the pocket of the United States 46
NATO: the pitbull gnashes its teeth 51
How the West went soft 56
Divide and rule: the same old colonial story 58
A cruel embargo 60
Hemming in Hamas 62
Comfort for the quislings 65

3 **Aiding the occupation** **67**
Speeding at night without headlights 72
Oslo: doomed from the start 74
The PA's life-support machine 78
Aid benefits the oppressor 79
The courage deficit 80

4 **The misappliance of science** 86
Oiling the war machine with euros 88
Merchants of death go green 92
The security deception 94
Beyond the pale of human tolerance 96
Small isn't always beautiful 97
Big Brother in Palestine 100
Satellites of war 101

5 **Profiting from Palestine's pain** 106
Obliged to shun, happy to serve 111
France's full circle 112
Furtively feeding the war monster 114
Benelux embraces a bloody trade 117
Double standards Dublin-style 118
Buying Israel's deadly wares 120
Moral bankruptcy 123
The racist railway 127
Volvo: a subcontractor for torture 128
A trade in deception 131

6 **The Israel lobby comes to Europe** 136
European Friends of Israel: enemies of truth 138
Transatlantic Institute: stifling debate with smears 142
B'nai B'rith: a maker of myths 145
European Jewish Congress: apologists for apartheid 148
A French taboo 150
Access all areas: the lobby in London 152
Israeli aggression harms Jews, too 156

Conclusion: confronting Europe's cowardice 159
Stop the suffocation of Palestine 160
Boycotting Israel: a tactic, not a strategy 163

Notes *167*
Useful contacts *190*
Index *191*

ACKNOWLEDGEMENTS

I very much appreciate the help I have received from the following people:

Roger van Zwanenberg and everyone at Pluto Press, Agnès Bertrand-Sanz, Angela Godfrey-Goldstein, Merav Amir, Martin Konecny, Richard Stanforth, Shir Hever, Ben Hayes, David Nichols, Jeff Halper, Hamdi Shaqqura, Charles Shamas, Majed Abu Salama, Nathalie Stanus, Michelle Pace, Nathalie Tocci, Brigitte Heremans, Pierre Galand, Amjad Shawa, Gizem Sucuoglu, Husam El Nounou, Wesam Ahmad, Khalil Abu Shammala, Steve McGiffen, Sanjay Suri, Miren Gutiérrez, Arthur Neslen, Stephen Gardner, Tom McEnaney, Rachel Henderson, Caterina Amicucci, Greig Aitken, Antonio Tricarico, Fakhri Abu Diab, Maher Hanoun and family, John Hilary, Kaye Stearman, Wendela de Vries, Patrice Bouveret, David Landy. Several others have helped me on condition of anonymity, I would like to thank them namelessly.

Special thanks to my parents Vincent and Mary Cronin and my parents-in-law Tom and Kathleen Carroll.

And extra special thanks to my wife Susan Carroll for her constant love and support and for tolerating my occasional grumpiness while this book was being written.

Note: the individuals listed above do not necessarily share the opinions I express in this book.

David Cronin

INTRODUCTION

It was not journalism's finest hour.

In August 2009, the Swedish tabloid *Aftonbladet* published a feature about the illicit international trade in human organs.[1] The article hopped from news that had recently broken in the United States to rumours that had circulated in the Middle East 17 years earlier. In the first case, a New York man faced charges of arranging the sale of a kidney from a donor in Israel. In the second, Israeli soldiers were said to have carried out autopsies on the corpses of young Palestinian men and then ripped out their organs for use in medical transplants. As there was no evidence of a link between the two sets of allegations – other than that Israel was mentioned in both – their juxtaposition was clumsy and crude.

Nonetheless, the newspaper deserves a little credit for highlighting a scandal that the Western media had ignored until then. During the Palestinian uprising or *intifada* between 1987 and 1993, many Palestinian families complained about the corpses of their sons or siblings being returned to them with missing body parts, after Israel had conducted post mortems without the families' consent. In 2002 and 2005, the institute where these autopsies took place – Abu Kabir near Tel Aviv – was investigated by the Israeli authorities over suspicions it had sold body parts to medical research centres. Yehuda Hiss, director of Abu Kabir at the time, admitted that the transfer of organs had occurred, and said that they belonged to Israeli soldiers who had been killed while on active service. But Hiss has never been convicted of any wrongdoing, and has continued working at the institute as a pathologist.[2]

The fact that there are many unanswered questions about this episode might help explain why *Aftonbladet* touched a raw nerve in Israel. Shortly after the article appeared, a campaign was launched imploring Israelis to stop buying IKEA furniture, Volvo cars and Absolut vodka. And the Israeli government demanded that the Swedish state censure Donald Boström, the author of the piece. After Carl Bildt, the Swedish foreign minister, not only refused to condemn the journalist but implicitly defended his right to express himself, the rage within Israeli officialdom soared once more. Avigdor Lieberman, Bildt's Israeli counterpart, drew a hysterical comparison between Stockholm's standoffishness and an infamous anti-Semitic tract from the early 1900s that warned of Jews planning to take over the world. He said:

> The story published this week is a natural continuation of the *Protocols of the Elders of Zion* and blood libels like the Beilis trial, in which Jews were accused of adding Christian children's blood to Passover matzot [flat bread]. It's a shame that the Swedish foreign ministry fails to intervene in a case of blood libel against Jews. This is reminiscent of Sweden's stance during World War II, when it failed to intervene as well.[3]

This diplomatic row was not a purely bilateral affair. Because Sweden had assumed the European Union's rotating presidency the previous month, it cast a pall over Israel's relations with the 27-country-strong European Union for a number of weeks.

It would be wrong, however, to deduce that such relations are constantly strained. On the contrary, Israel has developed such strong political and economic ties to the European Union over the past decade that it has become a member state of the European Union in all but name. Javier Solana, then EU foreign policy chief, recognised as much while visiting Jerusalem later in 2009, when he candidly admitted that Israel is considerably closer to the European Union than Croatia, even though the former Yugoslav state is on the cusp of formally joining the European Union. Solana said:

> There is no country outside the European continent that has this type of relationship that Israel has with the European Union. Israel, allow me to say, is a member of the European Union without being a member of the institutions. It's a member of all the [EU's] programmes, it participates in all the programmes.[4]

What Solana didn't acknowledge was that this deepening relationship is being built at the expense of human rights. While EU representatives routinely speak of how they are wedded to fundamental values such as human rights and democracy, their alliance with Israel is largely devoid of ethical integrity. This was illustrated by the Union's lily-livered response to the slaughter of around 1,400 Gazans by Israeli forces during December 2008 and January 2009.

Even though there was ample *prima facie* evidence to suggest that international law had been violated during that offensive – labelled 'Operation Cast Lead' by Israel – the European Union dithered on calling for an independent investigation. When the Union's foreign ministers met in January 2009, the statement that they issued merely committed them to monitoring the results of any such probe. It took until June that year before the European Union voiced support for the four-member team appointed by the United Nations to examine the violations. That support turned out to be short-lived.

The UN team, headed by a retired South African judge, Richard Goldstone, produced a thorough 575-page report that was sharply critical of the Israeli government. It concluded that there was 'no justifiable military objective' behind ten of the eleven cases it examined in which Israel had launched direct attacks against civilians in Gaza. It also found that an Israeli policy of imposing an economic blockade on Gaza until Hamas released an Israeli soldier it had captured in 2006 constituted a collective punishment of the strip's 1.5 million inhabitants (collective punishment is forbidden under international law). And it condemned Israel for tightening its grip on the West Bank both during and after its assault on Gaza; expropriation of Palestinian land, demolitions of their homes, exploitation of their natural resources were all stepped up by Israel over that period, as were the restrictions placed on movement between Gaza and the West Bank.

The report did not shield the rival Palestinian organisations Hamas and Fatah from criticism, either. Hamas was denounced for firing rockets on southern Israel; security forces working for the Palestinian Authority in the West Bank, which is controlled by Fatah, were accused of suppressing demonstrations against Israel's military actions and of unlawful arrest, detention and torture of people deemed sympathetic to Hamas.[5]

Even though Goldstone and his colleagues had been punctilious and even-handed, the European Union could not bring itself to collectively endorse their findings. Seven EU governments sided with the United States in rejecting the report outright when it was considered by the UN General Assembly in November 2009. These were Germany, Italy, the Czech Republic, Hungary, the Netherlands, Slovakia and Poland. Fifteen other EU states – including Britain, France, Spain, Sweden, Denmark and Finland – abstained. This left only five of the Union's 27 countries – Ireland, Cyprus, Portugal, Malta and Slovenia – supporting a resolution that called on both Israel and Hamas to ensure that credible and independent investigations are promptly conducted.[6]

The European Union's cowardice towards Israel is in stark contrast to the robust position it has taken when major atrocities have occurred in other conflicts. After the war between Russia and Georgia in the summer of 2008, for example, the European Union tasked an independent mission with ascertaining the facts behind that conflict and assessing whether international law had been flouted. Similarly, after several thousand civilians were reported to have been killed during the first half of 2009 as a result of Sri Lanka's war against the Tamil Tigers, EU foreign ministers urged that an impartial inquiry be carried out and that perpetrators of human rights abuses be brought to justice.[7]

BAD CONSCIENCE NO EXCUSE FOR BAD POLICY

Samir Kassir, a Lebanese journalist who was murdered in 2005, explained succinctly how Israel is allowed to evade responsibility for its crimes against humanity:

> Undeterred by Egypt since [President Anwar] Sadat's peace [accord with Israel, signed in 1979], convinced of America's unfailing support, guaranteed impunity by Europe's bad conscience, and backed by a nuclear arsenal that was acquired with the help of Western powers, and that keeps growing without exciting any comment from the international community, Israel can literally do anything it wants, or is prompted to do by its leaders' fantasies of domination.[8]

It is right that Hitler's efforts to exterminate Europe's Jews (as well as homosexuals and Roma gypsies) should be regarded as the most shameful stain on the continent's history. That today's politicians should continue to suffer from the 'bad conscience' Kassir referred to – even if they were either swaddling infants when the Holocaust took place, or not yet born – is in many respects proper. There will always be a moral duty on our governments to ensure that nothing remotely comparable ever happens again.

Yet the evils of the Holocaust cannot disguise the fact that the state of Israel was founded as a result of a gross injustice against the Palestinians, a people who had nothing to do with the Nazis' crimes. Nor can it disguise the fact that the initial injustice of destroying Palestinian villages, forcibly resettling and in some cases massacring their inhabitants, has been followed by an occupation of Palestinian land, the brutality of which intensifies with every passing year.[9]

Europe's enduring shame does not give it any grounds on which to exonerate Israel for its oppression of the Palestinians, just because Israel's ruling elite insists that it is a state to which Jews everywhere must bear allegiance. Nor can Europe allow itself to be duped by Israeli propaganda, which holds that the country's military might is necessary to avoid a repeat of the Holocaust. Avraham Burg, a former speaker in the Israeli parliament (the Knesset), has written audaciously of how the suffering of the Jews during the last century is being misused by Israel in a way that is becoming increasingly unhealthy for its society.

> For many years we have lived comfortably, thanks to a national hypocrisy that tries to contain two conflicting worlds: well-being and complaint, power and victimhood, success and trauma. Our private worlds are defined by physical security, personal comfort and even wealth, both as individuals and as a nation. Our state is well-established and powerful, almost without precedent since the destruction of the Second Temple. Yet for some acquired psychological deficiency, we try to hide this splendour by constantly whining – because we had a holocaust. We always want a stronger army because of the *Shoah*, and more resources from other countries' taxpayers, and an automatic forgiveness for any of our excesses. We want to be above criticism and attention, all these because of Hitler's twelve years, which changed the face of Europe and our face beyond recognition. It cannot go on like this forever. This inherent contradiction will smash its vessel, the state, and the society that contains it.[10]

EU ambitions to have a more strident and cohesive foreign policy have led it to pay ever-greater attention to the Middle East. Talk to any diplomat in Brussels and he or she is likely to vent some frustration at how the status of the European Union as Israel's top trading partner and as the largest donor to the Palestinian Authority has not been reflected by a commensurate role in the so-called peace process. For too long, many diplomats feel, the European Union has been relegated to being 'a payer rather than a player' in the Middle East.

To a certain extent, these frustrations have been lessened over the past decade. Although the European Union doesn't wield anything like the same clout as the United States, EU representatives are now heavily involved in high-level discussions about the Middle East. This has been particularly so since 2002, when a formal 'quartet' of mediators between Israel and the Palestinians was set up at a meeting in Madrid. The quartet's members are the European Union, the United States, the United Nations and Russia. This greater involvement has been facilitated, too, by a growing desire within Israel to cultivate stronger bonds with Europe, instead of relying almost exclusively on the United States to defend its interests abroad.

Some diplomats may speak out of genuine conviction when they suggest that the European Union is better-suited to being an honest broker than the United States. Yet the record shows there is no substantial difference between how Israel is pandered to by leaders on both sides of the Atlantic. If anything, some powerful EU figures have been more gung-ho in supporting Israeli policies than the United States, especially since the election of Barack Obama.

The debate over Iran's nuclear programme offers a case in point. As well as depicting the uranium enrichment widely assumed to be taking place in Iran as an existential threat, Israel has been dropping hints that it would be prepared to go to war against Iran. Israel's staunchest ally in Europe over this issue has been Nicolas Sarkozy. In September 2009, the French president effectively accused Obama of appeasement when he took issue with Washington's stated willingness to negotiate with Iran, implying that this stance had enabled the country to acquire the wherewithal for making a nuclear bomb. 'I support America's outstretched hand', Sarkozy told the UN General Assembly. 'But what has the international community gained from these efforts of dialogue? Nothing but more enriched uranium and centrifuges.'[11]

It is instructive that this belligerence has coincided with European efforts to shield Israel's nuclear weapons from scrutiny. The same month that Sarkozy made that comment, the International Atomic Energy Agency adopted a resolution calling on Israel to grant inspectors from this UN body access to its nuclear sites. Israel, the resolution observed, is the only state in the Middle East to have refused to sign up to the nuclear Non-Proliferation Treaty.[12] European countries declined to support this call, the first one directed at Israel that the agency had issued since 1991.[13]

ISRAEL'S CHARM OFFENSIVE

As well as undertaking military offensives against Gaza, the West Bank and Lebanon, Israel has been engaged in a sophisticated charm offensive. Determined that the country should not be only synonymous with incessant bloodshed, Israel has been cleverly presenting itself as one big adventure playground for artists and intellectuals. 'We will send well-known novelists and writers overseas,' Arye Mekel, a senior official in the Israeli foreign ministry, has said. 'This way, you show Israel's prettier face, so we are not thought of purely in the context of war.'[14]

Europe's media has often allowed itself to be seduced by this 'prettier face'. When 60 Israeli artists took part in the Nuit Blanche festival in Paris, *Le Monde*'s culture section devoted almost an entire page to the exhibition, organised by former Israeli diplomat Marie Shek. Accompanied by an image of a naked woman floating serenely in the Dead Sea, the feature celebrated the aesthetic qualities of Israeli art. No questions were asked about the ethics of making art against the backdrop of an occupation of which some of the artists doubtlessly had direct experience, given that military service is mandatory in Israel.[15]

EU institutions have been equally enchanted by Israel. More than representatives of any other country neighbouring the European Union, Israel's elite has studied carefully how the European Union functions and how to exploit both its external relations and domestic policies to maximum advantage. Diplomats in Brussels – grown men displaying all the outward signs of intelligence – have confessed to me that they were mesmerised by Israeli counterparts who were well-dressed and well-versed on the intricacies of EU rules and procedures. (I'm not making up the 'well-dressed' bit; officials have genuinely praised the sartorial elegance of their Israeli interlocutors.)

This charm – coupled with Israel's impressive performance in science and technology – has helped Israel present itself as a dynamic economy that Europe can ill-afford to ignore. The consequence has been that in most of the European Union's dealings with it, Israel is treated as any 'normal' industrialised country would be. The niggling fact that it is occupying the land of another people is either overlooked completely or dealt with in a highly inconsistent manner.

Whereas relations with most foreign countries are usually the preserve of just one or two departments in the European bureaucracy (typically external relations or trade), Israel is given a treatment that insiders describe as 'horizontal'. This means that numerous departments – ranging from transport to culture – are in charge of different aspects of the relationship with it. Inevitably, this has meant that officials handling dossiers that have a significant

Israeli input do not have the requisite knowledge of international law to deal with a government that habitually defies it.

Not surprisingly, then, there have been stark inconsistencies in the way that Israel has been treated, notably on issues concerning East Jerusalem. In internal documents, the European Commission has been sharply critical of Israel's ongoing efforts to render East Jerusalem free of Palestinians. One such report, that was leaked to the press in March 2009, stated that 'Israel is, by practical means, actively pursuing the illegal annexation of East Jerusalem.'[16]

In 2005, another report from the Commission had recommended that the European Union should 'support Palestinian cultural, political and economic activities in East Jerusalem' as one of several steps aimed at thwarting Israeli efforts to take over the entire city.[17] Ironically, however, the European Union has been actively supporting Israeli cultural, political and economic activities in East Jerusalem.

The Israeli Antiquities Authority (IAA) is among the beneficiaries of Euromed Heritage, an EU-financed programme which has been allocated €13.5 million between 2008 and 2012. The IAA's involvement comes despite how it is headquartered in the Rockefeller Museum in East Jerusalem, which the European Union formally considers to be occupied Palestinian territory.[18] Its involvement also comes despite how archaeology is being used as a pretext to uproot Palestinians so that more Israeli settlements can be built. The IAA has been playing a central role in assessing the archaeological value of the Silwan area of East Jerusalem, where the Israeli authorities want to expel 1,500 Palestinians from their homes in order to extend the nearby City of David Park, honouring a king reputed to have conquered the city three millennia ago.[19]

The IAA has been accused of exhibiting stolen artefacts across the globe. In 2009 the Royal Ontario Museum teamed up with the IAA to host a display of the Dead Sea Scrolls, even though the Palestinian Authority wrote to the Canadian government protesting at how these 2,000-year-old fragments were acquired illegally after Israel captured East Jerusalem in the 1967 war. Until then, they had been kept in the Rockefeller Museum, which was under Jordanian control.[20] I went to see this exhibition when I was in Toronto for a wedding; I spent a few hours fixated by the ancient texts and the audio-visual displays accompanying them but found not even one admission that they were obtained under controversial circumstances. I often go through an experience akin to hypnosis in a fascinating museum or art gallery. But I would expect EU officials to be more alert when dealing with bodies like the IAA; they should not be lulled into assisting illegal activities.

TAINTED BY TORTURE

Europe's unholy alliance with Israel has been forged partly as a result of the 11 September attacks on the Twin Towers and the Pentagon. Both Europe and Israel have identified Islamic militancy as a common enemy and resolved to cooperate in addressing its symptoms, while allowing its causes (notably the occupation of Palestine) to be aggravated. Once again, the cooperation that has ensued has prompted EU policymakers to renege on their commitments to vigorously defend human rights.

Convinced that intelligence from Israel would prove useful to detectives on this continent, EU governments mandated Europol, the Union's police office, to begin talks aimed at reaching a cooperation agreement with Israel in 2005. This mandate was given in flagrant disregard to the spirit of the 1995 convention under which Europol was established. That convention states that Europol may not process data obtained through methods involving human rights abuses.

Anyone who has flicked through Amnesty International's reports on Israel and the occupied Palestinian territories would know that it would be next to impossible for Europol to receive data from Israel that had not been gathered by using torture and other forms of ill-treatment. Amnesty has maintained that Israel has 'routinely tortured' Palestinians in its custody for over four decades. Techniques favoured by Israeli interrogators include the sharp twisting of the head backwards, sleep deprivation, sudden pulls to the body, beatings, fastening handcuffs so tight that a prisoner's circulation is affected, humiliation, threats and solitary confinement.[21] Sometimes a detainee's loved ones have even been forced to appear before him or her dressed in prison uniform to convey the impression that they too are being held or tortured.[22]

Israel has tried to rebut evidence of systematic abuse by pointing to its signature and ratification of the UN Convention Against Torture and by maintaining that Israeli law 'strictly forbids' all forms of ill-treatment in its prisons.[23] However, despite numerous complaints by detainees, the Israeli High Court of Justice did not rule against the use of torture during interrogations until 1999. That verdict came with the all-important caveat that members of the security forces could not be prosecuted for using unauthorised methods if they were dealing with a 'ticking bomb' case.[24] Human Rights Watch has observed that the Israeli attorney general has been all-too-willing to provide security agents with the legal cover they need to avail themselves of this loophole.[25] Furthermore, the Israeli courts remain unwilling to ensure that the law against torture is upheld. The Public Committee Against Torture in Israel has decided to reduce the number of petitions it brings before the country's Supreme Court seeking the repeal of orders of incommunicado detention – which clearly facilitates torture, as well as being inherently cruel. The committee took this decision after it and other organisations and individuals lodged hundreds of such petitions over many years, none of which were granted by the court.[26]

Police cooperation with Israel could also undermine European laws on data protection. I have seen a copy of a confidential report by the board of data protection officials that oversees Europol's activities. It concludes that 'direct connection' between Europol's headquarters in the Hague and the 45 databases administered by the Israeli police would breach the 1995 Europol convention. According to the report, Israel's protection of privacy legislation lacks provisions forbidding the 'excessive' collection of data by security forces or requiring that data is not stored indefinitely. Europol, by contrast, is bound by these principles.[27]

Israel's refusal to respect human rights standards that Europe officially holds dear has not prevented Europol from working as closely with Israel as it can. When I asked a Europol spokesman about the status of its negotiations in November 2009, he told me that a draft cooperation agreement with Israel has been completed and has been 'submitted to Europol's governing bodies for approval'. All he would say about the routine use of torture in Israel was that 'it is explicitly forbidden for Europol to process data which has clearly been obtained by a third state in obvious violation of human rights'.

This reply echoes the clauses relating to human rights in the Europol convention. But it seems to me that Europol is leaving ample wiggle room to allow data being processed in cases where abuses can be considered less than 'obvious'. Israel could, for example, offer political guarantees that torture is not used and it is conceivable that the EU authorities would regard these as sufficient, even if the proverbial dogs in the street know they are not. If Europol and EU governments were truly concerned about avoiding complicity in the violation of human rights – obvious or otherwise – they would never have sought a police cooperation agreement with Israel in the first place.

There are many other ways in which the European Union is

embracing Israel. This book examines how the relationship has been enhanced even as Israel has tightened its noose around Palestine (Chapter 1) and how Europe has happily kowtowed to America's neo-imperialist meddling in internal Palestinian politics (Chapter 2). It traces how EU aid programmes for Palestine have turned the Union into a proxy for the Israeli occupation (Chapter 3) and how some of the biggest beneficiaries of EU scientific and commercial ties with Israel are the arms firms that profit from Palestinian misery (Chapters 4 and 5). Finally, it offers a guide to the lobbying organisations that have helped convince European policymakers that it is in their interests to draw closer to Israel (Chapter 6), before concluding with a call for action against this unholy alliance.

Most of this book was completed before a senior Hamas figure, Mahmoud al-Mabhouh, was assassinated in a luxury Dubai hotel during January 2010. In an operation universally assumed to have been carried out by Mossad, the Israeli secret service, counterfeit passports were used so that the killers could masquerade as British, Irish, French and German citizens. After it was proven that some of these passports were fraudulent copies of ID documents held by Britons living in Israel, the London government expelled an Israeli diplomat from the United Kingdom. David Miliband, then the British foreign secretary, spoke of 'compelling reasons' to believe that Israel was behind the forgeries, and protested at how the incident 'represents a profound disregard for the sovereignty of the United Kingdom'.[28]

If Iran, North Korea or any other state considered hostile had abused European passports in this way, it is a safe bet that Britain would not be choreographing its protests with an effort to placate the regime in question. But a few weeks before Miliband was accusing Israel of insulting Britain, his boss Gordon Brown was busily kowtowing to the Knesset. In an opinion piece for the *Daily Telegraph*, the prime minister promised to amend a British law on universal jurisdiction, the principle under which serious crimes can be prosecuted in a British court no matter where in the world they are committed. Brown did not mention Tzipi Livni, the former Israeli foreign minister, by name but it is clear that his article was prompted by her decision to cancel a visit to London the previous December because a court had issued a warrant for her arrest on the request of Palestinian solidarity activists.[29] Brown wrote:

> There is already growing reason to believe that some people are not prepared to travel to this country for fear that such a private

> arrest warrant – motivated purely by political gesture – might be sought against them. These are sometimes people representing countries and interests with which the UK must engage if we are not only to defend our national interest but maintain and extend an influence for good across the globe. Britain cannot afford to have its standing in the world compromised for the sake of tolerating such gestures.[30]

It is a measure of the level of moral bankruptcy to which the higher echelons of the Labour Party had slumped after almost 13 years in power that Brown could dismiss so blithely the efforts made to hold Livni accountable for the crimes she had authorised in Gaza. Rather than applauding the litigants for their selfless actions, Brown trivialised them as mere 'gestures'.

None of the other European countries implicated in the Dubai passport affair took any steps that would have any lasting consequence for Israel. On the contrary, all of them gave their assent to Israel's membership of the Organisation for Economic Cooperation and Development (OECD) in May 2010. Israel's rationale for wishing to join this exclusive capitalist club is comparable to its courtship of the European Union. The more influential or prestigious bodies it can flirt with, the more Israel can insinuate that its acts of terror are carried out in the name of western 'civilisation'. As Yuval Steinitz, Israel's finance minister, commented: 'We are now receiving a very significant seal of approval'.[31]

Throughout the year that I have spent researching and writing this book, I have repeatedly heard EU officials defend their alliance with Israel on the grounds that the greater contact they have with Israel, the more opportunities they have to criticise the occupation of Palestine. This argument might have merits if the European Union seized those opportunities, yet the reality is that its protests against Israel's contempt for international law are becoming more timid and ineffectual. Worse, the increasingly practical nature of EU–Israeli cooperation has meant that the European Union has become increasingly accommodating of that illegality.

This accommodation has occurred without European citizens being asked for their opinion and without proper scrutiny by our elected representatives. In some cases – scientific research, for example – top-level EU officials have been dishonest about the precise nature of the cooperation to conceal how the Union is directly assisting the Israeli military-industrial complex which is seeking to perpetuate the occupation.

It is no exaggeration to say that Europe is abetting crimes against humanity in the Middle East. Ending this complicity will not be easy, but it can be done if enough people dedicate themselves to the task. The first step in achieving this goal is to inform ourselves about how the unholy alliance has been built.

1

BUILDING THE UNHOLY ALLIANCE

GAZA CITY, MAY 2009

A herd of scrawny goats appears amid the piles of rubble and the tangles of girders. For a few moments, these pitiful creatures seem to be the only sign of life. I am in one of the most densely populated places on earth, yet the destruction all around me lends it a hollow and desolate feel.

Through the cracked windscreen of a dilapidated Mercedes, I stare in disbelief at the pulverised remains of buildings where whole families lived. 'There, Merkava', my driver points, naming the brand of tank that flattened the house. 'There, F-16', he says to distinguish a separate building that had been attacked from the air.

Four months have passed since Operation Cast Lead, as Israeli officialdom calls its latest act of slaughter against the civilians of Palestine. Here in the Izbet Abed Rabo area of Gaza City – a Hamas stronghold, according to Israeli propaganda, as if that excuses everything – the men, women and children left homeless are living in the white tents of UN agencies. There is no sign that work on reconstructing their houses will start any time soon; Israel is refusing to allow essential building material into Gaza.

Practically everyone I meet tells me of how terrified they were during the last days of 2008 and the first few weeks of the New Year. 'On the first day of the war, I was in my office at 11.45,' says Amjad Shawa, who runs a human rights organisation. 'Suddenly everything changed; it was all bombs and ambulances. For five to six minutes, I couldn't recognise what was happening.'

Unable to contact his wife because the mobile phone network was not functioning, Shawa drove to his children's school. It had been damaged because of its proximity to the headquarters of the

Palestinian security forces, which had been bombed in the early stages of this no-warning attack. 'I found my children', he says. 'They just kept telling me the names of their classmates who were injured. They thought that because someone was bleeding, he was killed. For the first time my children – the youngest is six and a half, the eldest nine and a half – were asking: "What does it mean to die?" I am struggling to give my children a better life. And they are talking about death.'

Beside the Park of the Unknown Soldier – a sorely needed splash of floral colour in the heart of Gaza City – I am approached by Nahed Wasfy Wshah. He is a tall and friendly man bearing more than a little resemblance to the footballer Eric Cantona; his English is inflected with a slight drawl he acquired from living in Texas. Today, he lives in Al-Brij refugee camp about 10 km away but he is desperate to leave. After he asks me where I am from, he wants to know whether I can help him gain asylum in Ireland. His youngest son Mohammed was burned on his arms and chest when the camp – reputedly another Hamas stronghold – was attacked.

'My children, my daughters are still scared by the war', he says. 'Sometimes they wake up at night and start screaming. They say: "Daddy, take us away from here; there will always be war here.'"

Majed Abu Salama, a technology student, tells me of the colloquial name that Gazans have given to the buzzing of Israeli warplanes overhead, which constantly afflicts their eardrums like tinnitus. *Zanana*, they call it, comparing it winsomely to the sounds emitted by honey-bees. But he knows first-hand the destruction wrought by these flying instruments of death. He began 2009 huddled in his home as his family provided shelter to terrified neighbours. With his father, he operated a shift system, so that at least one of them would be on constant alert. At night one would sleep for three hours, and then be woken by the other.

One afternoon a family friend sought to take advantage of a lull in the attacks, which the Israeli authorities had announced. It was a false promise, as the man discovered. 'They killed him through a rocket, when his daughters and his wife were with us in my family's house', Salama says. 'It was terrible.'

Research by the Gaza Community Mental Health Programme indicates that the psychological effects of the attack are profound. Out of a sample of 374 children questioned, over 73 per cent thought they were going to die during the violence. Almost 68 per cent of the children – all aged between 6 and 16 – fear that a similar attack will occur in the future, and 41 per cent expressed a strong desire for revenge. Of parents quizzed in the initial stages of this study (unpublished at the time of writing), 82 per cent have observed that their children have been behaving aggressively since the attack and 52 per cent reported that their children had emotional problems.

'Everybody lost something in this war', says Husam El Nounou, a spokesman for the programme:

> Some lost friends and relations, some lost parts of their bodies. Others lost property and money; others a feeling of security and protection. It was a very cruel feeling. I've never felt so near to death as during that period. There was no place to where we could escape.

BRUSSELS, JANUARY 2009

The timing of Operation Cast Lead could scarcely have been more cynical. Within a month, George W. Bush would be handing over the White House to Barack Obama. This transition period in US politics gave Kadima, the main party in Israel's ruling coalition, an opportunity to exploit the country's military muscle in a blatant bid – unsuccessful, as it transpired – to win a forthcoming general election. No real pressure would be exerted by the United States, its key ally, to suspend the attack, the Israeli elite assumed correctly. Too busy honing his inauguration speech, Obama maintained a shameful silence.

Richard Falk, the UN investigator on human rights abuses in the Palestinian territories, has suggested that Operation Cast Lead might have set a new precedent for modern warfare. For the first time, an entire civilian population had been locked into a war zone, its borders sealed. 'No children, women, sick people or disabled people were allowed to leave', the veteran Jewish-American academic and campaigner stated in little-reported comments to the European Parliament.[1] 'For the first time, the option of becoming a refugee has been withheld.'

MORE DEFENSIVE THAN OFFENSIVE?

As the European Union's policymakers routinely describe human rights and democracy as their core values, surely they could be relied on to speak out against the carnage. Or could they? With the EU presidency changing hands every six months, the Czech Republic had just stepped into the metaphorical driving seat of the European

Union on New Year's Day 2009. Jiri Potuznik, the Czech press spokesman in Brussels, took it upon himself to declare the Israeli military operation as 'defensive, not offensive.'[2]

His parroting of the Israeli explanation for the war – that it was simply a response to Hamas' rocket attacks on southern Israel – did not go down too well in some European capitals. Nicolas Sarkozy's government, which reluctantly ceded the EU presidency at the end of December, was particularly irked that the comments were at odds with the tone of a message from a meeting of the EU foreign ministers held in Paris less than a week earlier. The ministers had urged a ceasefire on that occasion.

And so Potuznik swiftly issued a statement of clarification. 'Even the undisputable right of the state to defend itself does not allow actions which largely affect civilians', it read.[3] Superficially, this appeared more balanced and nuanced. Yet it still implied that the operation was retaliatory in nature – a claim that falls apart when subjected to a modicum of scrutiny.

By intimating that Operation Cast Lead was an act of self-defence, the EU presidency was misrepresenting – perhaps deliberately – the nature of Israeli violence. Whereas Israel uses violence as a tool of oppression, Hamas uses it on behalf of the oppressed. Hamas is a resistance movement. Its tactics can cause and have caused deaths and horrific injuries to innocents, and there are good reasons to argue that – like many acts of violence – they have been counterproductive. Still, Hamas is a symptom of the Israeli–Palestinian conflict and not, as some apologists for the Israeli establishment would have us believe, its cause.

Leaving aside the legal and philosophical questions about whether people living under occupation or the control of racist and colonial regimes have the right to resist – a right recognised by nearly every government in the United Nations through a 1987 resolution of its General Assembly – there are more prosaic reasons to dispute Israel's version of events.[4]

Far from Hamas having provoked Israel, it had observed a four-month ceasefire until 4 November 2008. On that day (probably by no coincidence, the same date as the US presidential election), Israeli troops made a raid on Gaza, in which they killed six members of Hamas. Unwisely, though not unsurprisingly, Hamas responded with a salvo of rocket attacks on southern Israel.

Known in Arabic as a *tahdia* (lull), the ceasefire had gone into effect in June 2008, after being brokered by Egypt. Jimmy Carter, the former US president, has written of his understanding that its terms committed Israel to dramatically easing the blockade it had imposed on Gaza since Hamas took control of the Strip in 2007. This would involve allowing 700 truckloads of supplies to be delivered to Gaza per day – roughly equivalent to deliveries before the 2005 withdrawal of Israeli settlers. (Carter qualified his remarks by saying he was unable to confirm the agreement with the Israeli authorities, as they were loath to admit that they had been in contact with Hamas.[5])

Rather than living up to its obligations, the amount of food, medicine and fuel allowed into Gaza reached only about one-fifth of the levels considered 'normal'. The Red Cross found that malnutrition had soared among Gazans to the extent that 70 per cent of its 1.5 million inhabitants were suffering a 'progressive deterioration' of access to food of sufficient quality and quantity to lead healthy lives.[6]

Despite the hefty evidence contradicting it, there are many in senior positions in the EU institutions who continue to accept Israel's propaganda. These include those who have access to all the material they need to make an informed judgment. Marc Otte, the Union's 'special representative' to the Middle East, sounded exactly like a mouthpiece for the Israeli government when I interviewed him in the summer of 2009. He apportioned all the blame for Operation Cast Lead on Hamas and its 'sponsors' in Iran and Syria. 'Gaza was a crisis waiting to happen,' Otte said. 'Do you think the Palestinians could continue to launch rockets on Israel without Israel reacting?'

Angela Merkel, the German chancellor, went even further, declaring that Hamas 'clearly and exclusively' bore responsibility for the attacks.[7] Along with Italy, the Netherlands and Romania, her government refused to call for a UN investigation into war crime allegations against both Israel and Hamas.[8] Sarkozy – his efforts to temper the extremism of the Czech position notwithstanding – shared Merkel's analysis (if that is the correct term). Although he labelled Israel's use of force as 'disproportionate' (a standard, and usually asinine, European Union response to state-approved atrocities), he insisted that the situation had been caused by 'irresponsible provocations' from Hamas.[9]

AFTER THE BOMBS, A BANQUET

Further indications that the most powerful leaders in the European Union were siding with the aggressor came on 18 January, a day after Israel called a 'unilateral ceasefire' (as the country's main newspapers dutifully dubbed it). Every death or injury caused in a war is a tragedy and an affront to humanity, yet it is beyond dispute that most of the victims of this offensive were Palestinian. A total of 1,417 Palestinians died over the course of the 22 days, according to Gaza-based human rights monitors.[10] Of these, 926 were civilians, including 116 women and 313 children. By contrast, 13 Israelis were killed, just three of whom were non-combatants.

If gestures of solidarity were required, it was surely the beleaguered residents of Gaza that were most deserving of them. In their wisdom, however, presidents and prime ministers from Britain, Italy, Germany, France, Spain and the Czech Republic chose instead to embrace the man who had ordered the onslaught. The six leaders converged on Jerusalem, where Ehud Olmert, the Israeli prime minister, hosted a gala dinner in their honour. Olmert's then successor-in-waiting Binyamin Netanyahu was also in attendance.

The symbolism of the event was not lost on the Israeli press. This was the single largest delegation of world leaders to visit Israel at one time since the funeral of its assassinated prime minister Yitzhak Rabin in 1995, the newspapers observed. 'Six world leaders dropped everything to come here and express their support for Israel's security,' an anonymous Israeli official told the *Jerusalem Post*.[11] 'That's not something that happens every day.'

Sated by Olmert's culinary delights, the European leaders once again accused Hamas of inciting the attacks and promised to work towards restricting the flow of weapons to the organisation. The question of halting the supply of weapons to Israel does not appear to have been discussed.

Within less than a week, Olmert would be telling journalists of how he had wept while watching images of a bombing in Jabaliya refugee camp, in which three sisters and their cousin were blown to pieces. The incident was one of the few in this war that had engendered a mild controversy within Israel, thanks to an anguished TV appearance by the girls' father and uncle Ezzedine Abu Al-Aish, a doctor. Olmert pledged that an investigation would be held to find out if any soldier had opened fired deliberately.[12]

In the absence of credible witnesses, it is impossible to verify if Olmert really did cry. Assuming that he is telling the truth, it is difficult to think of tears that have been shed with greater hypocrisy.

SPIN TRIUMPHS OVER SUBSTANCE

Unlike some national administrations, the European Commission is not brimming with highly skilled public relations professionals.

Nonetheless, the executive arm of the European Union notched up a success for the dark arts of spin during the final days of Operation Cast Lead. On 14 January, Ramiro Cibrian-Uzal, the Commission's ambassador in Tel Aviv, briefed reporters on the implications of the offensive for European Union-Israel ties. 'Everybody realises that it is not the appropriate time to upgrade bilateral relations,' he said.[13]

His words gave the impression that the European Union was taking a firm stance. Representatives from Britain's Labour Party welcomed his remarks during a debate in the European Parliament held the same day. Richard Howitt, a Labour MEP with a solid track record of speaking out on human rights issues, informed his colleagues that the European Union had put 'on hold' its talks on improving relations with Israel because the latter's army had killed 139 children and injured almost 1,300 others 'since the conflict began'.[14] (This death toll would, of course, climb.)

The picture was a bit more complex than the one Howitt painted. In June 2008, foreign ministers from both the European Union and Israel agreed that relations between the two sides should be raised to a new level of 'more intense, more fruitful, more influential cooperation'.[15] This decision followed a request made by Tzipi Livni, then Israel's foreign minister, a year earlier for her country to be integrated into the EU single market for goods and services and to be allowed take part in a wide range of the European Union's other political and economic activities. According to many observers, the proposal was designed to ensure that Israel enjoyed closer ties to the European Union than any other country outside the Union's borders. In effect, it would make Israel an EU member state in all but name (and possibly lead towards eventual membership of the increasingly powerful bloc). And because the plan included the holding of annual summits between European and Israeli leaders, diminutive Israel would be placed on a par with major economies like the United States, China and India in terms of its ranking in the European Union's external relations.

Livni met her EU counterparts again in December that year, when they confirmed their intention to go ahead with the upgrade. Israel's unilateral breach of its ceasefire with Hamas a month earlier was perceived as no more than a minor irritant by the EU side on that occasion. And while nothing was carved in stone, it was agreed that the paperwork needed to put the upgrade into effect would be completed by the summer of 2009.

Then the attack on Gaza took place. A top-level EU official told me that the offensive came as a 'nasty shock' and that Livni had given no inkling it was being prepared when she was in Brussels a few weeks previously. You could legitimately ask how well-educated civil servants were so naive as to think that a full-scale onslaught wasn't being considered when Israel had already undertaken attacks of a smaller nature a short time beforehand. But I have no reason to doubt that some officials who handle dossiers concerning the Middle East felt aggrieved at being kept in the dark.

The response of EU officials to the operation was based on pragmatism, not principle. Because of the new dynamic that had been created and the large demonstrations against the carnage internationally, they realised that they could not proceed with the upgrade as swiftly as planned. Preoccupied with the breaking news from Gaza, they could not give this multifaceted process the same level of priority. Contrary to what some newspapers indicated, no decision was taken to 'freeze' the upgrade as a protest.[16]

Karel Schwarzenberg, the Czech foreign minister at the time, explained the formal situation bluntly. The original upgrade proposal had been approved by all 27 EU foreign ministers, he noted, and reversing this move could only be done with these ministers' consent. 'It can't be changed at the word of a very respected representative of the European Union in Jerusalem,' he stressed.[17]

Apart from the not insignificant fact that the envoy he was alluding to was based in Tel Aviv, rather than Jerusalem, Schwarzenberg's assessment was accurate. More tangible proof that many EU officials were dealing with Israel on a business as usual basis came within a fortnight. Antonio Tajani, the European Commission's vice-president and a crony of the Italian prime minister Silvio Berlusconi, visited Israel in late January to discuss cooperation on air transport and satellite navigation. The script for a speech he delivered at the Ilan Ramon international space conference in Tel Aviv made no reference to the war in Gaza or to the broader problems of the occupation. Evidently, the opportunities afforded by the space sector were deemed to be of far higher importance. After all, it was 'a €90 billion world market, growing at the rate of 7 per cent per annum', as he reminded his audience.[18]

FALLING IN LOVE WITH LIVNI

Even if it sometimes appears that Israel regards the United States as the only ally worth having, its ruling elite has kept a close eye on how the European Economic Community (EEC) (the precursor of the European Union) has evolved ever since its inception. In 1958 – the year after the Treaty of Rome was signed by the six states that founded the EEC – David Ben-Gurion, Israel's first prime minister, predicted that this 'closely knit community would become a central force in world affairs'.[19]

The question of whether Israel is entitled to view itself as a European state inevitably arises at the level of barroom discourse each time the country participates in the Eurovision Song Contest (memorably won by Israeli transsexual chanteuse Dana International in 1998) or in the qualifying stages of the UEFA European Football Championship. While Israel's case may be flimsy on geographical grounds, it has been advanced with considerable brio on ideological grounds. Well before Israel achieved actual nationhood, Zionists declared their goal of setting up a Western-style state in Palestine. Theodor Herzl, in his hugely influential 1896 book *Der Judenstaat,* portrayed a Jewish state as 'the portion of the rampart of Europe against Asia, an outpost of civilisation as opposed to barbarism'.[20]

In academic circles, the idea that Israel should seek EU membership has been bandied about for some time. Alfred Tovias, a professor of international relations at the Hebrew University in Jerusalem, has contended at numerous symposia that this step is required on economic, political and security grounds. Geography should not be a barrier, he believes, pointing out that other countries outside the European continent such as Cyprus have been admitted to the Union.[21]

Although many Israeli politicians have alleged that the European Union has been too sympathetic towards the plight of Palestinians for their liking, there has been a growing recognition that more harmonious ties with the European Union would be desirable for reasons of *Realpolitik*. This dichotomy was exemplified by Silvan Shalom, who served as Israel's foreign minister under Ariel Sharon. In 2003, Shalom let it be known that Israel was mulling over the possibility of applying to join the European Union.[22] Ironically, this message was disseminated around the same time that an opinion poll suggested that 74 per cent of Israelis felt the European Union was biased towards the Palestinians. Shalom had reflected this widespread unease by stating: 'I find myself challenged to convince the Israeli people that the EU is a partner we can trust.'[23]

Leon Hadar, a former UN bureau chief for the *Jerusalem Post,* appears to take credit for inspiring Shalom's volte-face. In his book *Sandstorm*, Hadar recalls that he had written an article advocating that EU membership would be beneficial for Israel and that it was published (by the Cato Institute in Washington) the same week that Shalom had broached the subject with an EU delegation. Hadar wrote:

> Conditioning Israel's entry into the EU on its agreement to withdraw from the occupied territories and dismantle the Jewish settlements there would strengthen the power of those Israelis who envision their state not as a militarised Jewish ghetto but as a Westernised liberal community.[24]

His vision may sound appealing but the reality is that the European Union has been willing to accommodate Israel's wishes for ever-deepening ties in recent years, not only without a withdrawal from the occupied Palestinian territories but at a time when the occupation has become more vicious.

Tzipi Livni's assiduous courting of senior EU figures in 2008 offers something of a master class in Machiavellian duplicity. Despite being a protégé of Ariel Sharon, a man whose reputation for murder and destruction as an army general is largely unrivalled in his country's blood-stained history, she convinced the West that she was Israel's 'Mrs Moderate'. By accepting that she was genuine in striving towards the foundation of a Palestinian state alongside Israel, the European Union was prepared to gloss over the undeniable fact that the occupation worsened during her stint as foreign minister.

EU officials credit Livni for developing the 'upgrade' concept, although the Israeli press has indicated that three diplomats – Yossi Gal and Rafi Barak (both foreign ministry aides) and Ran Curiel (Israel's ambassador to the Union) – played a vital role in ensuring that the plan gathered momentum.[25] 'We've always wanted to help Livni,' a Brussels source, who took part in the discussions, told me. 'The upgrade business is something that she came up with, primarily for her own domestic purposes.'

And what could her real intentions be? According to my source, the upgrade will make it far more difficult for the European Union to condemn atrocities carried out by Israel in the future.

> It was very clever of them. If we try to criticise them, they will turn around and say 'how can you speak to us like that? That's not the kind of language you use with friends.' The fact we now have extremely close ties on paper means that we are not able to criticise them in public as we used to.

Duped into believing that she genuinely wanted peace, EU governments pandered to most of Livni's whims. One of their most egregious capitulations occurred in December 2008 when she demanded that there should be no formal link between the upgrade process and resolution of the Israeli–Palestinian conflict.

While Britain, Ireland, Belgium, Malta and Cyprus had indicated that they would not endorse an upgrade unless it was flanked with conditions relating to the 'peace process', they were all charmed and cajoled into submission. When Livni travelled to Brussels to meet EU foreign ministers she asked at one point that everyone else leave the room so that she could have private discussions with France's Bernard Kouchner, who was chairing the meeting. During their conversation, a deal was hatched whereby the upgrade accord would not bind Israel into making peace with the Palestinians. Instead, the EU side would merely issue a separate declaration underscoring the need for grappling with the conflict's thorniest issues (such as Israeli settlements in the occupied territories, the future of Palestinian refugees and the status of Jerusalem).[26]

Officials involved in the talks have confirmed to me that EU member states were willing to accommodate Livni in almost every regard as they wished to bolster her position within the Israeli political pantheon. A few months earlier Livni had taken over as leader of Kadima from Olmert, who had been mired in a corruption scandal. Most EU governments expressed a desire that Kadima would outpoll Binyamin Netanyahu's Likud in a general election slated for the following February and Livni would therefore become the country's new prime minister. Though the European Union is normally careful not to be caught interfering in the internal affairs of foreign countries, its governments were eager to do what they could to support Livni against Netanyahu, who had a reputation for being more hawkish and less open to dialogue. Kouchner was especially eager to shore up Livni in whatever way he could, according to well-placed sources.

'It was very explicitly mentioned by several member states that keeping a link to the peace process would not be helpful to her,' a Brussels-based diplomat said: 'It was a little bit weird. We are always talking about the importance of democracy. And we are supposed to be uncomfortable with taking sides in elections held in other open democracies.'

If EU representatives needed proof that the doveish image Livni sought to cultivate was a sham, all they needed to do was to examine data compiled by their own officials. Since 2003, the European

Commission has been working towards the goal of involving countries to the east and south of its external borders in many of its activities. Because Israel was the most economically advanced of these countries – which also include Ukraine, Jordan, Egypt, Tunisia, Lebanon, Morocco, Libya and Syria – it was in a position to benefit more than all others to whom this 'European Neighbourhood Policy' was addressed. Still, there was an important caveat: the 'action plan' that the Commission agreed with Israel committed both sides to working towards a durable peace in the Middle East.

In its 2008 annual report on relations with Israel, the Commission registered its disappointment that 'little concrete progress' had been made in addressing a range of issues during the previous year.[27] Specific concern was expressed about the expansion of Israeli settlements and checkpoints and the ongoing construction of the 347 km concrete wall that suffocates much of the West Bank, the planned demolition of Palestinian homes in East Jerusalem and discrimination against the Arab minority in Israel. The only positive note in the report's section relating to the Israeli–Palestinian conflict was that there had been a drop in fatalities, compared to the preceding twelve months. In 2007, a total of 377 Palestinians died as a result of violence (the corresponding figure for 2006 was 643), while the Israeli death toll came to 13 (down from 27 in 2006).

Nobody who studied this sober document carefully could be left in any doubt that it was Palestinians which were suffering the most, not Israelis (this observation is not to trivialise in any way the pain endured by Israeli victims of violence). A simple exercise in mathematics showed how the number of Palestinians killed in 2007 was 29 times higher than the number of Israelis killed. Yet when presenting the report's findings to a press conference, Benita Ferrero-Waldner, then the European commissioner for external relations, heaped lavish praise on Ehud Olmert's government. Describing it as a 'leading partner', she announced that Israel was 'closer to the European Union than ever before'. She also reminded journalists that a 'reflection group' was studying how relations between the European Union and Israel could be upgraded to a 'truly special status'.[28] (This group had been formed by Livni and Frank-Walter Steinmeier, the German foreign minister, a year earlier.)

I have obtained a copy of a letter that Ferrero-Waldner sent to Livni around that time. Dated 27 March 2008, it notes that a year had passed since Livni first sought closer ties to the Union. Ferrero-Waldner wrote:

> Your announcement to aim for a significant upgrade of our relations received a warm welcome from the EU and the subsequently established reflection group is beginning to bear fruit. Implementation of the European Neighbourhood Action Plan is progressing at cruising speed, and we are starting to identify further areas of common interest we might continue to work on. The upcoming meeting of the reflection group will provide an opportunity to exchange views about our common way forward. Rest assured that the Commission stands ready to support your objective of an ever closer relationship.

The letter read as if it was trying to set a new record for the amount of clichés and quirky syntax that can be crammed onto a single page. But there was not one word about Israel's human rights record or the wider political problems in the Middle East, despite oft-repeated assurances from EU officials that they broach such issues on every available occasion.

On the surface, Ferrero-Waldner's confidence in Olmert and Livni appears puzzling as the latter duo had failed to deliver on measures that she had requested. At the 'peace conference' that Bush hosted in Annapolis (Maryland) during November 2007, Ferrero-Waldner stated that a freeze on the construction of Israeli settlements in the West Bank would be a prerequisite for any progress towards a resolution of the conflict.[29] Not only did Israel ignore this request, it accelerated the construction of settlements. Just a week after Annapolis, the government decided to proceed with the building of 307 new housing units in Har Homa, a settlement between Jerusalem and Bethlehem. This was not a breach of a promise to the Palestinians to halt new settlement activity, the Israeli government claimed, as it did not regard the location as part of the West Bank.[30]

Any hopes that this could be an exceptional case were dashed in March 2008, when the Israeli organisation Peace Now published a report documenting how a 'Lego system' was being used to erect settlement buildings in the Palestinian territories as quickly and cheaply as possible. More than 500 settlement buildings were under construction in the West Bank (excluding East Jerusalem), according to the report, with work on 275 of them beginning since Annapolis.[31] And though much of the construction was being undertaken without permits, the government was continuing to authorise new buildings. For example, the Israeli interior minister had given the settlement Modi'in Illit the status of a city at the beginning of that month. Ehud Barak, the defence minister, had also approved the construction of at least 946 new housing units in the Palestinian territories around the same time.[32]

The report by Peace Now was one of many indications during 2008 that Israel was tightening its vice-like grip on Palestinians. In June, the then UN human rights commissioner Louise Arbour stated that Israel's stranglehold on the West Bank had stifled economic activity and denied freedom of religious expression by often preventing Muslims from attending prayers in mosques of their choice. The number of curfews imposed had increased substantially, she said. For the entire duration of 2006, the West Bank was under curfew for 696 hours, rising to 873 hours the following year. But in the first three months of 2008 alone, the total stood at 776 hours.[33]

In his book *The Breaking of Nations*, Robert Cooper, a British diplomat who has become one of the key intellectual thinkers behind the development of EU foreign and security policies, makes a pertinent observation about the centrality of Israel to Washington's worldview. 'Commitment to a country means having to live with whatever policies the government of the day there is pursuing,' Cooper, a former adviser to Tony Blair, wrote.[34]

The same argument can be applied to EU links to Israel. In deciding to proceed with the upgrade in 2008, the European Union was effectively acquiescing with the occupation, even if its public pronouncements were designed to give the opposite impression. The conclusion that the European Union rewarded Israel for behaviour it officially rebuked is, in my view, inescapable.

Saeb Erekat, the chief negotiator for the Palestinian government in the West Bank, has alleged that the ongoing construction of settlements 'poisoned the atmosphere' in talks he attended with the Israeli government as part of the 'Annapolis process'. Olmert 'was not committed to stopping settlement activity,' Erekat told *Newsweek* magazine. 'I'm not going to say he was lying. But he was playing games with us.'[35]

Erekat's analysis contrasted sharply with a statement made by Livni in December 2008, in which she insisted that behind closed doors 'this is the best year in terms of relationship between Israel and the Palestinians' since 2000.[36] Even though all available evidence pointed in the other direction, the European Union was willing to accept her version of events.

This was despite the occasionally dire warning that the European Union had issued at the highest level earlier in 2008. In March that year, Javier Solana, the then EU foreign policy chief, used what was for him uncharacteristically robust language about Israeli plans to build 400 new homes in the Givat Ze'ev settlement. Stating that 'we deplore' the announcement, Solana argued that it 'may put in jeopardy the peace process'.[37]

On more than one occasion before then Solana had said that 'the European Union has never and will never let the Palestinian people down'.[38] His vow assumed an increasingly hollow tone in 2008 as it became clear that the European Union was willing to do precisely that. In May of that year, Salam Fayyad, the Palestinian prime minister, urged that the European Union should not upgrade its ties with Israel because the latter's settlement activities were in 'flagrant disregard' of Palestinian rights.[39] Fayyad, as I shall discuss in the next chapter, has largely become a puppet of Israel and the United States, yet his observations on this occasion were faultless. The Israeli authorities had issued tenders for 847 new housing units in the Palestinian territories since Annapolis, an almost eight-fold rise on the 11 months preceding the conference, he noted. Meanwhile, at least 185 Palestinian buildings had been destroyed by Israel in the four months after Annapolis.[40]

A similar message was delivered to the European Parliament in December by Mustafa Barghouti, a veteran Palestinian politician. Formally improving European Union–Israel ties at this stage would be tantamount to the European Union giving its blessing to the occupation, he suggested.

> It would send a serious message that Israeli actions, starting with the siege of the Gaza Strip, the Judaisation of Jerusalem, the violations of human rights and the increase in the numbers of military checkpoints, are all policies acceptable by the European Union. It would also serve as an encouragement to the extremist parties in Israel.[41]

REWARDING A ROGUE

In his book *Disappearing Palestine*, Jonathan Cook, a writer living in Nazareth, makes a convincing case that Israel's actions in the Palestinian territories may constitute genocide (though he argues that the term 'politicide' may be more apt in this context). He wrote:

> 'Genocide' is widely, and mistakenly, assumed to refer only to an act of mass extermination of a racial or ethnic group akin to the industrialised murder of Europe's Jews committed by the Nazis. In fact, the word's legal definition is far broader.[42]

As Cook points out, the lawyer who invented the term genocide, Raphael Lemkin (a Polish Jew who fled to the United States during the Holocaust) had intended that it should not generally apply to the 'immediate destruction of a nation' but to 'a coordinated plan of different actions aiming at the destruction of the essential foundations of the life of national groups'. In 1943, Lemkin stated that the objectives of such a plan would include inflicting damage on the political institutions, culture, language, religion, health, economy or security of a national group.

The United Nations' 1948 Genocide Convention incorporated the core elements of that definition. It specified that genocide was a crime designed to destroy a national, ethnic, religious or racial group in whole or in part by, among other things, causing serious physical or psychological harm to members of that group or imposing intolerable conditions of life on them.

EU institutions claim to be staunch defenders of this convention, which requires all signatories to prevent and punish any crime of genocide 'whether committed in time of peace or in time of war'. In late 2008, for example, the European Commission declined to grant Nigeria a series of trade preferences it had applied for because the convention had not yet been ratified by the Abuja government.[43] (Many anti-poverty activists regard Brussels' stance in this instance as being motivated by a desire to retaliate against Nigeria for its refusal to sign a free trade agreement that the Commission coveted, than by a wish to censure it for not placing an international law on its statute books.) Yet although EU officials verged on the pedantic when insisting that an impoverished African country should respect the convention, they have not displayed any comparable rigidity towards a wealthy industrialised country like Israel.

Apartheid in South Africa would also have fulfilled several of the criteria for genocide stipulated by the United Nations. That Israel's treatment of the Palestinians bears many of the hallmarks of that meted out to the black majority in South Africa by its white oppressors is beyond serious dispute. That much was acknowledged by Henrik Verwoerd, the South African prime minister, as far back as 1961 when he observed that 'Israel, like South Africa, is an apartheid state' because Zionists 'took Israel from the Arabs after the Arabs had lived there for a thousand years'.[44] It is worth reflecting on how Israel counted on white-run South Africa as a friend to the point that the UN General Assembly passed a resolution in 1984 deploring 'the increasing collaboration by Israel with the racist regime of South Africa.'[45]

Indeed, the original Zionist plan to conquer Palestine was heavily influenced by the ideas lying behind white supremacy. As far back as 1927, Chaim Arlosoroff (who would soon become the leader of Mapai, the political party that dominates much of Israel's history) drew a parallel between how Jewish settlers tended to have higher material expectations than Arabs in Palestine and how Anglo-Saxons regarded themselves as superior to 'Bantu-Negroes' in South Africa. In the latter case, 'colour bar' laws were introduced so that blacks could be excluded from better-paid jobs. He wrote: 'It is not important whether we reject this politics or justify it. It is important here to highlight the economic reasons or social relations that led, rightly or wrongly, to the promulgation of Colour Bar laws.'[46]

One of apartheid's philosophers Jan Smuts compared his invidious ideology to Zionism, too. In 1919, the year he became prime minister, he told the South African Zionist Federation:

> The white people of South Africa and, especially the older Dutch population, has been brought up almost entirely on Jewish tradition. The Old Testament has been the very marrow of Dutch culture here in South Africa. That is the basis of our culture in South Africa, that is the basis of our white culture, and it is the basis of your Jewish culture; and therefore we are standing together on a common platform, the greatest spiritual platform the world has ever seen. On that platform I want us to build the future South Africa.[47]

Apartheid's most vociferous opponents have been struck by the similarities between the plight of the Palestinians and what black South Africans were forced to endure. After Desmond Tutu visited the occupied territories in 2002, the Anglican archbishop described the 'humiliation of the Palestinians at checkpoints and roadblocks, suffering like us when young white police officers prevented us from moving about.'[48] Nelson Mandela, writing in 2001, complained of a 'vulgar racism' pervading Israeli society, with opinion polls spanning several decades indicating that one-third of the Israeli population harboured feelings of hatred towards Arabs. Mandela accused Israel of pursuing 'apartheid policies', adding:

> Israel has deprived millions of Palestinians of their liberty and property. It has perpetuated a system of gross racial discrimination and inequality. It has systematically incarcerated and tortured thousands of Palestinians, contrary to the rules of international law. It has, in particular, waged a war against a civilian population, in particular children.[49]

South African government minister Ronnie Kasrils has gone further by arguing that the abuses perpetrated by the Israeli occupation were more extreme than those by the bigots that used to run his country.

> The South African apartheid regime never engaged in the sort of repression Israel is inflicting on the Palestinians. For all the evils and atrocities of apartheid, the government never sent tanks into black towns. It never used gunships, bombers or missiles against the black towns or Bantustans. The apartheid regime used to impose sieges on black towns but these sieges were lifted within days.[50]

Kasrils' view has been echoed by other long-standing members of the African National Congress. Shortly before she was appointed South Africa's minister of health in 2008, ANC stalwart Barbara Hogan expressed her shock at what she witnessed during a visit to the West Bank:

> Non-whites lived in separate zones but in South Africa there were never separate roads [for whites and blacks], a 'security barrier', check-points, different car registration plates or the confinement of people in demarcated zones.[51]

The Palestinian minority within Israel's internationally recognised borders also faces systematic discrimination. Olmert conceded as much in November 2008 when he lamented how whole sectors of the Israeli economy were closed off to Arabs, even though – numbering nearly 1.5 million – they comprised one-fifth of the country's population. 'It is terrible that there is not even one Arab employee at the Bank of Israel (out of 900 employees) and that in the Israel Electric Company Arabs constitute fewer than 1% of all workers,' he said, adding that the bias against his Arab compatriots 'has been occupying me greatly'.[52]

Olmert may have been lauded for his words by some Arab

members of the Israeli parliament or Knesset. His acknowledgement that this discrimination is rampant may be unprecedented but it would also appear belated and mealy-mouthed, given how he did nothing to ameliorate the position of Arabs within Israel and how he worsened the living conditions of their kinfolk in the occupied territories during his premiership.

Nor did Olmert rescind laws which guarantee Jews more favourable treatment than Arabs. Whereas Israel's famous 'law of return' grants anyone in the world the possibility to claim Israeli citizenship provided he or she had a Jewish grandparent, members of its Arab minority have been officially told that their blood relations in the West Bank or Gaza are enemies of the state. Under the citizenship law that came into effect in 2003, Israeli Arabs may not seek reunification with their families living in the occupied territories or in Syria, Iraq, Iran or Lebanon, all of which have been categorised as hostile to Israel.[53]

Although the right of access to healthcare is enshrined in Israeli law, in practice this has not been upheld for Arabs. A recent report by the Arab Association for Human Rights cited data indicating that the rate of mortality for Arab children has been twice as high as that for their Jewish peers since the state of Israel was founded. In 2007, seven out of every 1,000 Arab children died before reaching their first birthday, compared with three out of every 1,000 Jewish children. Human rights workers say this discrepancy may be at least partly explained by the fact that health services are less available and accessible for Israeli Arab mothers than for Jews.[54]

Israel's refusal to cherish its children equally is part of a lengthy litany of human rights abuses by successive governments. *Hasbara*, as state propaganda is known in Hebrew, would have us believe that Israel is run in strict conformity to a deeply moral code. Reality shows how it shares its distinction for resorting to practices that only someone with a perverted imagination could countenance with regimes routinely branded as evil in the West. In January 2009, Israel decided to resume its policy of demolishing the homes of any family where one of its members was accused of terrorism, after temporarily abandoning that policy four years earlier. Such demolitions violate the Fourth Geneva Convention, which guarantees that nobody can be punished for an offence that he or she has not personally committed. As Norman Finkelstein, a son of Holocaust survivors, points out in his book *Beyond Chutzpah*, the only other country which targeted the families of suspected criminals in this way was Saddam Hussein's Iraq.[55]

Israel is under a contractual obligation to the European Union to respect human rights. Until now the main legal basis of relations between the two sides is an 'association agreement' dating from 2000; in article two, respect for human rights is described as an 'essential element' of the accord. In the world of commerce, when one party to a contract breaches its terms, it is customary for the other side to begin legal proceedings. But despite the solemn undertakings given by Israel to the European Union, the European Union has reneged on its duty to hold Israel to account.

The European Union has been treating Israel as if it is a kind of Middle Eastern Canada: prosperous (in macro-economic terms at least), industrialised and sophisticated. Israel is all of these things, yet it is also illegally occupying the land of another people and carrying out crimes that fulfil the textbook definition of genocide. Israel's persistent refusal to accept that international law applies to it means that it meets all the qualifications for being considered a rogue state. Yet instead of treating it as a rogue, Europe has decided to reward it.

2

BOWING TO THE UNITED STATES

A story told among the foreign policy cognoscenti in Brussels offers a clue about how they perceive Israel. During Binyamin Netanyahu's first stint as prime minister in the 1990s, he agreed to meet a visiting delegation from the European Parliament. When reminded by a Spanish MEP that Israel's activities in the occupied territories had proven so contentious that even Bill Clinton's government was ill at ease with them, Netanyahu is reputed to have delivered a characteristically withering riposte. 'You Europeans only look at what is happening above the table,' he said (or words to that effect). 'If you looked under it, you would see that we hold the Americans by the balls.'

Whether Israel really holds the United States 'by the balls' is a moot point. While there is no shortage of evidence to indicate that the pro-Israel lobby wields enormous clout in Washington, it would appear too that the United States has used its alliance with Israel to copper-fasten its own colonial interests in the Middle East. Although there were many instances of tension between the United States and Israel in the first few decades after the latter's inception, it has been viewed as an increasingly important client state since the time when Richard Nixon was president; as it became clear that the Vietnam War was unwinnable, he developed a doctrine whereby the United States should avoid direct military confrontation in the 'third world' but instead rely on lackeys such as Israel or the Shah-led Iran to pursue its overseas objectives.[1] During the Cold War, the emphasis was squarely on tackling both Arab nationalism and Soviet influence, yet this did not mean that less attention was paid to the Middle East in the Pentagon or the State Department once communism collapsed in Eastern Europe. If anything, the opposite occurred.

The scholar Rashid Khalidi has noted that the neoconservatives who held sway during George W Bush's presidency had set themselves an agenda of creating 'a new form of American hegemony over the region, in collaboration with Israel'. (The agenda was spelled out in a 1996 paper that Richard Perle, later a senior figure in the Pentagon and a cheerleader for the Iraq war, wrote for Netanyahu; as well as advocating regime change in Baghdad, it insisted that the United States and Israel had an identical goal of 'peace through strength', an Orwellian code for permanent conflict.[2])

Commentators in the Israeli press have long contended that the state's survival rests on two main 'pillars': a strong army and a rock-solid alliance with the United States. But in February 2008, the *Jerusalem Post* observed that the Israeli government felt that a third pillar had to be installed: closer links to the European Union.[3] The realisation was the fruit of the cooperation between Israel and Europe as part of the 'war on terror' that George W Bush declared following the atrocities that took place in New York and Washington on 11 September 2001.

Because Bush's unilateralist impulses proved divisive, it was easy to think that there was a serious transatlantic rift during his first term in office. With Jacques Chirac in France and Gerhard Schröder in Germany vociferously against the war in Iraq (primarily for domestic political reasons), a surreal debate developed in late 2002 and early 2003. Newspaper editors started running stories about irate Americans renaming French fries 'freedom fries' and boycotting the wines of Bordeaux and Languedoc, along with letters about how Western Europe was ungrateful to the valiant GIs that had come to its rescue on the beaches of Normandy six decades earlier. The conversations I had with American diplomats around this period were some of the strangest of my life; I remember one making a serious case that the French public had no right to oppose the war because they had subjected him to second-hand tobacco smoke as he sat in a Parisian café the previous weekend. (I loathe smoking, incidentally, but can't see why nicotine addicts aren't entitled to question the wisdom of military aggression.)

Donald Rumsfeld's categorisation of countries that supported the United States as 'new Europe' and those who voiced reservations as 'old Europe' was in fact hugely misleading. Germany might have been the largest member of the 'old' camp, yet it was also home to the largest US Air Force facility outside US territory (Ramstein). And unlike fellow NATO member Turkey, Germany took no steps to prevent the United States from using its land and airspace to transport troops to the Gulf.

Chirac, meanwhile, intimated that a strong Europe was needed as a counterbalance to US military muscle. Nonetheless, he was not prepared to launch any credible challenge to US hegemony. Before any controversy erupted over plans to attack Iraq, France and the main institutions of the European Union (including the European Commission, nominally an entirely civilian body) had given their unqualified support to the bombardment of Afghanistan. Both France and Germany still have troops taking part in a force in Afghanistan under the command of NATO, a US-led alliance. Though the Berlin government has tried to convince a public wary of sending soldiers abroad that they are involved in a mission of 'stabilisation', the truth is that they are fighting an imperial war in a region rich with highly coveted energy resources. Arguably even worse, Germany is one of many European countries that connived in the human rights abuses that have been an integral part of the war on terror by enabling the CIA to use its airspace for secret flights carrying prisoners who were abducted and tortured.[4]

SARKOZY SWALLOWS, MERKEL MARVELS

If Chirac and Schröder sought to deceive their electorates that they were ushering in a new era of independence from the United States, then one of the few things their successors Nicolas Sarkozy and Angela Merkel should be commended for is that they have been more honest about their subjugation to Washington. In 2009, Sarkozy went so far as to reintegrate France fully into NATO's military structures 43 years after Charles de Gaulle sought to put some distance between his government and the alliance.[5]

Sarkozy's unity of purpose with the United States has been especially marked in his dealings with Israel. He has spared no effort in making amends for the record of Chirac, who was derided by the Israeli press for being too friendly towards Arabs (in 1996, Chirac sparked a furore in Israel when he remonstrated with security guards who tried to stop him mingling with crowds in Jerusalem's Old City; he was also the first foreign head of state to address the Palestinian Legislative Council).[6]

In June 2008, the *Jerusalem Post* hailed Sarkozy as the most pro-Israel French president since de Gaulle was elected in 1958; de Gaulle had announced that many Franco–Israeli ties, including nuclear cooperation, would be severed in 1967 as part of a reorientation of his country's foreign policy.[7] Much was made of Sarkozy's Jewish roots, particularly of how he is reputed to have only discovered that his Greek-born maternal grandfather Beniko Mallah had been a Jew after the man died in 1972. Sarkozy also won plaudits from many

Israeli commentators for a speech he had delivered to the French Jewish organisation CRIF in February that year, during which he lashed out at the Iranian president Mahmoud Ahmadinejad for the latter's bellicosity towards Israel. 'I won't shake hands with people who refuse to recognise Israel,' Sarkozy had said on that occasion, alluding to Ahmadinejad's 2005 reported comments about wanting to wipe Israel 'off the map'.[8] (A transcript of Ahmadinejad's remarks indicates that they may have been misinterpreted in the West; while he talked about removing Israel's 'occupying regime', he did not explicitly demand the state's destruction.[9])

When Sarkozy became the first French leader to speak to the Knesset since François Mitterrand in 1982, his mood music delighted Israel's political establishment. Most reports zoned in on his plea for obstacles to the free movement of Palestinians to be removed and for Jerusalem to be a shared capital of both an Israeli and a Palestinian state.[10] Yet these were merely reiterations of long-held EU positions. What was far more remarkable was how he effectively equated modern-day 'terrorism' with the Holocaust:

> After what Europe experienced, after the slaughter of the Jews, we can't tolerate anyone in the world saying he wants to wipe the state of Israel off the map. Today this threat has taken the form of terrorism. No people can live under the threat of terrorism. France is Israel's friend and France will always stand shoulder to shoulder with Israel when her security and existence are threatened. I have always thought this. I have always felt it in my heart of hearts and I will never compromise on this. And those who call scandalously for Israel's destruction will always find France in their way, blocking the path.[11]

Sarkozy had evidently swallowed huge dollops of his hosts' propaganda if he genuinely believed that the actions carried out by relatively miniscule Palestinian armed groups – however abhorrent some of their consequences may be – pose an existential risk to one of the largest military powers on the planet.

Whereas Sarkozy made at least a token effort to recognise the suffering caused by Israel in the occupied territories, Angela Merkel's address to the Knesset in March that year was an exercise in unadulterated grovelling. Raymond Deane, a composer and prominent member of Ireland's Palestinian solidarity movement, summarised her speech aptly as 'a compendium of banalities, lies, omissions, threats, and sycophantic bunkum'.[12]

It is understandable that Merkel underscored that Germany bears a historic responsibility towards the world's Jews, even if she was born after the Holocaust. It is understandable, too, that she would wish to mark the sixtieth year of Israel's statehood by visiting the country. But it is inexcusable that she rendered homage to its founders in an entirely partisan manner, without once recognising that Palestinians consider the destruction of their homes and villages by the terror gangs that forged the state of Israel in the 1940s as the '*nakbah*' (catastrophe). When she quoted Ben-Gurion's maxim 'Anyone who does not believe in miracles is not a realist', she failed to observe that he was simply repackaging the views of Chaim Weizmann, Israel's first president, who described the dispossession of Palestinians as 'a miraculous clearing of the land'.

Like Sarkozy, Merkel inferred that the crude Qassam rockets fired by Hamas were putting Israel's future in jeopardy. 'While we speak here today, thousands of people are living in fear and dread of missile attacks and acts of terror by Hamas,' she said, ignoring how a considerably higher number of Palestinians, living in considerably worse conditions, are terrorised by Israel.[13]

Because of the two countries' size and how they can frequently eclipse all other EU member states during the formulation of policy, the relations of France and Germany with Israel merit particular attention. They are not the only powerful players in the bloc, however, and the role of Italy and Britain, as well as medium-sized countries like the Netherlands, in driving the European Union closer to Israel should not be underestimated.

BERLUSCONI: A CHEERLEADER FOR THE OCCUPATION

The most nauseating example of a senior European politician kowtowing to Israel I have found has been provided by Franco Frattini, now Italy's foreign minister. In his former capacity as the European commissioner for justice and home affairs, Frattini attended the January 2008 Herzliya conference, Israel's most prestigious annual talkfest. Although the newspapers that Frattini probably perused on his flight to Tel Aviv would have informed him of how Israel had been stopping deliveries of food, medicines and fuel to Gaza's civilians, he did not once mention this siege in his speech (despite how a top UN diplomat Lynn Pascoe had berated Israel that same day for violations of international law).[14] Rather, he engaged in a favourite pastime of the pro-Israel lobby by contending that anything beyond the mildest criticism of Israel is tantamount to anti-

Semitism. Frattini gave a skewed reading of the Palestinian uprising or *intifada* that began in 2000. Without recognising that the rebellion had been provoked by Israel's unceasing suppression of elementary rights, he accused Palestinian militants of fomenting hatred against Jews in the Middle East and in Europe. Left-wingers in Europe were complicit in the development of a new wave of hostility towards Israel and Jews, he implied. There was no suggestion that any of this hostility might have been caused by Israeli militarism or that opposition to a government's policies is in no way the same thing as hatred of that country's people (does he feel that critics of his political master, Silvio Berlusconi, bear some deep-seated grudge towards the pizza or ice-cream makers of Florence or Naples?).

> For the three years of the second Palestinian *intifada*, many in Europe were reluctant even to acknowledge that the rising, insidious tide of hatred that Middle East violence has unleashed might be called 'anti-Semitism'. This European sickness had taken new roots and new forms. But things have changed. Governments have taken note and more action. This prejudice, this stance towards Israel and Jews has no place in today's Europe, must not have a place in today's Europe. It does not matter if it is presented as a side-effect of political grievances. It is simply unjustifiable. Full stop.[15]

It is deeply ironic that Frattini has been taking up the cudgels against the anti-Semitism which he appears to detect around every corner when he happily serves in a government boasting two extreme-right parties. One of these, the Alleanza Nazionale (National Alliance) is led by Gianfranco Fini, who has eulogised the fascist leader Benito Mussolini as the twentieth century's greatest statesman.[16] Furthermore, his direct boss Silvio Berlusconi has not displayed the sensitivity towards Holocaust survivors one would expect from someone in his position. In 2003, Berlusconi outraged the European Parliament when he advised a German Social Democrat MEP to audition for the part of a concentration camp guard in a movie.

Unburdened by anything resembling a principle, Berlusconi has nevertheless been quite happy to nurture ever-closer relations with Israel as part of a foreign policy that is largely dictated to him from Washington. Indeed, Berlusconi has been so supportive of Israeli might that the harsh remarks against Israel made by members of his predecessor Romano Prodi's centre-left government have been forgotten.

Whereas Prodi's foreign minister Massimo D'Alema had denounced Israel's assassination of Imad Mugniyah, Hezbollah's chief operations officer, as an act of terror,[17] Berlusconi's ruling coalition has endorsed some of Israel's most egregious abuses. Apparently so desperate to atone for the anti-Semitism with which his party was once synonymous, Gianfranco Fini, now speaker of the Italian parliament, has defended Israeli excesses more vigorously than almost any other senior European politician. He has supported the construction of the massive wall that Israel is using to suffocate much of the West Bank, despite how it has been opposed by the European Union and subsequently found illegal by the International Court of Justice in The Hague.[18] More recently, he has been a lone EU voice in approving calls by Avigdor Lieberman, Israel's latest foreign minister, for Arab citizens to be stripped of their rights unless they swear an oath of loyalty to the state. When Fini recommended that something similar should be introduced in Europe during a dinner marking Lieberman's first official visit to Rome, there was a moment of embarrassment before Lieberman piped up: 'You should know that when I said that in Israel, they wanted to hang me.'[19]

DUTCH COURAGE?

Fini's fandom for Israeli aggression is shared by Maxime Verhagen, the Dutch foreign minister at the time of writing. A right-leaning Christian Democrat, Verhagen would appear to be following a long-standing tradition in the Netherlands of sticking by Israel at all times. History partly accounts for this tradition: 70 per cent of Dutch Jewry perished in the Second World War and there is a tacit accord among many of the country's politicians that it would be disrespectful to their memory to lash out at a state regarding itself as Jewish. 'Israel has a special hold over Dutch society,' a diplomat from the Netherlands said to me. He continued:

> There are deeply-held beliefs in Dutch society of Israel being a small, vulnerable country bullied by perfidious neighbours. A lot of people who are not Jewish identify themselves as Jewish. It's a weird identification that doesn't happen in other countries. In Amsterdam, supporters of Ajax [football club] wave Israeli flags, including Moroccan youths. The way we discuss Israel is still a very simple way. We have had the same discourse for 20 years.

The Netherlands was at odds with other founding members of the

European Union such as France and Italy when it supported Israel in its 1967 war against Egypt, Syria and Jordan.[20] And while most countries that opened embassies in Israel after its formation in 1947 decided to locate them in Tel Aviv, the Dutch stationed theirs in Jerusalem until 1980, when a bill was passed in the Knesset proclaiming Jerusalem as the sole, undivided capital of Israel for eternity.[21]

Tightening Israel's grip on East Jerusalem might have been a step too far for the Netherlands, but the bombs that have rained down on Gazan civilians have not presented it with the same moral dilemma. In January 2009, Verhagen travelled to Sderot in southern Israel, to empathise with Israelis who came under fire from Hamas's missiles. 'Israel has no desire to see people suffer in Gaza,' he said. 'Israel left [Gaza under a 'disengagement' plan hatched by Ariel Sharon] and has no intention of going back in.'[22]

You could ask why he was so certain that Israel's government did not wish to see Gazans suffer, when he refused to travel a few kilometres further to see life in Gaza first-hand. Verhagen declined once more to go to Gaza, when he was in the region in June. This omission from his itinerary was highlighted by John Ging, head of the UN agency for Palestinian refugees (UNRWA), when he praised Verhagen's then government colleague, development aid minister Bert Koenders, for having the 'political courage' to actually set foot in Gaza.[23] Koenders, a Labour politician whose CV includes a stint as an aid worker in Gaza, is known to have a prickly relationship with Verhagen.

The clashing views of these two men, both of whom sat in the same ministry, underscore that the Dutch government policy on Israel is not monolithic. However, as the minister who came higher in the pecking order, Verhagen was the one who was taken more seriously in Israel. At home, he was also able to count on the support of his prime minister Jan Peter Balkenende, who blamed Hamas's rockets for causing Operation Cast Lead. 'There comes a time when Israel has to say: we have to react,' Balkenende, another Christian Democrat, said.

The Dutch premier from 1977 to 1982, fellow Christian Democrat Dries van Agt, should be commended for labelling Balkenende's stance 'incomprehensible'. Van Agt has expressed his astonishment at how politicians cut from the same ideological cloth as himself could support Israel, when the ratio of deaths was 130 Palestinians for every one Israeli killed. 'Just look at the advanced weapons used by Israel and the do-it-yourself weapons from the shed of Hamas,' van Agt added.[24]

Verhagen's effective encouragement of Israeli war crimes would not be so hard to stomach if it were not for how this position reeks of double standards. Verhagen has been punctilious in holding other countries to account on human rights issues. Rightly, he has demanded that Serbia's moves on joining the European Union should be made conditional on Belgrade's full cooperation with the international tribunal on the former Yugoslavia in The Hague.[25] As the high moral ground can be a very lonely place, perhaps this explains why Verhagen has stepped down from it to advocate that Israel should be offered EU membership. He appears unfazed by the contradiction inherent in seeking special treatment for Israel, when some of its leading politicians and generals have records blotted with killing sprees comparably heinous to those attributed to Radovan Karadzic and Ratko Mladic in the Balkans.[26]

FROM BLAIR TO BROWN: THINGS CAN ONLY GET BETTER?

If Germany and the Netherlands owe a historical debt to the Jewish people, then surely Britain owes a historical debt to the Palestinians. As its colonial overlord, Britain ruled over a Palestine that was 90 per cent Arab yet, in a gift to the Zionist movement, decided in 1917 that it should be the location of the 'Jewish national home'. Arthur James Balfour, the foreign secretary at that time, has recorded how steps to create a Jewish state would be taken without any consultation with the natives:

> The four Great Powers are committed to Zionism. And Zionism, be it right or wrong, good or bad, is rooted in age-long traditions, in present needs, in future hopes, of far greater import than the desires and prejudices of the 700,000 Arabs who now inhabit that ancient land.[27]

Whenever British and US leaders meet, it is a safe bet that the words 'special relationship' will be uttered on BBC news bulletins. It is far less likely that a journalist will appear on a TV screen to explain how this relationship involves the willing submission of the world's once pre-eminent imperial leviathan to the one that now occupies that position. That the United States sets the agenda in the Middle East and Britain and the rest of Europe must follow has been considered a truism in international politics for some time. The late Derek Fatchett acknowledged this when he was a junior foreign minister in 1998 with this assessment of how the European Union must play second fiddle in the so-called peace process: 'The European Union role has been to complement the [US] leadership.'[28]

With Tony Blair at the helm, Britain's position on the Israeli–Palestinian conflict became virtually indistinguishable from that of the United States. It is true that for a short period following Labour's 1997 election victory, the London government was prepared to arouse Israel's ire on a small number of occasions. When Britain held the EU presidency in 1998, its foreign secretary Robin Cook attracted violent protests from the Israeli right when he visited Palestinians aggrieved by the Har Homa settlement in East Jerusalem; he pleaded, too, with Binyamin Netanyahu's government to allow Gaza airport, a beneficiary of EU funding, to be reopened.[29]

Similarly, it is true that Blair tried to maintain a pretence for much of his premiership that he was determined to see progress towards peace. Faced with a Labour rank and file and a public mostly opposed to the invasion of Iraq, he sought to convey the impression that he had extracted pledges from Bush that the United States would devote greater attention to the Israel–Palestine dossier in return for British participation in the war. In reality, Blair resorted to nothing more than posturing, and few could have been surprised when his assurances – such as one given to the British Labour Party's 2002 annual conference that Israel would be pushed to comply with UN Security Council resolutions pertaining to the occupied territories – came to nothing. When Bush handed a memo to Ariel Sharon in 2004 agreeing that it would be 'unrealistic' to demand that Israel should withdraw completely from the West Bank, 'this sharp change in American policy brought no word of disapproval from Blair', according to Chris Patten, the former EU commissioner for external affairs. 'We were apparently to welcome the policy shift as a step forward along the road to peace.'[30]

In a highly unusual step, more than 50 retired British ambassadors wrote an open letter scolding Blair for 'abandoning the principles which for nearly four decades have guided international efforts to restore peace in the Holy Land' through his approval of a 'one-sided and illegal action' by Sharon.[31]

Jack Straw, who replaced Cook as foreign secretary after a 2001 general election, plumbed new depths as an apologist for Israeli aggression. This was particularly so after the 11 September attacks when he almost fully accepted Israel's arguments that its fight against Palestinian suicide bombers was inseparable from Bush's war against al Qaeda. When Sharon ordered troops to invade areas of the West Bank that were nominally under the jurisdiction of the Palestinian Authority in 2002, Straw said it was 'important to understand the huge pressures' on Israel. In uttering those words, he attempted to justify the strangulation of a people and the economy on which they depended, notwithstanding how Israel was resorting to collective punishment, an activity forbidden by international law. Straw sunk even lower when Israel carried out a massacre in the Jenin refugee camp. Although independent organisations such as Human Rights Watch found *prima facie* evidence that war crimes were committed by Israeli troops and that civilians were deliberately killed, Straw echoed Sharon's line that no international investigation was needed. Instead, the Israeli Defence Force – the army responsible for the massacre – could conduct its own probe. Ben Bradshaw, a minister at the Foreign Office, summed up this spineless position: 'In the case of Israel, being a country that has respect for the rule of law, we would expect it to carry out its own investigations.'[32]

Another display of Straw's contempt for international law and the institutions tasked with protecting it occurred when the question of Israel's 'security barrier' arose. Straw opposed the referral of the project to the International Court of Justice on the grounds that it would be preferable not to 'embroil' this body in 'a heavily political bilateral dispute'. His view may have been shared by the United States but otherwise he was on the extreme margins of global opinion. After the court ruled that this massive wall was illegal, 150 countries voted in favour of the verdict at the UN General Assembly; just six voted against.[33]

Blair again went to extremes in order to align British foreign policy with the United States during Israel's 33-day assault against Lebanon in 2006. While the war left almost 1,400 people dead and uprooted over 1 million from their homes, Britain backed the US view that Israel should be given space to carry out the slaughter for as long as it saw fit. (The war was a long-planned operation, primarily hurting civilians, yet Israel's top western allies portrayed it as legitimate retaliation for the capture of two Israeli soldiers by Hezbollah.) At a summit of the Group of Eight (G8) top industrialised countries in St Petersburg, Blair and Bush were adamant that a declaration to be issued at its conclusion omitted any criticism of Israel. Rather, they called on Hezbollah to release the two Israeli soldiers. The absurdity of that analysis was to be plainly seen less than two weeks after that summit when Israel bombed a residential building near the south Lebanese village of Qana. Twenty-eight civilians, half of them children, were killed, with harrowing images of their bodies being dragged from the ruins broadcast throughout the globe.

Labour MPs were known to be disgruntled with Blair's refusal to call for a ceasefire, and some commentators have cited their unease as a factor behind his decision to step down as premier. Chris Mullin, a veteran parliamentarian, encapsulated their frustration while addressing Margaret Beckett, then foreign secretary:

> Is it not just a tiny bit shameful that although we rightly condemn Hezbollah for what they have done, we can find nothing stronger than the word 'regret' to describe the slaughter and misery and mayhem that Israel has unleashed on a fragile country like Lebanon?[34]

Yet it was not until after Blair announced his plans to leave office in September 2006, that a government minister (Kim Howells, then in charge of relations with the Middle East) had the guts to acknowledge that his stance on the Lebanon war might have been wrong.[35]

Blair was not the first politician to have abused the trust invested in him by his voters, and will not be the last. Yet his co-option by the Israeli right looks all the more scandalous when set against the background of the lofty ideals he espoused in word, if not in deed. His justification for launching a military onslaught against Serbia over its alleged persecution of Kosovo's Albanians was that Britain 'could not allow in the case of Kosovo ethnic cleansing and genocide to happen right on the doorstep of Europe and do nothing about it'.[26] For reasons best known to him, he was nonetheless prepared to give *carte blanche* to Israel to conduct ethnic cleansing in occupied Palestine, it too located on the doorstep of Europe.

By spending his premiership, in the words of the intellectual Tariq Ali, 'constantly ensconced in the posterior of the American president', Blair came to be despised throughout the Middle East.[37] As a result of his policies, 'we Westerners now have 22 times as many military personnel in the Muslim world than the Crusaders had in the twelfth century,' Robert Fisk wrote.[38] With that baggage, Blair is one of the least suitable candidates imaginable to become an international envoy for the Middle East, yet the so-called quartet (the European Union, the United States, the United Nations and Russia) appointed him to such a role following his departure from Downing Street. In early 2009, I attended a meeting in Brussels where the film-maker Ken Loach poured brilliant scorn on an appointment that still beggars belief: 'They say that satire died when Henry Kissinger was given the Nobel Peace Prize. Well, it died again when Tony Blair was appointed a special representative for the Middle East.'

None of the tenacity that Blair displayed in helping to resolve the Northern Ireland conflict – one of his few positive contributions to humanity – has been on display in his new job. Though he visits the region infrequently (after beginning his job in June 2007 he waited until March 2009 before setting foot in Gaza), he has taken over an entire floor in the American Colony, the swankiest hotel in East Jerusalem, at the cost of more than $1 million per year.[39] Being low-key to the point of invisible, however, has not harmed the esteem in which he is held by Israeli hawks. In 2008, he was awarded a prize named after the Zionist businessman Dan David for his 'steadfast determination' to bring peace to the world.[40] A hagiography posted on David's website praised Blair's 'morally courageous leadership over Kosovo', yet omitted any reference to the invasion of Iraq.

'Things can only get better' used to be the campaign song of New Labour. Things did not get better in relation to the Middle East policy pursued by Gordon Brown when he took over from Blair as prime minister. Brown has an arguably more simplistic view of Israel than Blair. When visiting Jerusalem in 2008, he gave a dewy-eyed account of how his father belonged to the Israel committee of the Church of Scotland. The photographic images the elder Brown brought home from his pilgrimages to the 'Holy Land' left an indelible impression on the young Gordon. Speaking to the Knesset, he declared Israel an 'ancient promise redeemed' and the bond between it and Britain 'unbreakable'.[41]

The solidity of British support for Israel was exemplified during Operation Cast Lead. As the casualties in Gaza mounted, neither Brown nor his foreign secretary David Miliband publicly condemned Israel. The only difference between their position and that of Blair during the 2006 war in Lebanon is that they did not try to stop the European Union from collectively demanding a ceasefire. Brown hinted that everything was Hamas's fault, and essentially gave Israel all the encouragement it needed to continue its slaughter in the last week of 2008 by misrepresenting the attack as an act of self-defence: 'I understand the Israeli government's sense of obligation to its population.'[42]

EASTERN EUROPE: IN THE POCKET OF THE UNITED STATES

EU expansion into countries that used to be closed off by a mythical Iron Curtain has proven to be a boon for Israel. As a bloc the ten mostly ex-communist countries that joined the European Union in 2004 have been staunch defenders of US imperialism and, by default, Israel. Although conspiracy theories surface every so often in Brussels about US neoconservatives wishing to derail European integration, the Bush administration was enthusiastic about EU enlargement. In fact, Washington wanted it to go further and pushed the European Union to admit Turkey, a long-standing ally, into its ranks (full Turkish membership is being resisted by Germany and France, largely to pander to domestic constituencies hostile to Muslims and immigrants).

It is significant that this enlargement took place at a time when there was some disharmony between France and Germany on one side and the United States on the other and before Sarkozy and Merkel arrived to repair any damage that had been caused to Europe's status as a vassal of the United States. Noam Chomsky has put the process in a historical context:

> The United States has a real interest in undermining France and Germany because they are the industrial, commercial and financial centre of Europe. The rest is kind of periphery. The United States has had a deep concern back through the 1940s that Europe might strike out on an independent path. That's one of the reasons they were concerned about French president Charles de Gaulle, with his call for a Europe from the Atlantic to the Urals. And the forces that might impel Europe that way today are 'Old Europe'. That's one of the reasons the United States was very much in favour of expanding the European Union to include the former Soviet satellites, which it plausibly assumes it can control. And it's one of the reasons also why US policy-makers are so supportive of getting Turkey into the European Union – not because they love Turkey but because that's another way of diluting the influence of the powerful sectors in Europe and ensuring, they hope, that Europe will remain under US control.[43]

I was in Poland, the largest of the countries then awaiting EU entry, twice in 2003 and was astounded by the simplistic rationale used by politicians there to state their case in support of America's military machinations. The country's totalitarian past had clearly helped to stifle critical analysis if the inanities trotted out by the elite were anything to go by. Poles had to stand by the United States, I was told, because Woodrow Wilson had backed Polish independence as early as 1917 and because Chicago is home to the largest Polish community in the world. Barbara Labuda, who was imprisoned as a dissident during the communist era and was then working as a state secretary to the Polish president, drew a spurious parallel when explaining why it was right for her country to help the United States by sending troops to Iraq: 'I thought the support was necessary because we were liberating a nation that had lived in a concentration camp. To me, Iraq was like one big concentration camp; it was like Auschwitz.'[44]

It is correct that Polish politicians should belatedly apologise for how the country treated Jews in the past. Former prime minister Wlodzimierz Cimoszewicz has cited the 1946 Kielce pogrom, in which 42 Polish Jews who had survived the Second World War in the Soviet Union were murdered by a mob when they returned home, as proof of how Poland had been an 'evil stepmother' to Jews.[45] The legacy of that war only offers a partial explanation, though, about why Poland is unwavering in its support for Israel. Poland's subservience to the United States is a far bigger factor, as Jerzy Halbersztadt, director of a museum being built next to the Warsaw Ghetto memorial, has recognised. Commenting on the residual anti-Semitism in Poland ('no longer an issue particular to us in daily life'), he said: 'But Poles are more strongly pro-American and a side effect of this is that Poland also has the strongest pro-Israel policy, to which there is no opposition anywhere on the local political spectrum.'[46]

The platitudes rolled lightly off the tongue of Donald Tusk, the Polish premier, when he was in Israel during 2008. Flanked by Shimon Peres, Israel's Polish-born president, he made a bid for the much-coveted title of Israel's best friend in Europe. 'You won't find any European country more loyal to Israel than Poland,' Tusk said. 'If you have a problem with the EU, it is not with Poland.'[47] Eager to please his hosts, Tusk maintained that Ahmadinejad's reported threats against Israel 'disqualified him from being part of the international community' and implicitly linked Israel's oppression of Palestine with the war against the Nazis in order to justify it.

> There's no place for anti-Semitism and terrorism among honest and decent people. Combating them is our common duty. Nothing can erase history with its good and bad things from our memory, but we're for history to help rather than interfere.[48]

The Czech Republic has been vying with Poland in recent years to be considered a teacher's pet in terms of relations between the United States and the newest entrants to the European Union. A particularly lurid manifestation of how their elites were prepared to satisfy the United States' every whim came in 2008 when both Poland and the Czech Republic signed agreements committing them to stationing missile interceptors on their soil. That these accords were approved at a time of heightened East–West sensitivities due to a war between Russia and Georgia helped to revive latent tensions from the Cold War epoch.

Czech–Israeli ties cannot be viewed in isolation from the servility towards the United States that has become endemic among Prague-based politicians. 'It is a case of a friend of our friend has to be our friend too,' was the slightly convoluted explanation that a Czech diplomat offered me. The tone of friendship messages delivered by Czech politicians to Israel chimes so closely to the United States' that their scripts might as well have been written by White House aides. Here's what Alexander Vondra, then deputy premier, had to say during a 2008 conference on Europe and Israel in Berlin:

> The very idea of a Jewish national state originated in Central Europe, at times when other nations, including the Czechs, struggled for their emancipation. Today, the survival and well-being of Czechs and other Europeans is guaranteed by a voluntary union of like-minded nations, who are striving to enlarge the area of security and prosperity to their neighborhood. We should not deny the same right to a nation sharing with us not only a great part of its history, but also moral values, economic interests, and political institutions.[49]

That is not to deny that there are long-standing connections between the former Czechoslovakia and Zionism. The supply of weaponry resulting from a deal struck between Ben-Gurion's hand-picked envoys and Ludvik Svoboda, the Czechoslovak defence minister at the time, in January 1948 was of crucial importance to Israel during the war of independence/*nakbah*. British estimates suggest that Czechoslovakia reaped $28 million – a colossal sum in those days – from selling arms and military services to the Middle East in 1948, 85 per cent of which went to Israel.[50] A political science professor, Borivoj Hnizdo from Charles University in Prague, has contended that some communist states felt that courting Israel could enable them to have some influence in the Middle East:

> The existence of the state of Israel maybe wouldn't have happened, or would have happened in a very different way, if there hadn't been any help from Czechoslovakia at that time. Czechoslovakia's communist regime helped Israel very much in the spring of 1948. The political situation was very different in the Middle East. Israel was a new phenomenon and the new Soviet bloc and the Soviet Union didn't have a lot of official allies on the international scene. Czechoslovakia at that time was a founder member of the UN so it was a very good ally and for the Soviet Union and for Czechoslovakia it looked as if maybe Israel would be the centre, the core area of the new influence of the Soviet bloc in the Middle East.[51]

Following the 1967 war, the communist government broke off ties with Israel in line with the policy adopted by other Soviet satellites. Ties were to remain severed until 1990, yet Vaclav Havel acted swiftly to restore them once he came to power thanks to the oft-celebrated 'Velvet Revolution'. Havel chose Israel for one of his first foreign visits as president, where he tried to wax lyrical about how great a democracy his host country was. Around the same time, Havel delivered such a trite observation about the Cold War that it is hard to comprehend why he is considered an unassailable intellectual in some quarters. This battle, he contended, was between two superpowers, one (the Soviet Union) a nightmare, the other (the United States) a champion of liberty.[52]

To his credit, Havel was at least willing to encourage dialogue between Israel and the Palestine Liberation Organisation. Other Czech politicians, though, have joined the chorus line when Israel has been demonising Palestinian leaders. During a 2002 visit to Israel, the then Czech premier Milos Zeman was asked if he would compare Yasser Arafat to Hitler. 'Of course,' he replied. 'Anyone who supports terrorism, anyone who sees terrorism as a legitimate means, anyone who uses terrorism to cause the death of innocent people is a terrorist in my eyes.'[53]

Comparably idiotic comments have emanated from Mirek Topolanek, who became the Czech prime minister in 2006. A Thatcher-inspired right-winger with a colourful turn of phrase, he has echoed Zionist thinking by labelling Israel a 'civilisation in the onrush of barbarianism'.[54] As holder of the EU presidency in 2009, Topolanek attempted to resist pressure from some of the Union's other governments and the European Commission to delay work on the upgrading of relations with Israel because of its assault on Gaza.

Ignoring evidence to the contrary, he characterised Operation Cast Lead as a response to terrorism. Welcoming Shimon Peres to Prague in March that year, he listened to the Israeli president claim that his country is 'at the forefront of the war in terror' and was helping to prevent bombings in Europe. Topolanek responded by assuring Peres that he would continue 'to take a friendly and supportive stance with Israel' and 'a strong and resolute stance against Hamas and terrorism'.[55]

Karel Schwarzenberg, the Czech foreign minister under Topolanek, brags about how he has identified with Israel since his youth whenever an opportunity arises. One of the first embassies that Israel opened in 1948 was set up in the home of Schwarzenberg's parents, who were regulars at functions held by the pro-Israel organisation B'nai B'rith. Despite claiming that he put his personal affiliations to one side in order to act in a balanced way while representing the European Union, he declined to even echo the mild and clichéd criticism of Israel from those European leaders who describe Israeli actions against Palestinian civilians as 'disproportionate'. He said: 'I never use the word because I am not a judge. I am somebody who tries to achieve humanitarian aid and somebody who tries to achieve a ceasefire, not the judge of what actions are proportionate or disproportionate.'[56]

Mid-way through its EU presidency, a motion of no confidence in Topolanek's government was carried in the Czech parliament, triggering his resignation. He was replaced by a technocrat Jan Fischer, who was just as predictably biased towards Israel. When he visited the country in July 2009, Fischer steered clear of anything that could be deemed even remotely controversial in his talks with Netanyahu. He was photographed wearing a *kippah* (skull cap) at the Western Wall. But he could not bring himself to voice concern about the planned destruction of Palestinian homes that he could have learned about if he took a short stroll from there into the Silwan neighbourhood of East Jerusalem.[57] About 90 families there face being uprooted to make way for an archaeological park honouring King David.[58]

NATO: THE PITBULL GNASHES ITS TEETH

Tucked away in a nondescript part of Brussels, the headquarters of the North Atlantic Treaty Organization (NATO) is a monument to US hegemony. For all the talk about transatlantic tensions in recent years, the United States has been able to bolster NATO's place in global affairs and by extension ensure that America's grip on Europe remains tight. Suggestions that this situation might be anachronistic now that the Cold War is supposed to be over are seldom heard in the discourse of the West's key political institutions.

After communism started falling asunder in central and Eastern Europe, a small industry developed in think-tank land dedicated to the question of whether NATO remained relevant. By bombing Serbia without UN authorisation in 1999 and by setting up a 'stabilisation force' to fight a US-led war in Afghanistan in the early years of this century, the alliance showed that rather than going out with a whimper, it intends to keep gnashing its teeth as – in the words of the scholar Edward Herman – a 'US and imperial pitbull'.[59] Just as troubling, a pledge given by Ronald Reagan's government to the Soviet leader Mikhail Gorbachev that NATO would not encroach into the former communist countries in central and Eastern Europe has been reneged on.[60] Russia now finds itself surrounded by NATO members, with senior US figures keen on expanding the alliance further so that it includes Ukraine and Georgia.

Although a coterie of EU members remain outside of NATO, the connections between the two organisations continue to grow. Javier Solana, NATO's secretary-general in the 1990s, was rewarded for his key role in terrorising Serbia (some 500 of whose innocent civilians were killed by Western missiles, according to estimates by Human Rights Watch) with the post of the first-ever EU foreign policy chief ('high representative' in official parlance).[61] Solana helped pave the way for the signature of an agreement (known as 'Berlin plus') in 2003 that would allow the European Union to make use of NATO's hardware in EU military operations. So far the effects of this accord have been 'more political and psychological than operational', as a report by the European Policy Centre, a Brussels think-tank, put it, with decades-old tetchiness between Turkey and Cyprus hampering its practical application so far.[62] Such hitches aside, the European Union's Lisbon Treaty stresses that while the European Union has its own nascent military structures, it is ultimately subservient to NATO. The treaty specifies that for most EU member states NATO remains the 'foundation of their collective defence'. Susan George, an indefatigable political campaigner, has correctly argued that this reinforces the American president's role as Europe's commander-in-chief.[63]

Robert Cooper, a high-ranking EU official, has elaborated on how the *raison d'être* of Europe's armies is to shore up US domination:

> What is the point of the Belgian army today? It is not to defend Belgium since no one is going to attack it. Rather, it is to demonstrate a sufficient commitment to 'the West' that friends and allies, above all the USA, will be there if ever Belgium should need help.[64]

Similarly worrying, the Lisbon treaty requires the European Union to assist countries outside its borders to 'combat terrorism'.[65] This legally binding provision was added against the political backdrop of Israel striving to bring itself closer to both the European Union and NATO.

Israel's moves to snuggle up to NATO predate the 11 September atrocities. In April 2001, Israel became the first of seven countries taking part in NATO's 'Mediterranean dialogue' to sign a 'security agreement' with the alliance, designed to ensure that classified information shared by the two parties does not wander astray. But the bombing of the Twin Towers and the international 'anti-terrorism' agenda that resulted from it has been exploited assiduously by Israel, especially in its dealings with NATO.

Avigdor Lieberman, Tzipi Livni and Israel's army chief Gabi Ashkenazi have all visited NATO headquarters to press their case for closer relations. Their efforts bore fruit in December 2008 when NATO governments rubberstamped an 'individual cooperation programme' with Israel, enabling deeper intelligence-sharing between them, connecting Israel to NATO's computer networks and increasing the number of joint military operations. Livni used the occasion to boast that Israel is indispensable in the 'war against terror':

> All of the free nations of the world who understand the nature of the terrorist threat recognise the need to form a united front against it. Israel's standing in terms of military might and counterterrorist capabilities is recognised by the entire world, aptly conveyed by the expansion of cooperation between Israel and NATO that we witnessed this morning. The agreement is a practical expression of the values and responsibility shared by the free nations to preserve world security. It signifies genuine recognition of Israel's special contribution to the international fight against extremism.[66]

It is significant that this upgrade in relations with NATO was approved around the same time that the European Union also agreed to deepen its cooperation with Israel. While there is no immediate prospect of Israel joining NATO, the idea is continuously broached in political circles and many commentators see a clear link between it and Israel's greater involvement in EU affairs. The view of Israel among the majority of NATO members has also evolved considerably from an earlier period when US ties with Israel proved contentious. Some scholars, for example, cite the 1973 Yom Kippur War as one of the most challenging episodes in the alliance's history; when the United States sided with Israel on that occasion, most of the United States' NATO partners refused to grant it permission to use their airspace for flights to the area where the war was being fought.[67]

It is somewhat ironic that Lieberman, Livni's successor as foreign minister, is depicted as too extreme by the European media (though certainly racist, Lieberman's attitude towards Palestinians chimes with what huge numbers of Israelis say in private), when he is in some respects a Europhile. Lieberman has been pushing for Israel to be admitted into both the European Union and NATO. Returning home from a trip to Brussels in 2007, he told Israeli army radio that NATO had given his country the 'green light' to attack Iran at a time yet to be revealed.[68]

Some influential public figures have added their names to the call for Israel to be admitted into NATO. In 2007, John Edwards, then hoping to become the Democratic candidate for US president, told the Herzliya conference that it would be 'only natural' for NATO to one day incorporate Israel, given how the organisation's 'mission' was no longer confined to Europe. On the Republican hustings a few months later, former New York mayor Rudy Giuliani made a similar case.[69] Spain's ex-premier José-María Aznar has further advocated that NATO should be broadened to Israel, as well as to Australia and Japan.[70] And Rupert Murdoch has used one of the numerous media outlets that he owns to back Israel in this regard; in an opinion piece published in the *Wall Street Journal* in April 2008, he claimed that Israel has been 'fighting Islamic terrorism almost since its founding', and listed it among countries that share Western 'values'. (Other valiant defenders of liberty include Colombia, according to Murdoch, who neglected to mention its invidious record as the place where trade unionists are most likely to be murdered.[71])

Perhaps the most vocal and persistent advocate for better Israeli–NATO cooperation, though, has been Ronald Asmus. After serving as one of the key figures on European affairs in the Clinton administration, he went on to become head of the German Marshall Fund of the United States in Brussels. Along with promoting US corporate interests on the opposite side of the Atlantic, he put his name to a series of publications extolling Israel's democratic virtues. Asmus has said that as an American he is sympathetic to 'Israeli exceptionalism' – that poisonous doctrine which holds that Israel has a God-given right to ignore laws by which the rest of humanity are bound. Bringing Israel and other countries with a comparable level of economic development into NATO would, he believes, allow the alliance to 'fully and openly assume its true form: that of a free association of democratic countries that are committed to promoting an open and liberal way of life'.[72] Improving relations between Israel and the alliance, he has further contended, should not be made conditional on progress towards peace. With Iran widely assumed to be developing a nuclear bomb that would be pointed at Israel, Asmus feels that 'this is no longer the time for political correctness'.[73]

Asmus has undertaken his campaign for Israel to be accorded a special status by NATO at the request of friends in the Israeli political establishment. Nonetheless, his argument that relations with NATO should be delinked from the 'peace process' appears to be more extreme than the case put forward by senior Israeli officials themselves. Uzi Arad, the national security adviser to Binyamin Netanyahu, stated in July 2009 that he did not foresee any prospect of a peace accord with the Palestinians in the short term. But he added:

> We must strive to join NATO and to conclude a defence alliance with the United States. If there is an Israeli-Palestinian settlement that will lead to the establishment of a Palestinian state, membership of NATO and a defence alliance with the United States should be part of the *quid pro quo* that Israel will receive.

Notoriously bellicose ('I do not like wars between Jews; I prefer to direct the brute force energies within me at the goyim'), Arad has sought to give assurances that joining NATO would not hinder Israel from starting the wars that it has entered into with alarming regularity:

> Just as France and Britain possess capabilities even within the NATO framework, the same can be true with regard to Israel. Membership of NATO is a logical step and can provide us with a guarantee of mutual security and even add a layer to our own deterrence if the Middle East goes nuclear.[74]

Arad has been part of a group of Israeli officials which has been diligent in forging closer contacts with NATO in recent times. He has seldom squandered an opportunity to exploit Western fears over Iran's nuclear programme and how it could set off an arms race in the Middle East. He has been so successful in promoting a one-sided agenda that his interlocutors at NATO studiously avoid drawing attention to Israel's brazen hypocrisy. A state like Israel that has – if estimates cited by Jimmy Carter are accurate – amassed at least 150 nuclear warheads through a programme it has withheld from international scrutiny has no credibility in telling others that they must remain nuclear-free.[75] Yet it does not seem to have occurred to NATO strategists that there is a moral vacuum at the core of Israeli diplomacy. When Claudio Bisogniero, NATO's deputy secretary-general, gave a fawning after-dinner speech to Livni and other distinguished guests in Herzliya in 2007, he directed a message towards Iran that would have been more appropriately directed at Israel:

> A nuclear-armed Iran would deal a major blow to the international non-proliferation regime and could also produce a 'domino effect' throughout the Middle East as other states may feel compelled to develop nuclear technology as well.[76]

Jaap de Hoop Scheffer, NATO's secretary-general from 2004 to 2009, has successfully expanded the alliance's imperial tentacles. The US-led war that NATO has been fighting in Afghanistan has been assisted considerably by Israel's logistical cooperation and counsel on how to fight 'terrorism', he noted during a trip to Jerusalem and Tel Aviv in March 2009. US and Czech air forces have 'made use of Israeli technology, equipment, lessons learned, and doctrine and training on their way to Afghanistan,' he added.[77] What he didn't spell out is more revealing: Israel has helped NATO prolong a war, in which the principal victims have been Afghan civilians.

HOW THE WEST WENT SOFT

In the past, European governments have been willing to say things that Israel found to be unpalatable. In 1980, for instance, a declaration was issued in Venice by the nine countries that then comprised the European Community. It stated that Israeli settlements in the West Bank and Gaza were illegal under international law, insisted that the community could not accept any unilateral moves to change the status of Jerusalem, and urged negotiations between Israel and the PLO.

Menachem Begin, Israel's prime minister at the time, was so furious with the declaration that he likened it to Adolf Hitler's *Mein Kampf*:

> The declaration calls upon us and other nations involved in the peace process to bring in the Arabs' so-called PLO. For the peace that would be achieved with the participation of that organisation of murderers, a number of European countries are prepared to give guarantees, even military ones. Anyone with memory must shudder, knowing the result of the guarantees given to Czechoslovakia in 1938 after the Sudetenland was torn from it, also in the name of self-determination.[78]

Standing up to Israeli aggression is one thing. Taking a principled stand independent of US influence is quite a different matter, and this is something that the European Union has not been able to do collectively in any serious way since it became an important player in international diplomacy. Irrespective of who occupied the White House at any given time, the United States has done whatever it deems necessary to assert its primacy in the Middle East. That much has been clear since the Suez crisis of the 1950s, when Washington told its allies that it would not tolerate any behaviour which lacked its permission. After Britain, France and Israel attacked Egypt in response to the nationalisation of the Suez Canal, the United States triggered a run on the pound sterling. The consequences of this action were so severe that Britain withdrew from Egypt, with France and Israel following suit.[79]

In 1974 Henry Kissinger predicted that 'the Europeans will be unable to achieve anything in the Middle East in a million years'.[80] The evolution of the European Union into a more cohesive international force in the interim makes his prophecy seem just a little antiquated. Yet while the European Union may now have sufficient political and economic weight to offer prescriptions that differ from those of the United States without fear of repercussions, it has been unwilling to do so. As a result, European diplomats have been 'working on the margins of US-dictated policy', to quote a pamphlet from the Centre for European Policy Studies in Brussels.[81]

This much was vividly illustrated in 2006. That year the European Union undertook to strongly support the holding of the first elections to the Palestinian Legislative Council in a decade by dispatching a 185-strong observation mission (including 27 MEPs) to monitor the vote.

In January, Benita Ferrero-Waldner, then the external relations commissioner, spoke of assurances given by the Palestinian side that the elections would be able to take place 'free from violence and intimidation and according to international standards', and from Israel that it would allow polling to take place in East Jerusalem ('a difficult decision' for Israel to make given that it was in a pre-election situation too, she said).[82] When polling day (25 January) arrived, Israel placed 'rigid restrictions' on Palestinians in East Jerusalem to minimise voting but 'otherwise the election was orderly and peaceful', in the words of Jimmy Carter, who visited more than two dozen polling stations.[83] His assessment was shared by the EU monitoring team; in a statement the following day it described the exercise as 'another important milestone in the building of democratic institutions', recorded that voting had occurred 'peacefully and smoothly', welcomed an 'impressive' turn-out of 77 per cent of eligible voters and noted that the candidates from 'across the whole political spectrum' participated.[84] Edward McMillan Scott, a British Conservative MEP who took part in the monitoring, hailed the election as 'a model for the wider Arab region'.[85]

There was a snag: the result. To everybody's apparent surprise – not least the party's leadership, judging by anecdotal evidence – Hamas emerged as the winner, taking 74 of the 132 available seats, compared with 45 for its rival Fatah. 'I don't know anyone who wasn't caught off-guard by Hamas' strong showing,' said Condoleezza Rice, the US secretary of state at the time.[86]

DIVIDE AND RULE: THE SAME OLD COLONIAL STORY

In initial public statements, the United States indicated that it might be prepared to support the outcome of an election that it had wanted to take place, in line with its 'freedom agenda' of bringing democracy to the Middle East. 'Unpredictability is the nature of big historic change,' Rice noted. Yet when Hamas and Fatah tried to overcome their deep-rooted differences by forming a 'national unity' government, the United States refused to accept that they had a right to exercise their democratic mandates in this way.[87] Even though Washington had agreed that Hamas could take part in the elections, it would not countenance its involvement in government.

Israel would soon underscore its contempt for Palestinian democracy by rounding up that June 64 Hamas figures, including

Nasser Shaer, the deputy prime minister in the new government. As this was not enough to trigger the collapse of the government, the United States decided to intervene more directly. In October, Rice travelled to Ramallah, where she told Fatah leader and Palestinian Authority president Mahmoud Abbas that he must dissolve the government within a matter of weeks. The actions of the United States – which included covert supplies of weapons to Fatah, in collaboration with Israel – ultimately created the conditions in which the Palestinian territories would be split in two as part of a neocolonial 'divide and rule' strategy. Stoked by outside forces, the tensions between the two parties would rise to such an extent that the unity government could no longer survive. In June 2007, Hamas asserted its authority by taking over Gaza after a week-long battle with Fatah, which left at least 116 dead.[88] With Palestine polarised between '*Hamastan*' (Gaza) and '*Fatahland*' (the West Bank), the bitter rivalries persist.[89]

The European Union once had a more nuanced stance towards Hamas than the United States. Until 2003, the European Union distinguished between Hamas as a political party providing badly required social services in the Palestinian territories and its military wing, the Izz al-Din al-Qassam brigades. Whereas the latter had been included on the EU list of proscribed terrorist groups since 2001, the former was not. Yet following protracted lobbying by Israeli diplomats, the European Union modified its stance in September 2003 by deciding that Hamas in its entirety should be deemed a terrorist organisation.

The EU policy of designating groups (and often individuals) as terrorists has been closely linked to the US war on terror. At an 'emergency' summit ten days after the 11 September attacks, EU presidents and prime ministers identified the fight against terrorism as one of their top priorities and agreed to draw up a list of groups and individuals involved in terrorism. This move came despite the fact that the European Union at the time lacked a common definition of what constituted terrorist acts. It was not until the following June that a step was taken to formally rectify this anomaly. The common definition approved by EU member states then appeared to make sense, at first glance; activities identified as terrorist included those aimed at 'seriously intimidating a population' or 'seriously destabilising or destroying the fundamental political, constitutional, economic or social structures of a country.' But while there is a rich body of evidence available indicating that Israel's treatment of the Palestinians fulfils several of those criteria, the agreement of the

European Union was flanked with a crucial caveat. Actions carried out by the armed forces of a state were not covered, it specified.[90]

By placing Hamas on its terrorist list, the European Union ensured that it was to remain subservient to the United States in the Middle East 'peace process' (to use a term that has become increasingly meaningless). Even if Hamas had won an election which EU observers had categorised as fair and democratic, it soon became clear that it would be ostracised by the most powerful players in international affairs. Within five days of the election, the Middle East 'quartet' had issued an ultimatum to Hamas. Either it comply with a series of conditions laid down by the 'international community' (as the United States and its key allies are routinely described in polite company) or direct contacts with the Palestinian Authority would be frozen.

The conditions were that it renounce violence, recognise Israel and accept previous accords signed between Israel and the PLO. These were both unfair – the European Union and United States have never made their diplomatic relations with Israel subject to its cessation of violent attacks on Palestine – and ludicrous. Expecting Hamas to recognise Israel was especially unreasonable as under diplomatic rules only *bona fide* states can recognise each other and the Palestinian Authority does not represent a state. As part of a policy agreed at an Arab League summit in 1967, most Arab states – including many, such as the hardened human rights abuser Saudi Arabia, that have cordial relations with the West – refuse to recognise Israel. Why was Hamas being singled out and told that it, alone, must recognise Israel to have the mandate it had been granted by the Palestinian electorate respected internationally? Moreover, there was the important question of which Israel Hamas was being told to recognise: the one created with the United Nations' tacit blessing in the 1940s, or the one that is actively expropriating Palestinian land in East Jerusalem and the West Bank?

A CRUEL EMBARGO

Predictably, Hamas did not accept the quartet's conditions and it was punished as a result. Of course, it was not just Hamas representatives who bore the brunt of the sanctions imposed on them, but the ordinary people of Palestine. This was especially so with regard to the reaction of the European Union.

The European Union is the world's largest donor of aid to the

Palestinian Authority. In the next chapter, I will discuss how the European Union is effectively footing the bill for the occupation. Although I believe that the basis on which aid is given needs to be rethought, the nakedly political way in which the European Union suspended aid to the authority during 2006 cannot be accepted. As the courageous Israeli journalist Gideon Levy has observed, this was the first case in which a land under occupation was boycotted, instead of the occupying power.[91]

The effect of the international boycott of Hamas was that the Palestinian Authority's annual budget plummeted from $1.5 billion before the election to less than $500 million for 2007. Much of the resulting financial hardship was caused by Israel's refusal to transfer some $700 million in customs and tax revenues that it had collected on behalf of the Palestinians to the Authority. Yet anti-poverty organisations have also apportioned some of the blame for the humanitarian crisis which ensued to the EU aid embargo.

A survey by Oxfam published in June 2007 found that the number of Palestinians living on less than 50 cents a day doubled to over 1 million. Out of 2,500 households queried, one out of every 15 families had run up a debt exceeding $25,000 – nearly three times the annual salary of a teacher. Some 68 per cent of families in Gaza and 53 per cent in the West Bank reported that their debts – typically for water, electricity and food – had risen in the preceding year.

During the summer of 2006, the European Union took some steps to try to avert a humanitarian catastrophe by setting up a temporary international mechanism (TIM), designed to allow aid be delivered in a way that bypassed a Hamas-led Palestinian Authority. Yet immense damage had already been done because of the suspension of aid. In the case of 160,000 public sector employees, wages were paid either late or not at all.[92] Examining the effects of the aid embargo, the UN Conference on Trade and Development reported in August 2007 that 46 per cent of public sector employees did not have enough to meet their basic needs.[93]

The EU embargo on direct aid to the Palestinian Authority lasted for 15 months. Eventually, it was eased through the signature of a 'technical assistance' agreement with Salam Fayyad, then the Palestinian finance minister, in June 2007.[94] Within a week of that deal being formalised, Mahmoud Abbas would declare a state of emergency and sack Ismail Haniyeh of Hamas from his position as prime minister, replacing him with Fayyad. In doing so, Abbas appears to have strayed beyond his powers as president. Under the

Basic Law – the closest thing that the Palestinians have to a constitution – the president can remove a prime minister but cannot appoint a successor that does not represent a party commanding majority support. Nor does this law contain any provision allowing Abbas to establish an 'emergency government' shorn of Hamas, the party that had won the 'model' election of the previous year (to recall the verdict of an EU poll monitor).[95]

Fayyad enjoyed little popular support among his people. His party, the Third Way, held a mere two seats out of 132 in the legislative council. For the West, however, his ideological commitment to neoliberal economics conferred on him far greater importance than his poor electoral showing should have allowed. Holding a doctorate from the University of Texas, Fayyad had worked for the World Bank in Washington from 1987 to 1995 before returning home as the representative of the International Monetary Fund in Jerusalem. Since being appointed as finance minister by Yasser Arafat in 2001, he won plaudits internationally for helping reform an authority that had become synonymous with corruption. Tony Blair has become something of a Fayyad groupie, describing the unelected premier as 'absolutely first-class – professional, courageous, intelligent'.[96]

The huge question marks over the legitimacy of the emergency government notwithstanding, the European Union swiftly endorsed its establishment. In a statement reeking of contradictions, EU foreign ministers called for Palestinian 'national unity', while implicitly welcoming the dismissal of a government formed with that goal in mind. The ministers also assured Abbas of their 'full support' for his new administration and urged all parties to 'abide by his decisions'.[97]

The EU ministers were taking their cue from the United States and Israel. Condoleezza Rice had responded to Abbas's move by promising to resume direct contacts with the Palestinian Authority, while claiming that the people of Gaza were 'at the mercy of terrorist organisations' now that Hamas had taken control of the Strip. And Tzipi Livni, who had travelled to Luxembourg for discussions with her EU counterparts, indicated that Abbas was helping Israel pursue a strategy 'to make a clear distinction between the moderates and the extremists'.[98]

HEMMING IN HAMAS

These platitudes ignored how the West had wasted an opportunity to help steer Hamas away from violence. By refusing to respect the democratic mandate given to Hamas, the party was being offered no incentive to cease its attacks on Israel and to seek the attainment of its political goals by peaceful means. Chris Patten, the former European commissioner, has correctly argued that by pushing Hamas into a corner, the United States did exactly the opposite of what it had exhorted Britain to do with Sinn Féin in the context of the Irish peace process (namely to engage it in a dialogue that would eventually defuse a centuries-old conflict).[99]

Behind closed doors, some EU governments have expressed misgivings about the isolation of Hamas. In spite of Sarkozy's inveterate defence of Israeli aggression, France has admitted having secret contacts with the organisation; Yves Aubin de la Messuzière, a former ambassador to Iraq, held talks with two senior Hamas figures, Ismail Haniyeh and Mahmoud Zahar, during 2008, reportedly as part of efforts to better understand Hamas' policies.[100] Ireland, too, believes it is unwise to snub Hamas completely.[101] But neither of these countries has taken firm action to have Hamas removed from the terrorist list so that formal dealings with it can commence. As a senior EU official told me, the notion that Hamas must be regarded as terrorists has become 'something almost religious' for EU governments. 'We have locked ourselves into an idealistic situation that if principles are not adhered to the letter, then we can't engage [with Hamas],' the official added.

Endlessly dismissing Hamas as terrorist or extremist betrays a fickle grasp of the movement's history. When it was set up in the 1987, Hamas concentrated on its political and social welfare activities as the Gaza and West Bank branch of the Muslim Brotherhood in Egypt and Jordan. It is frequently – and conveniently – forgotten that Israel welcomed its inception, viewing it as a tool for undermining the PLO. It was not until 1993 that Hamas resorted to suicide bombings (a tactic it renounced in 2006), and it is clear that these attacks – with their undeniably appalling consequences – were a direct response to the growing brutality of the occupation. Back in the mid-1990s, Edward Said emphasised that the violence employed by Hamas and the comparable methods of Islamic Jihad must be understood as an expression of anguish and his words remain pertinent today:

> Their suicide missions, bomb-throwing and provocative slogans are acts of defiance principally, refusals to accept the crippling conditions of Israeli occupation and Palestinian collaboration. No matter how much secular people like myself lament their methods

> and their vision (such as it is), there is no doubting the truth that for many Palestinians these people express a furious protest against the humiliations, demeanments and denials imposed on all Palestinians as a people.[102]

Although it is guided by interpretations of the Koran with which many secular Muslims would take issue, there are no firm grounds to believe that Hamas wants to become embroiled in a clash of civilisations until the bitter end. Alistair Crooke, a specialist on Islamist politics and an erstwhile Middle East adviser to Javier Solana, has contended convincingly that Hamas is in many respects a moderate organisation.

> If you talk with any Hamas leader, they say 'Look, I don't get messages from God. I don't get instructions about who should be the Hamas candidate. We believe the Koran sets out principles by which a human being should live and we try to find a practical way in which to conduct our policies based on these principles.' That's not dogmatism. That's not irrationalism. It's not in any sense extremism.[103]

When I visited Gaza in 2009, I interviewed Sayed Abu Musameh, one of Hamas's founding members, in what remains of the Palestinian Legislative Council building. Though his adversaries may depict Musameh and his ilk as the epitome of evil, I found him to be a hospitable and thoughtful man. After I was introduced by his aide as 'Mr David from Ireland, the country of Mr Gerry Adams' (the Sinn Féin leader had visited Gaza a few weeks earlier), Musameh signalled his wish to visit Belfast to learn how the peace process there had reached fruition. He insisted that while he regarded Zionism as a racist ideology, he had nothing against ordinary Israelis or Jews, describing claims that Hamas is driven by a fanatical anti-Semitism as a 'big lie'. He stressed, too, that Hamas's rocket attacks on Sderot and Ashkelon were designed 'not to destroy Israel or to destroy Israeli people' but to 'make them notice our siege'. And to my surprise he expressed sympathy for pacifism: 'I hate all weapons. I dream of seeing every weapon from the atomic bomb to small guns banned everywhere.'[104]

As a general rule, I believe that journalists should be sceptical whenever they hear politicians making a statement of principle. That said, I am prepared to accept that Musameh reflects the views of many Hamas members who genuinely yearn for peace with Israel.

This is a view based not on how he can charm foreigners by saying the 'right' things for them (in decent English) but on how Hamas has offered a series of olive branches to Israel over the last few years. Tragically, all of these have been spurned by Israel in a way that perpetuates the conflict and the underlying injustice that fuels it.

COMFORT FOR THE QUISLINGS

Claims by Western leaders that they prefer Fayyad over a prime minister from Hamas because he is a moderate amount to little more than hypocritical cant. History is littered with examples of where the United States has supported politicians far more extreme than Hamas when doing so has been considered advantageous to its interests; it even backed Osama bin Laden when he fought the Soviet invasion of Afghanistan in the 1980s. A more reliable explanation for why Fayyad is a darling of imperialists can be found in a 59-page document titled *Building a Palestinian State* which he presented to a donors' conference for Palestine held in Paris in December 2007. It recommended a number of measures to lure multinational companies to Palestine, while simultaneously worsening the lot of its impoverished population. Public sector salaries would be frozen, the number of civil servants cut and the private sector would be turned into the principal engine of economic growth, it said.[105] Western governments were so impressed with this programme that they undertook to provide $7.7 billion in assistance, nearly $2 billion more than the Palestinian Authority had requested. The programme's attractiveness for them stems primarily from how it illustrated that Fayyad remained devoted to the free market fundamentalism to which he had been exposed in the World Bank and IMF. Indeed, some analysts have remarked on how his plan was almost identical to the 'structural adjustment programmes' that these institutions foisted on many African countries in the 1980s and 1990s, often exacerbating poverty by, for example, slashing expenditure on basic services like health and education.[106]

There was to be one sector that would be shielded from the machete that Fayyad was wielding over the Palestinian budget: security. Between 2008 and 2010, he proposed allocating $228 million to 'reform and transformation' of the security services, compared with $135 million for access to education and just $20 million on women's empowerment. The result of this excessive concentration on security is not that Palestinians are being made to feel safer; it is that Fayyad and Abbas have happily assumed the status of quislings by carrying out Israel's dirty work in the areas under their command. With the financial support of the European Union and United States, the Fatah-dominated authorities in the West Bank have been responsible for hundreds of arbitrary arrests of political opponents, the torture of detainees and the crackdown on freedom of expression (including the closure of media outlets).[107]

True, Hamas has perpetrated the same kind of abuses in Gaza and nothing in this book should be interpreted as suggesting that I favour one party over another. Rather, my objective is to highlight how the money of European taxpayers is being used to help drive a wedge between Palestinians in a way that provides a distraction from their common foe, the Israeli occupation. In colonial times, the European powers asserted their might through a variety of divide and rule strategies. The present-day ruling elites in Europe and the United States are helping Israel to hone such a strategy in Palestine.

3

AIDING THE OCCUPATION

With eyes that look like they are forced into remaining open, Javier Solana exudes an air of fatigue. This is not surprising; a hefty proportion of his decade as the EU foreign policy chief was spent criss-crossing time-zones as he pretended that he was addressing the root causes of the world's latest crisis. His frequent trips to the Middle East have helped him develop friendships that would appear unusual for an Iberian socialist, none more so than the bonds he forged with Ariel Sharon.

As Sharon saw the world through a prism of prejudice and facile equations, he was initially frosty towards Solana. Because Solana was Spanish, it automatically followed that he had to be pro-Arab, the military-turned-political leader reckoned. Through continuous contact, though, the dynamic of the relationship improved. A well-placed diplomat explained:

> Just before he went into a coma [in January 2006], Sharon told Solana, 'I made a mistake about you. I always tried to keep out the Europeans but I should have let you in.' Sharon said that he could see the EU as bringing something important to Israel.

One factor that may explain the success of the courtship was that Solana was prepared to treat many Israeli myths as statements of fact. When Sharon pushed ahead with his plan to withdraw Israeli settlers from Gaza, Solana inferred that he was making a significant gesture towards peace. Soon, it would become clear that the 'unilateral disengagement' (which also involved dismantling four settlements in the West Bank) was no more than a cynical smoke-screen; Kadima, the party that Sharon founded after he split from Likud, was to elaborate on the policy of 'convergence' (*hitkansut*, in Hebrew) which the Gaza 'withdrawal' effectively set in motion. This would involve abandoning settlements that were not considered of major strategic importance, while consolidating a hold on the large-scale developments such as Ma'ale Adumim, Ariel and Gush Etzion in the West Bank, as well as stepping up the dispossession of Palestinians in East Jerusalem.[1]

The other enormous myth peddled by apologists for Israel is that 'disengagement' was a step on the road to peace. Dov Weisglass, a senior advisor to Ariel Sharon, dispelled that myth by acknowledging that the Gaza manoeuvre was a charade. Its purpose was to stave off a potential peace accord by securing US recognition that major settlements in the West Bank would remain in place forever and that other issues would be placed on the back burner. In 2004 – when the plan was still being fine-tuned, Weisglass said: 'The disengagement is actually formaldehyde. It supplies the amount of formaldehyde that's necessary so that there will not be a political process with the Palestinians.'[2]

Solana is no fool; he had access to plenty of analysts who could have appraised him of Sharon's real agenda. Still, he chose to accept Sharon's bona fides at face value and to praise the prime minister for facing down the opponents of the plan within Israel. He said:

> Sharon kept his word and did so in an intelligent and professional manner. The IDF acted professionally, by the book and reduced the potential damage. There was a government decision here, approved by the parliament, and that is how a democratic country behaves. The law was implemented and that should be emphasised, considering the difficulty involved in the operation.[3]

A few months later Solana again appeared elated when the European Union was given a role in supervising the border between Gaza and Egypt, reportedly as a result of the 'disengagement'. In November 2005, Solana announced that the European Union would be assembling a team of 50–70 personnel (comprised of police, soldiers and others with experience of border patrols) to supervise an agreement to allow Palestinians to cross into Egypt from the neighbouring Gazan city of Rafah. 'This is the first time that a border is opened and given to the Palestinians themselves to control with the aid of a third party,' he said.[4]

The accord was never as generous as Solana insinuated. Israel was not surrendering control of the border crossing to the Palestinians; the Israeli security forces would be intimately involved in monitoring who was travelling in and out of Egypt. From an office in Kerem Shalom (another border post a few kilometres south, known to Palestinians by its Arabic name Karim Abu Salam), the

Israelis would be able to undertake video surveillance of Rafah and be supplied with the names of travellers.

In promotional material, Solana and other EU officials have continued to present the border assistance mission (BAM, to give it their preferred acronym) as a diplomatic triumph. For example, a 'factsheet' dated December 2007[5] says that some 440,000 people crossed over it in the 18 months that the EU team was present at the terminal, What the brochures don't divulge is that the mission has been at the total mercy of Israel, to the point that the European Union has become a 'subcontractor for the occupation', in the words of Eoin Murray, a Middle East specialist with the Irish anti-poverty group Trócaire.[6] The aforementioned 'factsheet' (the inverted commas are necessary, I believe) states that the crossing has been closed since Hamas captured an Israeli soldier Gilad Shalit in June 2006. Notwithstanding that, the EU team has maintained its 'full operational capacity' and can attend to other important business such as training Palestinian officials, it says.

The full picture is a little more complex. The subordination of the mission to Israel was evident from its inception. Each morning the EU personnel had to report to the Israeli security forces at Kerem Shalom; it was Israel, therefore, that decided whether the EU appointees could do their daily work. Following Shalit's capture, the Israelis decided to close the border frequently. Because this had profound consequences on the economic well-being of Gazans, the entire population of the Strip was made to suffer for the capture of one man. Such collective punishment is illegal under the 1949 Geneva Convention and, indeed, Solana has berated Israel on occasions for resorting to such tactics.[7]

Under these circumstances, the only correct thing for the European Union to do would be to pull out of the agreement setting up the mission. Instead, it has willingly accepted the Israeli line that the crossing must be closed, basing its staff in a seaside resort in Ashkelon in the vain hope that they might one day have something useful to do. The idea that these people are far from idle was scotched by Nigel Milverton, a former officer in the British army who has been helping to manage the mission. 'We've been sitting here doing nothing,' he told the *Jerusalem Post*.[8]

A joint report by Gisha, an Israeli organisation campaigning on freedom of movement issues, and Physicians for Human Rights, has illustrated how Israel has exploited the agreement relating to Rafah in order to continue its stranglehold over Palestinian life. This might seem like a deeply ironic conclusion, given that Ariel Sharon's government expended great energy trying to convince the world that it had relinquished control of Gaza. Yet the two organisations have detailed exhaustively how the impression that Palestinians were being put in charge of deciding who should leave and enter Gaza turned out to be false. According to their report, the agreement 'signalled the end of Israel's military presence at Rafah crossing but not the end of its substantial control over the crossing'.

Loopholes in the agreement meant that while any Palestinian was theoretically allowed to travel to and from Gaza, it was Israel that decided if they could do so. This was because each traveller had to be included on the population register for the West Bank and Gaza. Since 1967, Israel has taken responsibility for that register and any updates to it can only occur with Israeli approval. Israel has often been mean-spirited when deciding if people should be registered. After a new *intifada* began in 2000, Israel ceased registering the names of Palestinians living abroad (usually the offspring of refugees uprooted by Israel in the past) who married residents of the occupied territories and then moved there. Around 10,000 Palestinians – mostly women – are estimated to have remained in Gaza without being registered as a result of that decision. Because they were not eligible to acquire identification cards, they were unable to benefit from the agreement to open Rafah.

The closure of Rafah has affected almost every aspect of life for Gaza's inhabitants. Workers who used to travel to the Gulf states for employment can no longer do so; businesspeople have been forced to cease trading with Egypt; young people have been denied the possibility of studying in the West Bank (where most Palestinian universities are located) or further afield; and families have been kept apart because Gazans cannot see their relatives outside the Strip. The cruelty of this situation is more acute again in the case of people suffering from diseases. Obtaining spare parts for specialised medical equipment has become extremely difficult and sometimes impossible, with the result that machines that are essential for modern hospitals to function can go unrepaired if they are not working properly. In June 2008, Physicians for Human Rights discovered that 13 of the 72 dialysis machines in Gaza were out of order, hampering the service available to people diagnosed with kidney complaints. And while there have been some instances where Rafah has been opened to ensure that patients received treatment in Egyptian hospitals, its general closure has severely curtailed access to medical help, cutting many lives short. Estimating precisely how many deaths can be attributed to the closure is fraught; but the

Palestinian ministry of health has calculated that 265 people died between June 2007 and December 2008 as a result of the suffocation of Gaza, including the sealing-off of border crossings.[9]

Data gathered by the World Health Organisation, meanwhile, suggests that the rate at which patients were given permission to leave Gaza for treatment fell from 89 per cent to an unprecedented low of 64 per cent during the course of 2007. And with the arbitrary nature in which restrictions on access to Gaza have been implemented, being in possession of a permit was no guarantee that one could exit the Strip for treatment; human rights workers in Gaza have noted cases where people who had been cleared for travel were stopped at border crossings and not allowed to venture any further.[10]

Israel has signalled that the closure of Rafah and the restrictions on the transport of goods through Karni (the cargo terminal on the Israeli–Gaza frontier) are part of an experiment to observe how a primarily urban population responds to the incremental destruction of its capacity to live 'normally' (if that word can be used in the context of a brutal occupation). Dov Weisglass explained this policy concisely in 2006: 'The idea is to put the Palestinians on a diet but not to make them die of hunger.'[11] The petty-mindedness of these measures, which have helped malnutrition levels soar, were exposed in early 2009, when Israel decided that pasta could not be brought into Gaza, without issuing anything that could reasonably be called an explanation.[12] To ensure that they have basic supplies of food and household items that most of us take for granted, ordinary Gazans have had literally to develop an underground trade, relying on a network of tunnels in Gaza. The tunnels, which can take eight weeks to dig, are unsafe from several perspectives. About 40 tunnellers died in 2008 from cave-ins, while Gazans complain that the goods carried through them regularly exceed their sell-by dates.[13]

Hind Abu Shaban, a pharmacist in Gaza City, produced a lengthy hand-written list for me of medicines and medical supplies she could not obtain because of the blockade. These included Flucan, an antibiotic used to fight fungal infections in people with weak immune systems (such as those ravaged by cancer), saline solutions (for cleaning wounds), ear drops and treatments for head lice. The latter complaint had become prevalent, she said, as people huddled together in each other's homes at the time of the war.

It is true that the European Union has called on Israel to allow Gazans access to any medical treatment they require. But that is not enough. Article 1 of the Fourth Geneva Convention stipulates that all signatories must do what they can to ensure that it is respected in all circumstances. International humanitarian law analysts consider this as an unambiguous obligation on each party to ensure that the convention is upheld both by that party directly and by others.[14] By agreeing to keep the border assistance mission on standby in a situation where Israel is subjecting Gazans to collective punishment – and by tacitly accepting that the aggressor (Israel) sets at least some of the rules under which the mission will operate – the European Union would appear to be acquiescent in a massive injustice. Unless it can rectify the situation (and all the indications are that it has failed to do so), the mission should be terminated.

SPEEDING AT NIGHT WITHOUT HEADLIGHTS

The question of how much aid the European Union should give to Palestine and how that aid should be administered is a vexed one. Because Western powers, including several now belonging to the European Union, crafted the UN plan to divide Palestine into separate Arab and Jewish states in the 1940s, they have a clear historic responsibility to the people affected by subsequent events. And with poverty and unemployment widespread, there would seem to be a profound moral duty on wealthier countries to provide Palestinians with some degree of sustenance. The duty seems pronounced in the case of Gaza, where a merciless blockade has made 80 per cent of the population dependant on external help, an increase of 17 per cent from 2006.[15] Cutting off that lifeline would prove fatal to many and doing so should not even be contemplated.

That said, the European Union has obligations to international law and its own taxpayers, too. As I belong to the latter category, I feel that we have a right to know how our money can and does assist the Israel occupation. My feelings, incidentally, are not based on esoteric considerations; the principle that freedom of information is a basic human right was recognised by the UN General Assembly at its very first session in 1946. A resolution passed then declared this right as 'the touchstone to all the freedoms to which the United Nations is consecrated'.[16]

David Shearer, head of the UN Office for the Coordination of Humanitarian Affairs (OCHA) from 2003 to 2007, has highlighted how the Palestinians have proportionately received more foreign aid than any other people on earth since the Second World War.

After the *intifada* broke out in September 2000, donor governments doubled their aid levels to more than US$1 billion per year, which breaks down at about $300 for each person in the occupied territories. The way that this high level of giving has been sustained is equally noteworthy. Even as levels of aid to other parts of the world afflicted by conflict – like Kosovo and Afghanistan – have dropped, the amounts allocated to Palestine have remained high.

While this would appear to reflect the importance that Western governments attach to the need for stability in the Middle East, it does not automatically follow that they have the best interests of ordinary Palestinians at heart. In a paper he co-authored with the lawyer Anuschka Meyer, Shearer wrote:

> Contrary to most perceptions, aid is not necessarily positive or benign. Pouring an immense amount of aid into a conflict without either the structure of a peace agreement or a solid analysis of its impact is comparable to speeding along a road at night without headlights.[17]

Arguably the most important point in relation to the whole question of aid is that under international law it is the occupying power that is responsible for meeting basic needs in Gaza and the West Bank, and not foreign governments. The 1907 Hague Regulations set out broad principles relating to land that has been occupied by force; they confer on the occupying power an obligation to take care of the welfare of the population under its yoke. Article 43 of those regulations says that a power which has seized a certain territory 'shall take all the measures in his power to restore and ensure, as far as possible, public order and safety'.[18]

This principle was fleshed out further by the Fourth Geneva Convention, which stipulated that the occupying power is responsible for making sure that the population under its control have adequate supplies of food and medicine, as well as that the education needs of their children and their access to essential services are provided for. The convention requires that Israel must allow UN agencies or impartial organisations like the Red Cross to help the local population in cases where they do not have sufficient supplies. But the relevant provisions (Articles 59 and 60) stress that such agencies cannot relieve the occupying power of its obligations or operate in lieu of the occupying power. It was for that reason that the Red Cross ended a food distribution programme in the West Bank during 2003, citing concerns that if it kept an emergency aid scheme going indefinitely, it would be assuming responsibility for tasks that Israel was legally required to perform.[19]

Since 1993, the year when Yitzhak Rabin and Yasser Arafat supposedly ushered in a new era of peace with a handshake on the White House Lawn, the European Union has been the largest aid donor to the Palestinians. The trend whereby the financial backing for implementing the so-called Oslo Accords would come from Europe was established at a Washington conference that December. Of the $2.4 billion pledged on that occasion for supporting the 'peace process', 38 per cent of that sum was committed by the European Union.[20] The role of the European Union as paymaster is often seen as part of a division of labour tacitly agreed with the United States. Under it, the United States drives the political agenda in the Middle East forward (or backwards, depending on one's perspective), while Europe foots the bill, particularly for any damage caused by Israel. Jacques Chirac is among the political figures to have vented his frustration with this arrangement; after the United States backed the Israeli bombardment of Lebanon (codenamed Operation Grapes of Wrath) in 1996, he said: 'The United States cannot expect to call all the shots and then expect Europe to pay.'[21]

After a few years of this arrangement, a concerted effort was made by EU diplomats to break out of this mould. Perhaps the most tangible manifestation of their desire to do so came in 1996 with the appointment of Miguel Angel Moratinos, formerly Spain's ambassador to Israel, as the EU 'special representative' for the Middle East 'peace process'.

The evolution of a more cohesive foreign policy for the European Union might have increased its collective assertiveness. It is rare nowadays to hear a serious discussion about the Middle East, without some allusion to the latest statement by a senior EU figure. Paradoxically, the European Union has not properly used the leverage granted to it by virtue of its status as the Palestinians' main donor in order to strive for changes in Israeli behaviour.

OSLO: DOOMED FROM THE START

Nine years after the Rabin–Arafat handshake, Chris Patten lamented that 'the promise of Oslo has not been delivered'. The blame for this failure, he said, lay on both sides. Israel had rapidly expanded its settlements in the occupied territories and refused to withdraw from the West Bank, while 'extremist forces' on the Palestinian side had resorted to violence 'with the clear aim of sabotaging any Israeli–Palestinian peace deal'.[22]

What Patten didn't say – and what few EU representatives will acknowledge, at least publicly – is that the Oslo Accords were doomed from the start. The rise in popularity of Hamas, which became an increasingly trenchant critic of Oslo, cannot be attributed to an aversion to peace. Rather, it signified a deep-rooted unease among Palestinians at the flaws of the Oslo process. These flaws were summarised neatly by Alastair Crooke in his book *Resistance*:

> What Hamas is doing – in dramatic fashion – is to put a finger on a key failure of the Israeli-Palestinian political process since the Oslo accords were signed in 1993 – which is the singular omission of any clear outline of Palestinian rights.[23]

Far from loosening Israel's stranglehold of the Palestinians, Oslo reinforced it in a number of critical respects. Israel kept control of points of exit from and entry to the occupied territories, as well as of water resources and large settlement blocs in the West Bank. And whereas it undertook to withdraw its army from some parts of the West Bank (though with the possibility that soldiers could return at any point), 75 per cent of its troops were allowed to remain, while 62 new military bases were provided for.[24] Israel could also halt the development of an independent Palestinian economy by, among other things, setting up Israeli banks in the occupied territories without approval from the Palestinian Authority or deciding on what tariffs should be levied on imports.[25]

In what was probably Arafat's greatest disservice to his people, the Oslo Accords were negotiated without the Palestinian side having any legal advice. Not surprisingly, then, Arafat's team was easily outmanoeuvred by the Israelis, who persuaded it to accept the designation of different areas of responsibility in the West Bank. Crucially, such cities as Ramallah, Bethlehem, Jericho, Nablus and Qalqilya were placed in Area A, which theoretically meant that the Palestinian Authority could exercise full control over them. Though this area incorporated the principal centres of population, it only accounted for 3 per cent of the West Bank's land. By far the biggest chunk of the West Bank – Area C, or 73 per cent of the land – remained under Israel's control.

It is true that the composition of these areas was modified in 2000, so that Area A covered 17.2 per cent of land, Area B (where the Palestinian Authority took charge of public order but Israel was still responsible for overall security) 23.8 per cent and Area C 59 per cent. But as the Israeli scholar Neve Gordon has highlighted, Area A was heavily partitioned – to travel from Jenin to Bethlehem, Palestinians would have to navigate their way through an infuriating network of Israeli roadblocks. No such divisions applied to Area C. 'The areas in which Palestinians had full control were like an archipelago, while the areas controlled by Israel were strategic corridors that interrupted the territorial contiguity of the West Bank,' Gordon added.[26]

Raja Shehadeh, founder of the Ramallah-based human rights organisation Al Haq, has contended that Oslo gave a 'great boost' to the Israeli settler movement. Amid the poignant paeans to his native land in his book *Palestinian Walks* (winner of the 2008 Orwell Prize), he unravels the conventional 'wisdom' that Oslo was a genuine bid for peace. Many years earlier, Israel had hatched a plan to settle 80,000 Jews in the central region of the West Bank by 1986, yet, despite offering handsome economic inducements, only 6,000 had installed themselves by the target date. The reluctance of Israelis to move to the West Bank was eroded after Oslo because the Israeli government could convince them that the Palestinian Authority had agreed to designate Area C for Israeli settlements. As a result, settlers now felt 'safe enough to invest in the settlements and move their families with them,' according to Shehadeh.[27]

Overall, the number of settlers in the occupied territories rose from 240,000 in 1993 to 380,000 in 2000. The same period saw the confiscation of 35,000 acres of Palestinian land and the building of about 20,000 new housing units for settlers, with the pace of such construction accelerated considerably in the late 1990s, at the time when talks ostensibly aimed at thrashing out a final peace deal were under way.[28] In order to ensure that the settlements were interlinked, Israel developed a series of roads between them. Their construction, too, involved the theft of Palestinian farmland on a staggering scale.[29]

Ma'aleh Adumim, one of the biggest Israeli settlements in the West Bank, illustrates how fully Israel exploited the opportunities presented by Oslo. Though originally set up in the 1970s, it was to expand over this period, with the result that its population has grown from 15,000 in the early 1990s to 35,000 today (and, by some projections, this could double again in the not too distant future).

Little expense has been spared in enticing Israelis to move there. Even as the sweltering heat of a late April afternoon left me parched, the flowers on the roundabouts leading into this mini-California were in full bloom, a testament to how per capita the settlers guzzle more than five times as much water as the average Palestinian and twice as much as someone living inside Israel's internationally recognised boundaries. Thanks to government subsidies, the settlers are able to buy twice as big an apartment as their budgets would allow them elsewhere. Many are Jewish migrants from the United States, Ethiopia or France, who have become Israeli citizens. 'The people here are economic settlers and the government wants them here permanently,' Angela Godfrey Goldstein, a campaigner with the Israeli Committee Against House Demolitions, told me during a tour of the settlement. Pausing at a picnic site to take in a panoramic view of the surrounding Biblical landscape, she pointed downwards: 'We call that an apartheid road. No West Bankers can go on it; they know they will not get through the checkpoint.'

The late Tanya Reinhart, a linguistic professor at Tel Aviv University, drew a parallel between the Oslo Accords and a linchpin of institutionalised racism in South Africa. Under a 1959 law promoting 'self-government' of the black majority, a number of Bantustans were set up. The rhetoric about granting autonomy to blacks notwithstanding, the white government in Pretoria kept a tight grip on all matters relating to mining and other forms of resource exploitation, security and foreign policy.[30]

Similarly, Oslo has been followed by concrete steps to prevent Palestinians from developing a viable economic infrastructure – independent of Israel – in the West Bank and Gaza. For many years, Palestinians were pushed into a situation where they depended on low-paid work in Israel for subsistence. That possibility has generally dried up – to a drastic extent in the case of the blockade of Gaza, where workers are denied access to Israel. Meanwhile, industrial estates, usually with lax environmental standards, have sprung up near Israeli settlements. Involved in such activities as meat packing, chemical production, marble cutting and furniture manufacture, these plants are managed almost exclusively by Israelis.

By agreeing to bankroll the Palestinian Authority at the 1993 donors conference, EU representatives may have thought that they were laying the foundations of a Palestinian state. In reality, they were helping to institutionalise a system that would further the dispossession of the Palestinian people and postpone indefinitely the prospect of them being granted nationhood.

THE PA'S LIFE-SUPPORT MACHINE

Another consequence of the Oslo process is that it stymied the realisation of plans to help the emergence of an independent Palestinian economy. Whereas the European Union had hoped in the early 1990s to finance economic development projects, the situation evolved in such a way that it now primarily pays to keep the Palestinian Authority on a life-support machine. It is commonly believed that this transition from aid with a long-term objective to that of an emergency nature occurred after the *intifada* broke out in 2000. In fact, it started much earlier. The roadblocks and bureaucratic restrictions imposed by Israel in the 1990s hampered the delivery of aid and turned the execution of long-term development plans into a logistical nightmare.[31]

The World Bank has estimated that in 2000, the amount of development aid given to the Palestinian Authority was seven times greater than the amount of emergency assistance. Two years later, emergency exceeded development aid by a ratio of five to one.[32] But Anne LeMore, a researcher on the politics of aid to the Palestinians, has shown how the shift to relief assistance began in the 1990s. Between 1994 and 1996 nearly half of all external aid (more than $600 million) went to short-term aid, primarily because of an economic crisis that pushed poverty and unemployment levels upwards. The lack of focus on longer-term development hurt Palestinians badly; in 1999 their per capita spending levels were at the lowest they had been (in real terms) at any time since 1980.[33]

Sara Roy, a Harvard academic who coined the term 'de-development' to describe the decline of the Palestinian economy, has argued that the absence of any meaningful emphasis on human rights in the Oslo accords is of key relevance here. The underlying assumption throughout the process was that if Oslo failed, the occupation would remain intact. No alternative for facilitating a solution that respected international law was envisaged. The accords themselves, she has explained, make no reference to Israel being an occupying power and having responsibilities under international law as an occupying power:

> While blame for Oslo's failure can be assigned to many parties, including the Palestinian Authority, the principal factor lay in Israel's ongoing and deepened occupation of Palestinian land and resources. Hence, the unwillingness of the donor community, including the European Union, to challenge Israeli measures

> proved particularly damaging. There were certain factors informing donor actions but one was particularly important: a consensus among donors that Israel was not pressured in any public or even private way.

Roy attributes this aversion to confrontation with Israel to a fear that Israel would walk away from the peace process if it felt that it was being harried:

> The logic of international law was abandoned in the interest of maintaining a failed political process. In fact, as conditions worsened in the occupied territories because of increasing economic restrictions and a tightened closure regime, donors were forced – as early as the mid-1990s – to redirect their funding from donor to emergency relief, something they were loath to do. Again, this was done to keep the peace process alive.[34]

The illusion that Israel had benign intentions with regard to the Palestinian economy in the 1990s was shattered in a 2006 report by the United Nations Conference on Trade and Development:

> The Palestinian territory has effectively remained since 1967, and even since 1994, under the economic and political control of an occupying power. The latter has in turn hardly recognised any responsibility for the growth and development of the Palestinian economy, notwithstanding the perceived common interests of economic cooperation in the 1994-2000 period. The development potential of the Palestinian economy has therefore depended on the trade regime, fiscal and monetary policies and labour mobility criteria, which the occupying power can regulate in the light of its own sovereign interests.[35]

AID BENEFITS THE OPPRESSOR

One of the more perverse side-effects of EU aid to the Palestinians is that it has brought many benefits to the Israeli oppressor. The United Nations has estimated that 45 per cent of all foreign aid to the Palestinians finds its way back into the Israeli economy. To administer the aid, legions of diplomats and consultants on good salaries and with high disposable incomes are either permanently stationed in Israel or make regular trips there. Israeli industries are able to flourish free from any Palestinian competition. And Israeli companies are paid for providing goods and services to donors. Unlike their Palestinian counterparts, Israeli truckers are unimpeded from driving across checkpoints to deliver aid. Other Israeli firms sell food to international donors, who find it more economical to buy from Israelis than to pay customs on food from neighbouring countries (even when the food there is cheaper).[36]

A particularly troubling example of how the European Union has been abetting Israeli crimes relates to its funding of fuel supplies to Gaza. In 2008, the Israeli energy company Dor Alon was given nearly €97 million by the European Commission to supply industrial diesel for energy generation in Gaza. Dor Alon has actively facilitated the Israeli policy of subjecting the entire population of Gaza to power cuts as a form of collective punishment, officially in response to Hamas' rocket attacks. Not only did Dor Alon ration the amount of fuel it delivered in 2008 – in November that year, Israel refused to allow the fuel into Gaza for an entire two weeks – it adjusted the bill it sent to the EU executive accordingly.[37] Despite these adjustments and the knowledge that Dor Alon was carrying out the instructions of an occupying power and that it also runs a network of petrol stations and convenience stores in the illegal settlements of the West Bank, the Commission kept on paying the bills. Charles Shamas from the Mattin Group, an organisation in Ramallah that monitors EU–Israel relations, summed up how the European Union had become an accomplice to a blockade that it nominally opposed:

> The European Union has to give aid lawfully. That means a good faith effort not to conform to the wrongful acts of others. In this case, the EU is giving effect to wrongful measures by Israel. You can't really credibly call on Israel to correct its behaviour if you are adjusting what you do to fit into that behaviour.[38]

THE COURAGE DEFICIT

Privately, EU officials acknowledge that the aid policies they are implementing have become hugely problematic. 'Are we subsidising activities that should fall on Israel as a consequence of its responsibility as an occupying power?' a well-placed Brussels source said to me. 'The answer is unquestionably "yes".' Higher up the EU hierarchy, though, commissioners and government ministers have not taken steps to rectify the situation. Doing so would mean confronting the Israeli occupation with a little more than pious declarations. That would require a modicum of courage, a quality generally found wanting in senior EU figures.

The courage deficit is especially vast with respect to the damage of EU-funded projects by Israel. Between August 2001 and November 2008, Israeli attacks on the occupied territories inflicted damage worth more than €44 million on aid provided by the European Union, according to data collated by the European Commission's office in East Jerusalem. At a minimum, another €11 million worth of damage was caused to EU-financed infrastructure in Gaza when Israel bombed the strip in December 2008 and January 2009.[39]

Doubtlessly such figures err on the side of caution. They also vary widely, depending on which EU official one talks to; Brussels sources cited estimates of €22 million for damage between 2000 and 2008, half the total calculated by their colleagues stationed in Jerusalem. Seven years earlier – in March 2002 – the Commission released figures suggesting Israel had destroyed completely or partly €19 million worth of EU aid since the *intifada* began in 2000.[40] Given the scale of Israeli violence against Palestinians in the interim and the status of the European Union as top donor, it is hard to believe that the actual harm caused in monetary terms over the intervening years isn't greater than the statistics indicate. Officials admit that the figures almost certainly underestimate the scale of the damage because not every EU government is vigilant in monitoring what happens to its aid. 'Some member states were very cooperative and tell us what they have lost,' an official involved in assessing the damage said. 'Others didn't want to know.'

As this is taxpayers' money, it is a no-brainer that everything should be done to pressurise Israel into paying compensation. The EU foreign ministers effectively recognised as much in January 2002, when they issued a statement saying they reserved 'the right to claim reparation in the appropriate fora'. But two months later Chris Patten threw in the towel by complaining that legal action would be 'horrendously complicated' for the European Union to initiate because once aid was delivered to its intended beneficiary (in most cases here, the Palestinian Authority), legal ownership of the aid was transferred to that beneficiary.[41]

The Commission is not a monolithic body and there are diverging views on the feasibility of legal action among its staff. Although the European Union might have no luck in prosecuting Israel for all the damage it has caused, there would appear to be ample scope for pursuing test cases in the hope that an important precedent could be set. A number of cases have been identified by Commission officials where damage had been inflicted by Israel before all the paperwork conferring ownership of the aid on its intended beneficiary had been completed. In one such instance, €64,000 was allocated by the European Union to help the Dutch anti-poverty organisation Oxfam-Novib assist olive farmers in the West Bank. While officials believe they would have a solid basis on which to launch legal proceedings in that case in an international court, they bemoan how they would not be able to win the necessary support for doing so from the higher echelons of the Commission.

Furthermore, there have been isolated examples in the past of Israel agreeing to compensate donors. In 2003, Israel destroyed a warehouse in which the World Food Programme (WFP) was storing aid. Israel agreed to give foodstuffs such as cooking oil back to the WFP, claiming it was a 'humanitarian gesture'. This proves that it is possible to receive compensation from Israel; the fact that there have not been more instances of compensation is almost certainly down to the reluctance of donors to hold Israel to account.

I asked Benita Ferrero-Waldner, the EU external relations commissioner from 2004 to 2009, why she had never sought compensation from Israel. Her reply amounted to a piece of abject capitulation to Israeli aggression:

> The question of compensation is legally a very complex one. Besides, the records show that the majority of damage was to projects financed by the EU member states, in which case it is up to the member states to decide what legal action to take. The European Commission has sought, and will continue to seek, explanations from the Israeli authorities whenever there are Commission-funded projects which have been destroyed or damaged. But to halt the cycle of destruction and reconstruction, we need progress towards the creation of the future Palestinian state and thus peace in the Middle East.

Mustafa Barghouti, a well-known Palestinian politician, does not bear the same responsibility towards European taxpayers that Ferrero-Waldner did during her time in Brussels. Nonetheless, he defended their interests more valiantly than most officials actually tasked with that job have done when he asked several members of the European Parliament: 'Are EU taxpayers really happy to reconstruct what US taxpayers have paid to destroy?'[42]

I am sure that most taxpayers would be appalled if they were aware that their hard-earned cash was being used to perpetuate a vicious cycle of destruction and reconstruction. As part of this cycle, the United States gives roughly $3 billion in direct support to Israel per year, about one-sixth of the total US foreign assistance budget and the equivalent of 2 per cent of Israel's gross domestic product. As 75 per cent of this support is in military aid, almost every action that harms Palestinian life or property should be considered a joint United States–Israel initiative.[43] While principles of justice would indicate that compensation for this harm should be paid by those who caused it, the European Union has instead been willing to pay bills that should have been sent to Tel Aviv or Washington.

In May 2004, for example, Israel's despicably misnamed Operation Rainbow in Gaza destroyed around 300 houses and left 3,800 people homeless. According to Agnès Bertrand-Sanz, a specialist on the Israeli–Palestinian conflict with the anti-poverty organisation Aprodev, some international donors at the time wished to make their displeasure with the bombing known by stating that they would not pay for the houses to be rebuilt. But this protest did not materialise because the United States declined to sign a letter to that effect. Instead, the European Union decided to allocate just over €1 million to provide temporary accommodation for the victims, with Poul Nielson, then the EU commissioner for humanitarian aid, stipulating that 'these funds do not absolve the occupying power of its responsibilities to uphold international humanitarian law'.[44]

A comparable point was made by Nielson's successor Louis Michel during a subsequent Israeli attack on Gaza. The European Union is 'not there simply to pay for the damage', Michel said in January 2009, while the bombs were still falling on the Strip's inhabitants.[45]

Less than six weeks after Israel called off its military assault, Michel's colleague Ferrero-Waldner attended a donors' conference for Gaza in the Egyptian coastal city Sharm El-Sheikh. Keen to exploit the public relations potential of the event to the full and to assuage a European public horrified by the carnage in Gaza, she bragged of how the European Union was the largest provider of funds to the Palestinians and would 'mobilise' €440 million for them over the course of 2009. Her prepared script contained one sentence about how 'we must seek guarantees to end the "destruction–reconstruction" cycle' but did not recommend how this could be achieved. Paradoxically, she then announced that the European Union was willing to keep the cycle in motion by once again financing repairs to Palestinian homes.[46] (As it transpired, she was not able to honour this pledge as Israel prevented cement and other construction materials from going to Gaza on the spurious pretext that Hamas might use them to dig tunnels for smuggling weapons.)

ECHO, the European Commission's humanitarian office, correctly says that its job is to provide emergency assistance to people who need it irrespective of the political situation in any region where it is operating. In Gaza, its work – and that of partner organisations – has been severely impeded since the economic blockade was imposed by Israel. Ensuring that Gazans have proper water and sanitation has been identified as a top priority by ECHO, yet it has been unable to improve the situation because Israel will not allow vital equipment into the Strip. Even as UN workers warned in January 2009 that Operation Cast Lead had left the sewage system in Gaza on the brink of collapse, Israel stopped a French-made purification system from being delivered.[47]

It is true that the European Union has made diplomatic protests at the obstructions. In early 2009, the Czech government and the European Commission wrote a joint letter to Tzipi Livni and some other Israeli ministers, complaining that only 200 truckloads of aid were allowed to enter Gaza per day, when aid agencies had estimated that at least 500 were required. 'Your government gave us assurances regarding access of humanitarian aid and aid workers to the Gaza Strip,' the letter said. 'Since then we have not witnessed much improvement of the overall restrictions.' But the letter also had an element of dark comedy by suggesting that Israel really had the best interests of Gazans in mind, despite how it had bombed many of them to smithereens. 'Addressing the plight of ordinary people in Gaza and supporting the Palestinian Authority in its relief efforts are our priorities and as, we understand, also yours,' it added.[48]

Of course, the European Union was right to spell out its concerns to the Israeli government. But merely sending a polite letter is inadequate on its own and nobody can really be surprised that it did not ameliorate Israeli behaviour in any way. The refusal of the European Union to move towards more robust action, particularly by suing Israel for the damages and obstructions it has caused to EU aid programmes, means that it is failing to defend international law. As a result, the European Union is flouting principles that it nominally regards as sacrosanct. An EU 'security strategy' endorsed by its governments in 2003 emphasises that a core aim of its policies and activities is to uphold international law. 'There is a price to be paid, including in their relationship with the EU' for countries that 'persistently violate international norms' or 'place themselves outside the bounds of international society', the document says.[49]

To prove that it means what it says, the European Union has imposed sanctions against a raft of 'rogue states' or regimes that have displayed a contempt for elementary civil liberties, including Iran, North Korea, Zimbabwe and Belarus.[50] But even though Israel is a serial abuser of international law, it has not had to pay any price in terms of its relations with the European Union. Rather, the European Union has allowed itself become a figleaf for an illegal occupation. Using its taxpayers' money to keep Palestinians alive is commendable in itself. Doing so in a way that lets Israel off the hook is certainly not.

4

THE MISAPPLIANCE OF SCIENCE

Israel's prosperity – serious inequalities in its society notwithstanding – and its apparent resilience in the face of a global slump are doubtlessly things that many EU politicians find attractive. Since 2000, the overriding objective of the European Union is supposed to have been to build the world's 'most competitive and dynamic knowledge-based economy' by 2010. This goal, repeated ad infinitum during tedious conferences, is known as the Lisbon strategy because it was formally approved by EU leaders at a meeting in the Portuguese capital. The strategy has proven neither desirable nor attainable. Remodelling Europe so that it could outperform the United States would have required the dismantling of social protection and labour laws in many countries to make it easier for multinationals to 'hire and fire' on a whim. And besides, the rise of China meant that the idea of a European quest for world domination would soon appear quaint.

A key component of the Lisbon strategy was that 3 per cent of EU gross domestic product should be devoted to scientific research and development (R&D). While the European Union has struggled to meet that target, Israel has successfully allocated almost 5 per cent of its GDP for such purposes. That works out as proportionately twice as much as the United States allocates to R&D and about 2 per cent more than Japan. By according a high priority to science, Israel was able to present itself as an ideal candidate for participation in the EU Framework Programme for research, which enjoys a budget of over €53 billion for the 2007–13 period. In 1996, Israel became the first country from beyond EU borders to be fully integrated into EU funding programmes for research.

Today, the European Union is second only to the Israel Science Foundation, a 'non-profit' organisation headquartered in Jerusalem, as the top source of research funding for Israel. Although Israel has been required to contribute to EU programmes, it has had handsome returns on its investment. For what EU officials call the

Fifth Framework Programme, which ran from 1998 to 2002, Israel paid in €154 million and received back €164 million. For the sixth programme (2002–06), Israel contributed €191 million and gained €204 million. The seventh programme lasts until 2013, and officials administering it told me they hope the Israeli participation will be worth at least half a billion euros.

Scientific research is the largest single area of EU–Israel cooperation, and Israel has milked the system diligently. 'Today, there are as many papers signed by Israeli scientists with European scientists as with American scientists,' a diplomat based in Tel Aviv said. 'That was not the case ten years ago. We couldn't be closer to Europe. The next step would be membership of the European Union.'

To manage this cooperation, Israel has set up an office with the less than catchy moniker the Israel-Europe R&D Directorate for the EU Framework Programme (ISERD). Its staff, some of whom travel from Tel Aviv to Brussels virtually every week, represent a cross-section of different Israeli government departments. According to the ISERD website, the relevant ministries involved are industry, trade and labour, finance and foreign affairs, as well as the Council for Higher Education.

The absence of the ministry of defence from that list suggests that all of the research in Israel financed by the European Union is of a non-military nature. Conscious that there would be outrage among the European public if they thought that their tax was helping Israel develop ever more sophisticated and lethal weaponry, the European Commission has insisted that its work with Israel is of a purely civilian nature. When I quizzed Janez Potocnik, the EU commissioner for scientific research from 2004 to 2009, about this, he said that there had been lengthy discussions among EU governments about the extent of cooperation with Israel and that assisting the military had been ruled out. He said:

> Defence is not part of the seventh framework programme. We have space and security as themes for the first time [neither were included in previous versions of the multi-annual programmes]. But there is nothing that would be defence-related in any context.

Potocnik's explanation was Jesuitical and deceptive. As someone who has travelled to Israel, he must know that it is not a country where a neat distinction can be drawn between civilian and military life. If he is under any illusions, all he would have to do is take a train from Tel Aviv to Ashkelon on a Sunday morning and observe whole carriages teeming with young conscripts, many of them with machine guns draped nonchalantly over their shoulders as if they were sports bags. That Israel's militarisation encroaches into almost every area of its society is a fact that the nation's authorities appear determined to suppress (in sharp contrast to the carefully cultivated image that Israel is the only country in the Middle East that cherishes freedom of expression). In 2009, activists belonging to the feminist organisation New Profile had their computers confiscated in police raids. The group had struck a raw nerve in the Israeli establishment after protesting at how the army and education systems were in cahoots by arranging to have one uniformed officer stationed in every school and how the top brass went on to run companies and, in many cases, the government once they had left the army.[1]

Objectively, it is understandable that Israel would try to prevent an unpalatable truth from being aired. Israel values the myth that its army is the most moral in the world and challenges to this central tenet of state propaganda are increasingly becoming taboo. As Israelis are constantly bombarded with this propaganda, it is no surprise that all bar a brave minority of them accept its veracity; 98 per cent of Jewish Israelis supported Operation Cast Lead in Gaza, according to pollsters.[2] But senior EU politicians like Potocnik should be able to see beyond the propaganda and realise that it is virtually impossible to support scientific research in Israel without its fruits being used for military ends.

Not surprisingly, his assurances have turned out to be worthless. European Commission sources have confirmed to me that staff working for the Israeli ministry of defence have taken part in discussions relating to the use of EU scientific research funds. This became clear when conscientious Commission officials asked questions internally about the motives of certain Israeli interlocutors who were, in the words of one Brussels-based scientist, 'exerting a huge amount of pressure for a proposal to go through'. As part of a tacit policy of trusting the Israeli authorities, the Commission does not normally carry out background checks on Israeli officials that it deals with. 'These guys [defence officials] are present in the system,' a Commission insider told me. 'It is unbelievable that their backgrounds aren't checked.'

OILING THE WAR MACHINE WITH EUROS

Another frightening weakness in the Commission's oversight relates to research projects that are designed to invent new weapons. The Commission's staff say that they are under a contractual obligation to appraise the institution's hierarchy of any proposals for funding which appear to be of a 'dual use' nature (civilian projects that can easily be tweaked for military purposes). Yet though the surrounding issues are considered to be of an ethical nature, the Commission leaves it to the discretion of individual staff to decide whether there might be a military dimension to a certain project. Despite how the Commission's core activity is supposed to be the making of rules, it has not introduced firm regulations or unambiguous guidelines to ensure that staff can perform the difficult task of sniffing out inventions that are destined to kill and maim. When I asked the Commission how many applications for funding from Israel had been identified as being of a 'dual use' nature, I was told:

> To date, there have been over 1,800 proposals with Israeli participation. The number of proposals that could be considered as dealing with 'dual use' depends on how that term is defined and it is to be noted that the Commission does not systematically make a judgement on this question.

Indeed, there are strong indications that the Commission positively encourages applications that have a clear military dimension. The introduction to a paper that the Commission published outlining the first 45 'security research' projects to be assisted from the EU budget says:

> The relationship between defence technologies, on the one hand, and security technologies, on the other, is particularly noticeable in the field of R&D, with technologies that show potential developments in both areas (Dual Use). At both research and industrial development levels, synergies are possible and desirable.[3]

Israel's burgeoning arms industry has had no problem taking advantage of this contradictory and muddled approach to ethical matters. Ten of the initial 45 'security research' projects were undertaken with the participation of Israeli firms, academic or state institutions, with Israel appointed as leader or coordinator in three of these cases. Most of the projects draw on experience that Israel has gleaned from abusing elementary rights.

The projects include:

- Developing a Crisis Communication Scorecard (CrisComScore): The Ben Gurion University of the Negev – a 'proudly Zionist institution', in the words of its current president Rivka Carmi – is taking part in this effort to help public authorities develop public and media relations strategies for the 'war on terror'.[4]

- Foresight of Evolving Security Threats Posed by Emerging Technologies (FESTOS): Its prospectus reads like the plot of a science fiction movie: imagining the year 2030, the task is to identify what technology could be used then to pose a threat to society. But its objective of developing 'early warning signals' fits neatly into the post 9/11 discourse. Tel Aviv University is the Israeli partner.
- Innovative and Novel First Responders Applications (INFRA): Shabtai Shavit, chairman and founder of Athena GS3, spent 32 years working for Mossad, the Israeli secret service, culminating with a period as its director from 1989 to 1996. Following the 11 September attacks, he travelled to the United States to advocate that it should be prepared to sacrifice civil liberties, advice that the Bush administration was all too willing to heed.[5] His firm is part of the Mer Group, which has provided surveillance equipment to illegal settlements in East Jerusalem, as well as checkpoints and army bases in the West Bank. As Athena GS3 is run by a team that 'harnesses decades of expertise in understanding the mind of the terrorist', it should offer plenty of valuable insight to this project, which hopes to develop communications systems that the emergency services will be able to use in tunnels or other environments where mobile phones tend to be unreliable.[6]
- Security Research National Contact Point Network (SEREN): Matimop, the Israeli industry centre for research and development, is a partner to this project addressing what the Commission euphemistically calls 'sensitivity issues' for security research. The network being formed here is supposed to raise awareness about the EU's activities in this area as part of efforts to guarantee that new inventions are 'mission-oriented'.[7]

The pivotal role played by Motorola Israel in an EU project bearing the supposedly funky name iDetecT 4All merits special attention. Motorola's long history of involvement in Israel bears some similarities to its investment in apartheid South Africa, where the US multinational won a lucrative contract supplying the police and army with two-way radios. It was not until the anti-apartheid movement persuaded New York legislators to threaten Motorola with the loss of a similar contract for cops in the Big Apple, that it sold off its South African subsidiary.[8]

Often described by human rights activists as the technology wing of the Israeli army, Motorola chose Israel as the first place to set up a base outside North America as far back as 1948. Five decades later, it was garlanded by then prime minister Binyamin Netanyahu, who presented it with the Jubilee Award to recognise companies that have contributed most to the Israeli economy.

The *Israel Defense Sales Directory 2009–10*, as published by the Israeli ministry of defence, lists Motorola as the 'leading Israeli company in developing and manufacturing a wide range of electronic fuses for aircraft and bombs and guided munitions'. The directory adds that Motorola Israel is 'considered to be the fusing systems house for the Israeli Airforce and for leading Israeli defence industries like IAI [Israel Aerospace Industries], IMI [Israel Military Industries] and Rafael [the former state weapons development authority] for a wide range of projects'.[9] This directory was compiled before a campaign mounted by human rights activists successfully pressurised Motorola into selling the unit that produced the fuses in question. Motorola's Government Electronics Department was bought by the Israeli firm Aeronautics Defense Systems in April 2009.[10]

Components bearing a Motorola label were found by Human Rights Watch investigators who examined the remnants of bombs dropped on Gaza during Operation Cast Lead.[11] Motorola-made fuses are also fitted into the type of bomb with which Israel killed at least 28 civilians, most of them children, living in an apartment block in Qana, Lebanon, in 2006. The weapon in question was a Mark-84 bomb, the largest of the Mark-80 series of bombs. A ministry of defence document prepared for Israeli companies taking part in a 2008 air show in Chile says that Motorola's '980 low proximity altitude fuse is intended to provide a proximity function for the Mk-80 high explosive bomb series'. This function 'increases dramatically weapon effectiveness against soft and light targets', the document says.[12]

From a technological standpoint, one of Motorola's greatest achievements is that it pioneered a highly sophisticated encrypted voice and data system for the Israeli security forces. Known as Mountain Rose, this $100 million system went operational in 2004 and has been used both in operations in the occupied Palestinian territories and in the war against Lebanon.[13] Documents prepared for the Israeli delegation to the aforementioned Santiago air show say that the system was originally envisaged by technical experts in the Israeli military about 18 years earlier. The Motorola system was found to be 'far superior' to alternative technology examined by the Israeli army, the document says.

The same document also gives details of a wide area surveillance system (WASS) developed by Motorola. Using radar technology, this system is designed to 'monitor and protect the perimeter of sensitive areas in order to provide early warning of any intrusion'. A 'typical deployment' of this system would 'include 10 radar sensors and 4–5 day/night cameras all connected to a command and control centre'. The system can 'work over land and water and detect a variety of targets: crawling, walking and running people, vehicles, boats and swimmers'.[14]

Reports in the Israeli press indicate that a Motorola radar system worth US$158 million has been installed in 47 Israeli settlements in the West Bank since 2005. According to the *Jerusalem Post,* the Israeli justice ministry has granted permission for the radar stations required for this system to be built on Palestinian land. The project has helped replace the rudimentary fences and barbed wire that previously 'protected' Israeli settlements with a 'virtual fence' that befits the twenty-first century, the newspaper suggested.[15]

It is likely that work being financed by the European Union will make use of this technology. A project description of iDetect 4All drawn up by the European Commission says that it is expected to improve the capability of existing security systems to detect people or objects that could threaten 'critical infrastructure'.[16]

MERCHANTS OF DEATH GO GREEN

Not all of the EU finance that Motorola Israel is accessing falls under the heading 'security research'. The company has also led two projects on road safety which have been allocated a combined total of €5 million in EU funding.[17] Its knack for securing funding from different sections of the EU scientific research budget is something that it shares with Israel Aerospace Industries.

In 2007, IAI was welcomed into the bosom of the European Union when it was accepted that it would take part in the 'Clean Sky' initiative. Boasting a budget of €1.6 billion between then and its completion date in 2014, this is one of the largest scientific research projects ever funded by the European Union. As aviation has been a rising source of greenhouse gas emissions in recent years and the carbon dioxide released at high altitude is widely considered as more damaging to the environment than that released at ground level, it would be wrong to quibble with its stated goal of developing less ecologically destructive aircraft. But the initiative's green packaging cannot conceal how many of the firms benefiting from it are weapons manufacturers. They include Thales, Dassault, EADS, Safran and Saab (while best known for its cars, 80 per cent of the Swedish company's revenues are from defence activities). Half of the funding for the scheme is being provided by the Commission, the remainder by industry.[18]

EU commissioners might be able to convince themselves that Israel Aerospace Industries is a cuddly company, determined to save the planet. But pro-Israel propagandists are not so naive. In an article about IAI's participation in 'Clean Sky', Israel21c, an online news service run by a self-proclaimed educational foundation devoted to presenting Israel in a favourable light, gives a useful potted history of the firm, along with a litany of its other recent activities:

> With 15,000 employees and sales in 2006 of over $2 billion, IAI is globally recognised as a leader in the development of both military and commercial aerospace technology. Established in 1953, IAI has applied the skills and experience it has acquired in catering to Israel's security needs, to become a world leader in aircraft conversion and modernisation programmes, unmanned air vehicles (UAVs), communication programmes and defence electronics. IAI systems currently in use by the Israel Defence Forces are upgraded F-16, F-15 and F-4 aircraft, Yasur 2000 and upgraded CH-53 helicopters, Dvora patrol boats, Gabriel sea-to-sea missiles, and the Phalcon Early Warning aircraft. The Arrow anti-tactical ballistic missile, Israel's answer to the threat of short and medium-range ballistic missiles, is currently in development at IAI, in cooperation with the Israel Ministry of Defence and the US Ballistic Missile Defense Organization.[19]

The same article quotes Arnold Nathan, a director for research and development at IAI, who says: 'IAI's contribution [to "Clean Sky"] is well-recognised and significant. In 20% of cases we run the whole project. They see us as people with initiative and expertise on a technological level.'

IAI chairman Yair Shamir (a son of former prime minister Yitzhak Shamir) has effectively acknowledged that all of this 'valuable' expertise has been built up because of the company's commercial interests in the occupation of Palestine:

> Billions of dollars were injected into the defence industry during the 1970s. When the students at Technion (the Israel Institute of Technology) rubbed themselves up against electronics or information technology, it was almost exclusively for military use. At the same time, the army created elite units for developing technological tools internally. Firms like IAI, Tadiran and Elbit integrated this knowledge into their work before developing activities dedicated to the civilian sector.[20]

It is to be hoped 'Clean Sky' will prove beneficial for the environment. But it would be a bitter irony if any ecologically sound aircraft that result from the project are principally designed for war-making. To suggest that this could be the outcome is not idle speculation. Among the aims of the initiative are to substantially reduce noise from aircraft. You don't have to be a military strategist to grasp that a silent plane could be considered advantageous in catching an enemy off-guard or – as Israel has done repeatedly – bombing a home before the family inside it has a chance to evacuate.

Under the terms of IAI's participation, the company will be able to apply for patents on discoveries made during the project. Once granted, these patents will confer on it a monopoly right over new aircraft or components invented with the aid of public finance. There will be nothing – apart perhaps from international law – to tell the IAI or its clients in the Israeli Air Force that it cannot use the fruits of EU-funded research to murder Palestinians. The European Commission has stated that so long as the innovations are 'applicable to civilian aircraft', they will be 'for the company to deal with as they wish'.[21]

THE SECURITY DECEPTION

Assurances that the European Union does not finance defence projects from funds reserved for scientific research are at odds with statements made by Philippe Busquin, Potocnik's predecessor as the EU commissioner for science. Following the 11 September atrocities, Busquin expressed a strong desire for the European Union to become involved in military research. 'I think that this distinction between civil and military research has become more and more artificial and expensive,' he told a dinner party held in the European Parliament's

Brussels headquarters during 2003. 'The threats to security don't consider this distinction.'[22]

To bolster his case for spending EU money on military research, Busquin set up an advisory 'group of personalities'. Of its 25 members, eight were representatives of arms companies such as BAE Systems, Thales, Finmeccanica, EADS and Ericsson. By contrast, there was not one human rights organisation invited to take part in its deliberations.

Subsequent claims that the European Union funds 'security' rather than 'defence' projects appear dishonest when one reads the report from these 'personalities', *Research for a Secure Europe*. Published in March 2004 (shortly after the horrific bomb attacks on commuter trains in Madrid), it recognised that until then the European Union had not specifically funded defence research, but advocated that it should begin doing so:

> The dividing line between defence and civil research funding, the absence of specific frameworks for security research at the European level, the limited cooperation between member states and the lack of coordination between national and European efforts exacerbate the lack of public research funding and present major obstacles to achieving cost-effective solutions.[23]

Pandering to fears of al Qaeda attacks on European soil and to perceptions that the European Union was ill-equipped to deal with them, the report contended that at least €1 billion should be allocated to 'security research' per annum from 2007 onwards. The Commission acted swiftly on this recommendation; Romano Prodi, then the institution's president, announced that security research would be funded during the 2007–13 period, saying that the 'tragic events' in Madrid underscored the necessity to be prepared to avert threats of mass violence in the future. And though the report made it clear that such research should straddle the lines of demarcation between civilian and defence activities, the Commission would opt to use the word 'security' as a euphemism for anything that could be considered military in nature. The magazine *Defense News* explained the rationale behind this decision:

> Firms are angling to get in on the ground level of a radical reorientation of EU financial support for security and defence projects. With the launch later this year of half a dozen so-called security test cases, the European Union will move directly into defence

research, even though that object is being couched for political reasons under the term 'security'.[24]

While Israel may not have been represented in the 'group of personalities', it was to have a significant role in the discussions that followed on from the group's recommendations. In 2007, Germany, then the holder of the EU presidency, and the European Commission announced their intention to set up the European Security Research and Innovation Forum (ESRIF). Tasked with drawing up a '20-year vision' for security research, the forum has 65 members broken into two groups: 'supply' and 'demand'. Israel's state Counter Terrorism Board was one of the few bodies from outside the European Union invited to join the forum, taking part in the 'demand' group. The Israeli army and emergency services and the University of Tel Aviv are being consulted, too, about the forum's activities.[25] An interim report by the forum, published in 2008, indicated that more state funding for security research would enhance the profitability of firms involved in this sector, specifically for makers of surveillance technology. It argued that a 'security label' should be introduced as part of efforts to harmonise laws and standards applying to the use of such equipment.[26]

BEYOND THE PALE OF HUMAN TOLERANCE

IAI's participation in the EU programme is by no means limited to research ostensibly aimed at protecting the environment. Rather, it is taking part in more than 50 EU-financed projects. Among the seven of these projects that IAI has led so far is one relating to unmanned aerial vehicles, or drones as they are more commonly known. This project, the Civil Applications and Economical Effectivity of Potential UAV Configurations (CAPECON), was put in charge of drafting a blueprint for flying these pilotless military planes in civilian airspace by around 2015.[27] Elbit, another manufacturer of UAVs, is similarly soaking up EU funds, through the €3 million Simulation of Crisis Management Activities (SICMA) project. Nominally designed to help health professionals deal with emergencies, it is being spearheaded by the Italian arms company Finmeccanica.[28]

Thomas Bingham, a top-ranking British judge, garnered some – though not nearly enough – press coverage in 2009 when he intimated that UAVs should be placed in the same category as landmines and cluster bombs – weapons that are so cruel 'as to be beyond the pale of human tolerance'. After the United States had admitted in May that year that 26 Afghan civilians had been killed in a series of UAV attacks, Bingham said: 'It may be – I'm not expressing a view – that unmanned drones that fall on a house full of civilians is a weapon the international community should decide should not be used.'[29]

The UAV technology that the United States and other NATO forces employ in Afghanistan and Pakistan has been finessed by Israel, with the Palestinian territories and sometimes neighbouring countries like Lebanon as its chosen laboratories. Though the United States used drones for reconnaissance missions in south China and Vietnam in the 1960s, Israel was the first country to make regular and widespread use of them by its armed forces. Indeed, it was after studying Israel's experience with these weapons during its 1982 war against Lebanon that the United States decided that its navy should have a UAV capability.[30]

Despite their invidious nature, the European Union has been eager to nurture the development of more sophisticated and deadly drones. At present, drones are banned from flying in civilian airspace, largely because air traffic controllers feel it would be unsafe to allow them to do so. Undeterred by such pesky matters as public safety, the European Defence Agency (an EU body tasked with goading EU governments into increasing military expenditure) signed a deal with France, Germany, Italy, Spain and Sweden in June 2009, whereby the agency would oversee efforts to enable drones to fly alongside normal passenger jets as part of a €50 million research programme.[31] A month earlier *Jane's Defence Weekly* reported that an informal division of labour had been agreed between the EDA and the European Commission. Under this, the Commission would fund research aimed at allowing UAVs 'to autonomously move across Europe's controlled airspace'.[32]

For obvious reasons such work is being done furtively; there is no desire on the part of the Brussels elite to tell EU citizens that aircraft used in attacks on Palestinian civilians could soon be flying above them.

SMALL ISN'T ALWAYS BEAUTIFUL

For equally obvious reasons, the European Union does not draw much attention to the true nature of its cooperation with Israel in the field of nanotechnology. I have no doubt that the study of matter on atomic and molecular scale is one of the most exciting disciplines for scientists to be involved in nowadays. And it is quite possible that nanotechnology will lead to important breakthroughs in medicine. But I also have no doubt that Israel's intention to become a world leader in nanotechnology is being driven by a desire to use its results malignly.

That much has been acknowledged by Israel's current president Shimon Peres. Despite being a Nobel laureate for peace, Peres appears keen that Israel's scientific know-how should help keep the country on a permanent war footing. Following the frustration voiced by many hawks with Israel's inability to destroy Hezbollah in the 2006 war in Lebanon, Peres, then deputy prime minister, argued that sophisticated new weaponry would be required to fight such wars in the future. In a syndicated opinion piece, he contended that the arms which Israel had at its disposal were more geared towards fighting national armies than organisations resorting to guerrilla tactics. 'It would be senseless to use a plane or helicopter that has cost millions of dollars for the purpose of chasing a lone terrorist, or a small group of terrorists,' he wrote, adding:

> A terrorist might be deterred by the knowledge that new surveillance tools have been developed that could identify him, even in a large crowd; that his weapon could be detected without his knowledge. This kind of deterrent could be based on miniaturised arms or on remote-control robots operating on the battlefield; perhaps even on a type of intelligence hitherto unknown, grounded in revolutionary nanotechnology.[33]

Peres was asked by the government to chose 15 scientists that would help realise the vision of deploying such weapons as 'pearls of wisdom' – tiny sensors intended to sniff out suicide bombers.[34] Some $230 million was to be invested in nanotechnology over the next five years, so that Israel would have the wherewithal to kill an armed militant hiding in a civilian area, without having to bomb the entire neighbourhood, newspapers reported (reinforcing the myth that the Israeli army would never harm a civilian deliberately). This precision could be achieved through 'bionic hornets', which should become the diminutive successors to the UAVs with which the United States has killed al Qaeda operatives (and, lest we forget, innocent civilians) in Afghanistan.[35]

The strategy reviews undertaken following the war in Lebanon brought some media attention to Israel's objectives for nanotechnology research. Yet such research had been going on for some time prior to that. In 2001, the Israel National Nanotechnology Initiative (INNI) was formed by senior representatives of several government departments. A quick glance at the composition of its board of directors confirms that it is inseparable from the country's military establishment. Among the directors are Moshe Goldberg from the Israeli Ministry of Defence and Giora Shalgi, former president of Rafael, the state weapons development authority.

In 2002, the INNI set out its 'vision' for the future of nanotechnology in Israel, noting that it was one of the few industrialised countries lacking a national policy on this scientific discipline (something that was soon rectified). While the Ministry of Defence was prepared to bankroll research for 'targeted applications' (a euphemism for killing machines), Israel would not be able to afford to rival the United States, which was investing $1 billion per annum into nanotechnology, on its own. Collaboration with 'global partners' was therefore necessary to obtain funding, the INNI advocated.

Step forward the European Union. Between 2007 and 2013, the European Union has earmarked €3.5 billion in support for nanotechnology under its Framework Programme for research. Israel's eagerness to obtain as much of that sum as it can has been underscored by how Dan Vilenski, a board member of INNI doubles up as the chief Israeli representative to the EU programme. When I spoke to Vilenski he was reticent about the relationship between nanotechnology and the Israeli military. Though he conceded that military factors lay behind Israel's initial interest in the field, he claimed that only about one-quarter of all nanotech activities in Israel had a security dimension, before making the faintly ludicrous case that there is a 'big difference between fighting terrorism' with nanotech and its military applications. 'As far as I know, nanotechnology is not for killing people,' he said. 'It is for fighting terrorism by things like identifying explosives.'

Vilenski's reticence appears to be in keeping with a conscious effort by Israeli officialdom to accentuate the peaceful uses of nanotechnology. As deputy prime minister, Peres might have been happy to brag of plans to modernise warfare with mini-weapons. As president, however, he presented Pope Benedict XVI with a 'nanobible'. This Hebrew version of the holy book – the size of a grain of sand and requiring an electron microscope to be read – was the work of the Technion in Haifa.[36] As the pontiff was visiting the Middle East to promote the cause of peace, it is easy to understand why nobody drew his attention to how the Technion has few rivals in terms of academic institutions focused on military research.

Conveniently ignoring Peres's remarks in 2006, Israel's more recent public relations about nanotechnology has indicated that the related work is almost entirely benevolent. When *Newsweek* described several Israeli establishments as 'centres of excellence' in 2007, Ynet, a website run by the Israeli daily paper *Yediot Ahronot,* declared that 'the world salutes four Israeli scientists'. One of these, Hossam Haick from Technion, was credited with inventing an electronic 'nose' for diagnosing cancer; this won him an EU grant of €1.7 million. The Ynet article dealt solely with the medical applications of nanotechnology.[37]

Likewise, the European Commission does not wish to have much public attention drawn to how its Israeli partners view nanotechnology as a tool of war. A search on Cordis, an EU-funded news service about scientific research, did not yield any articles on the military dimensions of nanotech in Israel. The only hint that it was linked to the 'war on terror' came in a story about the invention of a 'whiskered robot rat' through a project launched in 2008, to which the European Union had contributed over €5 million.[38] That august journal *Playboy* told its readers that 'future applications for this technology could include using robots underground, under the sea, or in extremely dusty conditions, where vision is often a seriously compromised sensory modality.'[39] The Commission has indicated that the futuristic rodent will be helpful in search and rescue missions but with several Israeli institutes ensconced in this project, it is a safe bet that it will be of use for offensive purposes, too.

BIG BROTHER IN PALESTINE

Alarmingly, EU representatives are not prepared to accept that they are facilitating Israel to develop technology for the express intention of abusing human rights. When I asked a senior EU diplomat in Tel Aviv – to whom I spoke on condition of anonymity – if there was a danger that EU scientific research activities would make it complicit in the most brutal aspects of the occupation, the most he would concede was that 'we are complicit with Israeli settlements'.

This was an admission that some EU grants have gone to Israeli researchers based on occupied land. In a 2004 report, the Euro-Mediterranean Human Rights Network gave details of how researchers based in the Golan Heights and the Jordan Valley had benefitted from EU funding for science. A university in Ariel, an Israeli settlement in the

West Bank, is also known to have received EU support. This participation in EU activities completely contradicted statements that only bodies within Israel's internationally recognised borders were entitled to cooperate with the European Union. Peter Hain, Britain's one-time Europe minister, had explained the political and legal situation:

> The EU–Israel Association Agreement provides for cooperation between the EU and Israel in a number of areas and also allows Israel to participate in a number of EU programmes. The EU has repeatedly condemned settlement activity in the occupied territories (including East Jerusalem). It is illegal under international law and an obstacle to peace. Therefore, institutions from the Israeli settlements will not be eligible to participate in any EU cooperation or programme.[40]

After they were made aware of how grants they were administering were going to Israeli settlements, EU officials pledged to do what they could to avoid this problem recurring. But Palestinian solidarity activists say that the promises from the European Union have been purely verbal and that no concrete proof has been offered to show that firms in the settlements are being excluded. Activists who have examined the rules set by the European Union also say that they are extremely easy to circumvent. All a firm in the settlements would have to do is set up a front company in Tel Aviv or another Israeli town or city, and it could apply for EU funding, without EU officials knowing that its real work is done on occupied land.

Important though this matter is, the likelihood that some firms in the settlements are pilfering EU resources under false pretences should not be considered the biggest scandal relating to EU scientific cooperation with Israel. If anything, this issue pales in comparison with the wider question of how the research programmes have been shaped by an ideological agenda aptly summarised by the civil liberties organisation Statewatch as 'Big Brother meets market fundamentalism'.[41] Without having been consulted, the EU taxpayer could well be helping Israel acquire the tools it needs to tighten its stranglehold on Palestine.

SATELLITES OF WAR

Tough questions must be asked, too, about why Israel and the European Union have become allies in space. In 2004, both sides reached an agreement at a meeting in Jerusalem on enabling Israel to take part in Galileo, the EU satellite navigation system.[42] By undertaking to contribute around $25 million to the project over the coming five years, Israel won itself a seat on the board steering it, meaning that it would be the first non-EU country apart from China involved (India has subsequently come on board, too).[43] Oded Eran, Israel's EU envoy at the time, stated that his country's primary interest in this accord was to win lucrative industrial contracts.[44] But it is impossible to believe that Israel's real interest here is not the military potential of the programme.

No doubt, the truth is closer to that intimated by *Globes*, the Israeli business daily. A *Globes* guide to Israel's technology prowess says that Israel's space programme is the result of a 'military imperative'. Some of its roots can be found in Ronald Reagan's highly controversial 'Star Wars' plan for a 'missile defence shield'. The Arrow anti-ballistic missile which Israel reportedly developed in response to how Iraq hit Tel Aviv with Scud missiles during the 1991 Gulf war had its genesis in Star Wars, for example.[45]

Furthermore, it should be pointed out that Israel made considerable progress with space exploration long before Europe was investing seriously in this area. Israel was the eighth nation in the world to develop and launch satellites, beginning with the Ofeq spy satellite (indisputably a military project) in 1988. Promotional blurbs published by the European Commission on Galileo indicate that EU officials are somewhat in awe of Israel's success in space, and that they want Europe to emulate it.[46]

Galileo was originally conceived as a means of reducing Europe's dependence on the US Global Positioning System (GPS). A 2002 paper from the European Commission predicted that satellite navigation for cars would soon be as commonplace as mobile phones, with some 250 million European users by 2020. With the United States unwilling to share ownership of GPS with a foreign power, authorisation for foreigners to use the system required special permission from the Pentagon. While the dominance of GPS had not caused practical difficulties in Europe until then, it could in the future, the paper suggested, particularly if the United States opted to impose charges on countries that used the system. 'As our economic dependence on GPS grows, Europe can be held to ransom on all issues related to its use of GPS and might be obliged to pay governmental levies to the US in the future,' it said. 'Europe cannot accept this.' The paper concluded that Galileo should be a civilian system 'independent from GPS but interoperable with it', bringing tangible benefits for the road system, rescue missions and environmental monitoring.[47]

The suggestion that Galileo would be confined to the realm of the civilian was never really credible. France, Western Europe's top spender on space exploration, was especially adamant that greater attention should be paid to space on this continent. Marking the fortieth anniversary of the establishment of the French National Centre for Space Studies in 2001, Jacques Chirac said: 'The United States spends six times more public money on the space sector than Europe. Failure to react would inevitably lead to our countries becoming first scientific and technological vassals, then industrial and economic vassals.'[48]

Chirac's crony Jacques Barrot, then a European commissioner, is reputed to have noted that Galileo could be 'interesting' for the military in 2006 (the French word *intéressant* can mean both 'interesting' and 'attractive'). Addressing a meeting of EU transport ministers in Luxembourg, he reportedly said:

> Galileo was supposed to be a civilian system only but I wonder whether we shouldn't question that. Using it for military purposes, for defence purposes, would be very interesting in terms of paying for the infrastructure and investment.[49]

The militarisation of the project helps explain why governments have been willing to stump up the money needed for it. Initially, Galileo was hailed as the European Union's first large-scale 'public–private initiative', with two-thirds of the €2.1 billion projected costs for its deployment phase between 2006 and 2008 supposed to come from private companies.[50] Yet after delays were encountered in the project and the commitment of the eight firms taking part in it was queried by Barrot and his aides, EU governments stepped forward to finance it entirely from the public purse.[51] The viability of the project appears to depend on its military aspects; a recent survey by the European Commission suggested that military clients would comprise about half of all those who would have access to Galileo's encrypted signals.[52]

Chirac's vision of cutting Europe free from US domination in space notwithstanding, the European Union en bloc has been careful to avoid confrontation with Washington. Paul Wolfowitz, one of the most jingoistic neoconservatives in the Bush administration, wrote to the European Union in late 2001 to spell out his demands that Galileo's signals must not be allowed interfere with US military operations.[53] With Britain particularly emphatic about the 'need' to kowtow to Wolfowitz, EU officials undertook that Galileo would be effectively turned off when the United States demanded it. This commitment was solidified with a transatlantic accord in 2004, which allowed the United States to block European signals at times of war, without disabling Galileo completely.[54]

Because of the aforementioned delays in the project, China and India are said by space policy analysts to be expressing doubts about whether they can remain as partners.[55] By contrast, Israel has so far not wavered in its support for Europe's forays into the final frontier. As well as Galileo, Israel is involved in a second EU satellite navigation system. Formerly known as Global Monitoring for Environment and Security (GMES), this newer system was rechristened Kopernikus in 2008. Although it is promoted primarily as a valuable resource in tracking the effects of climate change and other ecological disasters, Europe's security elite are known to be examining how it can assist in military missions. Meanwhile, civil libertarians are perturbed at how Kopernikus offers considerable potential for zooming in on individuals, as well as how it plans to utilise UAV technology.[56] A qualification in rocket science is not required to see how it could prove advantageous for Israel in hounding Palestinians.

Never distracted from geo-strategic issues, Israel has been closely following EU deliberations on space and defence policy. The Lisbon Treaty, a repackaged version of the EU constitution rejected by French and Dutch voters in 2005, is designed to give a new impetus to EU military ambitions. Along with stipulating that EU governments will increase their defence expenditure (that it contains no requirements to boost spending on health or education speaks volumes about where EU priorities lie), the treaty contains little-noticed but significant provisions on space exploration. For example, it names the European Space Agency (ESA) in Paris as the official body handling EU space activities, including those with a military dimension.[57] Israel, already a participant in many of the agency's projects since 2003, hopes to sign a formal cooperation agreement with the ESA in the near future.[58]

Israeli entrepreneurs were also cock-a-hoop when the European Parliament voted to drop its long-held objection to the militarisation of Galileo in 2008. *Israel Valley*, the newsletter of the Franco–Israeli chamber of commerce, underscored the significance of this move:

> The Israelis are associated with this programme which allows

> them to be part of consortia of European companies tasked with putting the project in place. The spin-offs for Israel will be important for its 'Silicon Valley'. Very attached to the construction of a national industry that is solid and relatively independent in the domain of space, Israel considers all partners as welcome on the condition that the transfers of technology will be real.[59]

Time will tell if the transfers materialise. Regardless of whether they do, there is every reason to be suspicious of Israel's motives.

5

PROFITING FROM PALESTINE'S PAIN

If proof was needed that corporate lobbyists are to a large extent dictating the European Union's agenda, it could be found in abundance on 28 October 2008. On that date the European Commission handed over several floors of its high-rise Charlemagne building in Brussels to the employers' confederation BusinessEurope. The immaculately dressed executives who participated in the event were treated like royalty by a procession of senior politicians and officials reciting mantras about why their commitment to free trade should remain undiminished despite the perilous state of the world economy.

Of the plethora of companies represented at the conference, one had a particularly unenviable reputation: Caterpillar. For more than four decades, the US multinational has been supplying Israel with heavy vehicles knowing full well that they are used in the destruction of Palestinian homes. Its fearsome bulldozers flattened the dwellings of refugees when Israeli forces carried out a massacre in Jenin during 2002, leaving 4,000 people, a quarter of the refugee camp, homeless. A year later one was used to crush the brave peace activist Rachel Corrie to death when she placed her body in front of a Gazan home that was about to be razed.[1]

After years of dithering, the Church of England eventually announced in February 2009 that it was divesting from Caterpillar, in which it held shares worth £2.5 million.[2] But despite making several claims in recent times that it supports the concept of 'corporate social responsibility', the European Commission has no qualms about accepting policy recommendations from a firm like Caterpillar. Top-level EU officials did not utter one word of disquiet at the BusinessEurope conference about how Caterpillar profits from the occupation of Palestine. They merely nodded in affirmation as Michael Baunton, one of the company's vice-presidents, made a bizarre case for why its vehicles should be exempt from air pollution controls wherever it operates. 'There is regulation that is well-meaning that should not apply to us,' he said.[3]

Sadly, Baunton was preaching to the converted. Two years earlier the Commission formally undertook to pursue an aggressive strategy designed to remove any 'barriers' that multinational firms encountered when doing business in any country. Titled *Global Europe*, the strategy identified laws designed to protect people and the environment in foreign markets as irritants for entrepreneurs and vowed to fight against them.[4]

The deepening of Europe's political and economic relations with Israel cannot be divorced from this neo-liberal blueprint. That much became clear in November 2007, when the 'EU–Israel business dialogue', a forum in which senior businessmen (with perhaps one or two women) could brainstorm on how best 'barriers to trade and investment' can be stripped away.

What the promotional material for the dialogue doesn't tell you is that many of the Israeli companies taking part are involved in activities in occupied Palestine, in some cases activities that the European Union has formally criticised. Here are some examples:

- Elbit has been a crucial supplier of electronic equipment to the 'apartheid wall' Israel is building in the West Bank. The Norwegian government viewed this involvement as so serious that in September 2009 it decided that a state-owned pension fund should withdraw its $6 million investment in Elbit because the wall had been ruled illegal by the International Court of Justice.[5] 'We do not wish to fund companies that so directly contribute to violations of international humanitarian law,' Norway's finance minister Kristin Halvorsen said.[6] Elbit also makes unmanned aerial vehicles (UAVs) and other weapons for the Israeli army.
- The Saban Capital Group is run by Haim Saban, a media proprietor holding dual US–Israeli citizenship, who featured at number 261 on the *Forbes* list of the world's billionaires for 2009. He is one of the controlling owners of Bezeq, the telecommunications company providing services to Israeli settlements in the West Bank and Golan Heights, as well as to the Israeli army's bases and checkpoints in the West Bank. Bezeq's subsidiary Pelephone similarly provides mobile phone services to the Israeli army and has installed around 100 antennae and other communication facilities on occupied Palestinian land, according to the

Coalition of Women for Peace, an Israeli feminist organisation that monitors the activities of companies in the occupied territories.[7]

- Bank Leumi, Israel's second biggest bank, has branches in a number of Israeli settlements in the West Bank. It gives mortgages to settlers buying houses on occupied land. And it partly controls Paz Oil and SuperPharm, which operate petrol stations and pharmacies in West Bank settlements.
- Steimatsky, a major chain of book shops, has outlets in the Israeli settlements of Ariel, Ma'ale Adumim and Pisgat Ze'ev.

The establishment of the EU–Israel business dialogue was, according to the European Commission, the fruit of conversations between Ehud Olmert and Günter Verheugen, then the EU commissioner for industry, that began in 2005.[8] By establishing this body, the European Union was placing tiny Israel on a similar footing to other much more populous countries with which it has entered into similar dialogues (the United States, Russia, Japan and India). On one level, this appears extraordinary. But from a hard-headed business perspective it probably makes sense, given that Israel rivals Silicon Valley as a centre of science and technology. As Verheugen said, when encouraging EU-based companies to engage more with Israel, where the high-tech industry contributes around 7 per cent of GDP: 'There is a huge economic potential that is not yet fully exploited.'[9]

The first chairman of this dialogue epitomises how tech-savvy Israel is. Yossi Vardi is best known for pioneering instant messaging on the Internet through his firm ICQ, which was snatched up by AOL for a princely $400 million.[10] Vardi appears to be not only an expert on instant messaging but on tailoring messages to suit different audiences. At times, he has sought to identify with peaceniks by hinting that he regards the occupation of Palestine as bad for business. Chatting to a *New York Times* correspondent in between sips of cabernet sauvignon, he said:

> The place is crazy – a technology boom beside a very unacceptable political situation and chaos in Gaza, where most of the population is living on under $2 a day. It's not right or sustainable. You know, power corrupts and occupation is the ultimate manifestation of power. There are no checks, no balances. Occupation, after 40 years, corrupts absolutely.[11]

Perversely, Vardi has also conceded that Israel's prowess in the technology field is inextricably linked to the occupation. In a BBC report, he contended that the 1967 War was of pivotal importance to industrial development in Israel because it led to a situation where the country had to overcome a sense that it was ostracised, particularly by France, which switched from being Israel's main supplier of arms to imposing an arms embargo on it. He said: 'The two real fathers of Israeli hi-tech are the Arab boycott and Charles de Gaulle because they forced on us the need to go and develop an industry.'[12]

Just as the Internet was spawned at least partly as a result of military-related research in the United States, Israel's technology sector is the by-product of a weapons industry. An Israeli government decision to prioritise the development of arms manufacturing following the 1967 war was pursued with considerable brio. By 1975, this industry supported 45,000 jobs, or 5.5 per cent of the total labour force. And in order to assert its military supremacy over Arab neighbours, Israel deliberately concentrated on the more cutting-edge side of arms development. Over the decades, the Israeli corporate elite has cynically exploited the security situation in its region and more globally. Israel Livnat, the head of Elta Systems, a leading defence electronics firm, has summarised the underlying strategy deftly: 'Israel has been meeting the challenge of terror for decades before 9/11 and in those years of hands-on, real-time experience in overcoming terror lies our country's first competitive advantage.'[13]

Naomi Klein's book *The Shock Doctrine* traces how Israel's technology and military nexus has helped shield it from some of the afflictions besetting the global economy. Initially, Israel was concussed as a result of the 'dot.com' crash of 2000; by June the next year, tens of thousands of workers feared unemployment as about 300 high-tech firms verged on bankruptcy. An unlikely alliance of right-wing economics and al Qaeda then came to the rescue. First, the Israeli government boosted military expenditure by almost 11 per cent (partly financed by money saved through savage cutbacks in social welfare) and encouraged executives to shift their focus from information technology to that geared towards surveillance. Next, the attacks on the Twin Towers and the Pentagon were a boon for their order books. The way that Ariel Sharon took advantage of those atrocities to present Israel's oppression of the Palestinians as an indispensable part of the international 'war on terror' propelled Israel forward to such an extent that within three years it was rated one of the world's top performing economies.

As Klein wrote:

> The timing was perfect. Governments around the world were suddenly desperate for terrorist hunting tools, as well as for human intelligence know-how in the Arab world. Under the leadership of the Likud Party, the Israeli state billed itself as a showroom for the cutting-edge homeland security state, drawing on its decades of experience and expertise fighting Arab and Muslim threats. Israel's pitch to North America and Europe was straightforward: the War on Terror you are just embarking on is one we have been fighting since our birth. Let our high-tech firms and privatised spy companies show you how it's done.[14]

Selling more than US$5 billion worth of arms in 2007, Israel ranks fourth in the worldwide 'top 100' table of national and regional weapons vendors compiled by the Stockholm International Peace Research Institute.[15] Only the United States, Russia and – taken as a bloc – Western Europe outperform it. In recent years, it has even overtaken Britain, historically the workshop of the arms world, as a weapons exporter.[16]

Israel's resilience in the face of recession has won praise from capitalism's best-selling fanzine the *Economist*. Spared the ignominy of having to bail out banks, Israel has not been entirely unaffected by the paroxysms that swept through Wall Street in the autumn of 2009, yet continues to record robust growth. Although its unemployment rate has grown from 6 per cent to 8 per cent at the time of writing, its GDP per capita is higher than that of some European countries, such as Portugal, and five times that of neighbouring Egypt. The economic recipe followed by Yuval Steinitz, Israel's finance minister and a prominent member of Likud, reads like it was drawn up by the Republican Party in the United States: slash income and corporate tax, raise VAT, expel 'illegal' foreigners and, even as you cut other areas of spending, mollycoddle the military. While its technology sector is not indestructible, Steinitz is confident that Israel will remain an important producer of both computer software and military hardware.

> If I put money in ordinary peoples' pockets, they'll spend it on imported goods and foreign holidays. Our own economy doesn't produce consumer goods for them to buy. We make know-how and software, chips for Intel [the US technology giant] and

computers for irrigation, chemicals, stents for heart surgery and pilotless drones.[17]

OBLIGED TO SHUN, HAPPY TO SERVE

Theoretically, Israel is the kind of country that the EU weapons industry is obliged to shun. In 1998, EU governments signed up to a code of conduct on arms exports. Ten years later – in December 2008 – the same governments eventually made this code legally-binding. It requires each EU member state to assess each application for exports based on eight criteria. These include the record that the country of destination has on respect for human rights and international humanitarian law and whether or not the country is prone to becoming embroiled in an armed conflict or is situated in a volatile region. Clearly, if both the spirit and the letter of this code were properly applied, EU countries would not sell a single weapon – or even a component of a weapon – to Israel.

Grubby issues of *realpolitik*, though, have meant that many EU states ignore their obligations and merrily sell to and buy instruments of death from Israel. This has even occurred at times of heightened tensions in the Middle East. In the middle of Israel's attacks on Lebanon in July 2006, Germany surreptitiously signed a deal to supply Israel with two Dolphin submarines, capable of carrying nuclear warheads. With one-third of their cost paid for by Germany, some newspapers reported a month after the contract was clinched that the $1.3 billion submarines were superior to those already belonging in Israel's arsenal as they could remain submerged for longer. A few members of the opposition Green Party denounced the deal on the grounds that no guarantees were given that the submarines would not be used to carry nuclear weapons; this contravened Germany's stance on nuclear non-proliferation, the Greens argued.[18] Originally not expected to be ready for delivery until 2010, Germany nonetheless reportedly delivered them to Israel in the autumn of 2009, heedless of how Israel had just been accused of perpetrating war crimes in Gaza by the UN-appointed investigator Richard Goldstone. These U212s would bring the number of submarines at Israel's disposal to five and they could greatly assist Israel in attacking Iran, according to the newswires.[19]

Official EU data also indicates that elite consciences were generally not pricked by the atrocities committed by Israel in Lebanon. An analysis carried out by Caroline Pailhe from the Belgian arms trade watchdog GRIP demonstrates how the number of licences granted for exporting EU arms to Israel rose from 439 in 2005 to 610 in 2006 and to over 1,000 the following year. It is true that the actual value of those licences fell from €145 million in 2005 to €127 million in 2006 before climbing to €199 million in 2007. But Pailhe has calculated that at 0.9 per cent, the proportion of arms exports to Israel out of all EU arms exports throughout the globe was at its highest level since 2003. She also examined the number of licences refused and found that there was no significant fluctuation, compared with previous years. At 27, the number of licences denied to Israel in 2006 was 13 higher than the previous year, but only one higher than the refusal rates for both 2003 and 2004.[20]

It is true that the European Union is a much less important arms vendor for Israel than the United States. Whereas US supply of weapons to Israel is measured in billions (between $1.5 billion and $2.6 billion per year in the 2003–07 period) that of key European states is measured in millions. Yet that does not mean EU weapons sales are negligible. On the contrary, 11 of the top 20 weapons dealers to Israel are EU member states, they are France, Romania, Britain, Poland, the Czech Republic, the Netherlands, Spain, Germany, Slovakia, Finland and Italy.[21] Three applicants for EU membership – Bosnia, Serbia and Albania – also feature in that ignominious league table.

FRANCE'S FULL CIRCLE

There is a sense of full circle behind France's status as the top European supplier of arms to Israel (the value of French arms sales to Israel more than doubled from €57 million in 2003 to €126 million in 2007). In the 1950s France helped arm the fledgling Israeli state, and Shimon Peres continues to gloat about how he placed crucial orders with Paris in that period.[22] Appointed director of the ministry of defence when he was only 30, Peres was such a regular visitor to France that he was given his own office in the prime minister's headquarters. By the end of 1955, France, particularly the company Dassault, was the key supplier to the Israeli Air Force. And after France bought a patent for a process of uranium enrichment developed in Israel during 1953, France became an important player in helping Israel acquire the know-how for making nuclear weapons.[23]

Historians say that General de Gaulle was fearful that the United States would learn of Franco–Israeli nuclear cooperation and that he ordered France to desist in the early 1960s. Later that decade –

in 1967 – de Gaulle declared that France would refuse to support any state in the Middle East that took up arms against another one and as a result weapons sales to Israel ceased.[24] More recent French presidents have had no such reservations. Under Chirac – his pro-Arab posturing notwithstanding – and Sarkozy, French arms sales to Israel have grown exponentially. Sarkozy has appeared untroubled by the immense double standards inherent in his appeals to Russia not to sell weapons to Iran and his willingness to nurture an arms trade with Israel that has aggravated tensions throughout the Middle East.[25]

French arms sales to Israel did not resume at any significant level for quite some time after the seven-year embargo imposed by de Gaulle was lifted. Indeed, there were only two major Franco–Israeli contracts of a military nature reported between the end of the embargo and the mid-1990s. Yet business was soon to become more brisk. Between 1996 and 2000, France supplied major weapons worth $50 million to Israel. These shipments included several Panther helicopters, that were partly funded by the United States.[26] Boasting advanced radar and an electro-optic observation system, the Panthers have replaced the Dolphin helicopters used by the Israeli navy.

While de Gaulle – no doubt unintentionally – was a catalyst in encouraging Israel to build up its own domestic arms industry and to become a huge US client, the Israelis have subsequently realised that not all their desired equipment can be obtained from the United States. As a result, France has become an important source of lasers and specialised equipment for reconnaissance. The links between France and Israel have also been bolstered by an accord on greater technological and industrial cooperation that Alain Millon, then the French defence minister, secured when he visited Israel in 2000.[27]

That agreement was reached a few months before the Palestinian *intifada* erupted that September. In response to the rebellion and the upsurge in Israeli state violence, France and Germany indicated that they were suspending weapons sales to Israel.[28] With the exception of a small number of export licence refusals, however, Israel has had no problem buying military goods from the two countries.

The standard line from Paris is that it does not generally sell actual complete weapons systems to Israel, merely components of weapons. Patrice Bouveret, a veteran campaigner against the arms trade, has exposed this stance as a sleight of hand. 'Even if they are only components, they are used directly by the Israeli army,' he said.[29]

The destructiveness of such components was demonstrated by Operation Cast Lead. By searching the wreckage in Gaza, Amnesty International investigators found electrical components labelled 'made in France'. These were integrated into the Hellfire AGM missiles manufactured by the US company Hellfire Systems, a joint venture of Lockheed Martin and Boeing. According to Amnesty, they appear to have been used in the attack by Israel against a graduation ceremony taking place at Gaza's police headquarters in late December 2008.[30] More than 40 unarmed policemen who had been lining up in a parade were killed as Israel bombed from the air, marking the start of its offensive. Under the Geneva Convention, these men should have been treated as if they were civilians because they were not taking any direct part in hostilities.[31]

FURTIVELY FEEDING THE WAR MONSTER

In July 2009, it was reported that Britain had decided to revoke a few licences for military exports to Israel after discovering that some British-made equipment was used in Operation Cast Lead. While sources from the British Foreign Office were quoted as saying that such use broke both British and EU export rules, they insisted that no general embargo was being introduced and that relations with Israel were 'strong and constructive'. The deals that would be affected primarily related to replacement parts for an Israeli navy gunboat, the Saar 4.5 Class Corvette. These constituted only five out of more than 180 contracts held by British firms for feeding the Israeli war monster.

Not without reason, Avigdor Lieberman, Israel's foreign minister, responded to this news by saying 'there is no need to get excited'.[32] A few months earlier, Britain had categorically ruled out a full-scale weapons ban. Mark Malloch-Brown, then a minister at the Foreign Office, told fellow members of the House of Lords:

> Imposing sanctions would advance neither Britain's influence nor the prospects for peace in the Middle East and in our view is not the best way to engage or to influence Israel. We have been very clear that, in accordance with EU arms export criteria, no arms exports are granted where there is a clear risk that those arms could be used for internal repression or external aggression, and that is surveyed very closely. We continue to monitor this very carefully.[33]

It is staggering that someone of Malloch-Brown's calibre – in his previous guise of UN diplomat, he was credited with drawing up the Millennium Development Goals of drastically reducing extreme poverty – could imagine that arms sold to Israel will not abet repression and aggression. His mealy-mouthed explanation of why arms sales are 'necessary' typifies the kind of double-speak which the Labour government virtually perfected. Two years before Tony Blair came to power in 1997, the Conservative government signed an agreement with Israel on deepening military cooperation between the two sides. No moves were made to cancel it after the transfer of power occurred, despite how Labour had pledged to bring an 'ethical dimension' to the blood-soaked foreign policy that Britain has pursued for centuries.

The Palestinian *intifada* afforded an excellent opportunity to show that this 'ethical dimension' amounted to more than a soundbite. And, of course, the opportunity was squandered. As the severity of Israeli state-violence increased, so too did British arms sales. In 1999, arms sales to Israel were worth £11.5 million; by 2001, this had almost doubled to £22.5 million. Much of the weaponry dispatched – small arms, grenade-making kits and equipment for warplanes and tanks – would have been useful to an Israeli army hell-bent on terrorising a civilian population in occupied Palestine.[34]

Saferworld, an advocacy group on conflict resolution issues, has calculated that in the decade following Labour's 1997 election victory, Britain approved military exports of over £110 million to Israel. Yes, there was an increase in the number of refusals for export licences to Israel in 2002 after it emerged that Israel had used modified Centurion tanks (originally sold to it in the late 1950s) in the occupied territories, breaking a promise to Britain that it would not do so. Yet the increase in refusals seems to have been temporary and tokenistic. While 91 licences were refused or revoked in 2001, only 26 were the following year. Worse, the number of approvals grew in 2006, the year of the Lebanon war. Over 200 licences were authorised that year, the highest since 2001.[35] A claim by Bill Rammell, another Foreign Office minister, that no approvals were granted for components of F16s, tanks or helicopters following the war in Lebanon should be treated with circumspection, as clearly plenty of British materiel found its way to Israel nonetheless.[36]

David Miliband, until recently the British foreign secretary, has bragged of how Britain's arms export criteria are 'amongst the strongest and most effective in the world'.[37] But greater candour was offered by one of his predecessors, Jack Straw. In July 2002, Britain gave its blessing for 'head-up displays' manufactured by BAE Systems to be delivered to Lockheed Martin in the United States, which then fitted them into F-16 airplanes destined for Israel. Apparently fearing that these deliveries would fall foul of the EU code of conduct, Britain issued new guidelines on the 'incorporation' of components into weapons made abroad, in order to circumvent the code. (These guidelines were endorsed by the European Union as a whole a few years later.[38])

Straw, ironically a peace activist in his youth, made clear that he viewed lucrative deals with the United States as more important than the human lives these components would help to end and blight. Anxious to avoid jeopardising Britain's involvement in the 'Joint Strike Fighter' project that Lockheed Martin was leading, he said:

> The government has judged that the UK's security and defence relationship with the US is fundamental to the UK's national security. Defence collaboration with the US is also key to maintaining a strong defence industrial capacity. Any interruption to the supply of these components would have serious implications for the UK's defence relations with the United States.[39]

There are strong indications that military cooperation with Israel not only continued throughout Labour's three terms in office but intensified during crucial periods. In May 2002, the London government admitted – in response to a parliamentary question – that 13 members of the Israeli defence force had been trained in Britain over the preceding year.[40] In August 2006, a cross-party grouping of MPs queried why Britain authorised exports to Israel worth £22.5 million in 2005. And US planes transporting weapons to Israel around the time of its offensive against Lebanon were allowed to refuel in British airports.[41]

As discussed in Chapter 2, Tony Blair's obduracy meant that the European Union could not formally call on Israel to cease bombing Lebanon in 2006. Although there was widespread international revulsion at Israel's actions in that war, Britain stepped up its arms sales to Israel over the next few years. In the first three months of 2008 alone, Britain rubber-stamped military exports of almost £20 million to Israel. This was 18 times greater than the licences granted in total for April–June 2006, the three months leading to the Lebanon war. More importantly, it meant that Israel would have a bloated arsenal at its disposal when planning to attack Gaza.

Al Haq, a human rights group based in Ramallah, is taking legal action against Britain over its close ties to Israel. Its lawyers have compiled an impressive list of UK companies that have made parts of Apache helicopters. The firms include SPS Aerostructures in Nottinghamshire, Smiths Industries in Cheltenham, Page Aerospace in Middlesex and Meggitt Avionics in Hampshire. The description of the Apache's awful prowess by Shawan Jabarin, director of Al Haq, indicates that any firm that helps build an Apache is contributing significantly to the occupation:

> The Apache is not just equipment. For Palestinians it's a symbol of indiscriminate military violence. From a young age, every Palestinian child learns to distinguish the Apache's sound and to associate it with assassinations, destruction and blood on the street.[42]

BENELUX EMBRACES A BLOODY TRADE

Several other EU governments have policies on arms transfers to Israel characterised by ambiguity and duplicity. In November 2003 the Dutch foreign minister Jaap de Hoop Scheffer – soon to be appointed NATO secretary-general – stated that his country did not allow weapons sales to Israel. Nonetheless, the Netherlands has displayed a lax attitude towards the transit of weapons through Schiphol, its principal airport. As 'friendly' nations do not require a permit to bring their cargo onto Dutch territory, the United States has had no problem landing planes laden with weapons in the Netherlands en route to Israel. Peace campaigners have estimated that in 2005 and 2006, 160 million bullet parts and tens of thousands of cartridges and fuses passed through Schiphol, with no discernible lull in the regularity of these transits during the war in Lebanon. Furthermore, the apparent ban on weapons sales to Israel does not hinder Dutch firms from doing business with US arms-makers who then sell their wares to Israel. So it comes as no surprise that the Hellfire rockets, Apache helicopters and F16 fighters that traumatise Palestinian children contain components made by such firms as Stork Special Products in Zwolle, 120 km north-east of Amsterdam, as well as by the Dutch electronics behemoth Philips.[43] Nor does the ban extend to 'dual-use' equipment, with the result that chemicals, including samples of the poison gas Soman, have been developed through Dutch–Israeli cooperation and Dutch night-vision technology, which can easily prove valuable to an army of occupation, has been exported to Israel.[44]

Over the past few years El Al has swapped Schiphol for Bierset airport, near the Belgian city of Liège, as the hub for its cargo activities. El Al now has two or three flights from the United States to Israel, via Bierset, each day. Even though Belgium's federal government announced in February 2009 that it was halting the exports of weapons to Israel, this measure doesn't seem to apply to arms passing through the country, about which there is little transparency.[45] It is safe to assume, then, that El Al's cargo is often not benign.[46]

DOUBLE STANDARDS DUBLIN-STYLE

In the Republic of Ireland, there is widespread public sympathy with the plight of the Palestinians. In response to that sympathy, successive Irish governments have sought to convey themselves as some of Israel's harshest critics. In 1980, Republic of Ireland foreign minister Brian Lenihan outraged Israel when he broke a taboo during a visit to Bahrain by recognising Yasser Arafat's PLO as representatives of the Palestinian people and called for the establishment of an independent Palestinian state (it took more than two decades before a US president could utter those words). This, according to the journalist Robert Fisk, led Israeli officialdom to regularly vent its spleen with Irish troops serving as UN peacekeepers in Lebanon at the time. Alleging that these soldiers were constantly drunk, the Israelis dubbed them the 'Johnnie Walker Irish' after a whiskey of that name (ironically distilled in Scotland).[47]

The Republic of Ireland's defence of the Palestinian underdog became increasingly superficial as it transformed itself into the fastest growing economy in the European Union in the 1990s. The much-vaunted Celtic Tiger was built on a willingness to entice the most unscrupulous of foreign investors to the Republic of Ireland through tax sweeteners. Amid the new guests to the country were companies that supplied the US military industry with sophisticated software. Data Device Corporation used facilities provided by the publicly funded Industrial Development Authority in Cork, for example, to make material for Apache helicopters that were then sold on to other US firms, known to do business with Israel.[48] The company stated proudly that its 'data bus' products enabled 'complex electronic subsystems to interact with each other and the online flight computer'.[49] Jeff Halper, a long-standing Israeli human rights activist, put it more succinctly when I met him in Jerusalem. He said that the 'brain' of the helicopters was made in the Republic of Ireland.[50] Staff in Intel, the manufacturer of computer chips, have also confirmed to me that Israeli firms do constant business with its European headquarters in Leixlip, about an hour's drive from Dublin. Many of the Israeli firms concerned are involved in the arms industry, the sources confirmed.

Although the Republic of Ireland is not officially aligned to any military power, it continues to help the US occupation of Iraq and Afghanistan by letting US warplanes refuel in Shannon airport. It is known, too, that killing machines en route to Israel have stopped over in the Irish mid-west. In February 2006, a US cargo plane carrying three Apache helicopters landed at Shannon and remained there overnight before resuming its journey to Israel.[51] Later that year, the Irish Department of Foreign Affairs said that the country's airports should not be used to transport weapons to Israel.[52] Granted in the wake of the Lebanon war, such assurances were too late to repair the damage that had already been done by helicopters fitted with Irish components and refuelled on Irish soil.

The Republic of Ireland has also supported Israel's military industry in recent years by buying its wares. Over the past few years, Ireland has offered something of a cover for French neo-colonialism by providing the force commander for an EU operation in Chad, otherwise dominated by French troops and tacitly designed to shore up the regime of Chadian military dictator Idriss Déby.[53] During that mission the Irish army used mini-UAVs made by the Israeli company Aeronautics Defense Systems. In 2007, the Republic of Ireland bought two Orbiters (as these drones are called), each costing $550,000.[54]

Another Israeli firm Rabintex Industries won a €2.5 million contract in 2006 to supply Irish soldiers with 12,000 helmets. Denunciations of the Israeli tactics in Lebanon that year and more recently in Gaza emanating from the Irish Department of Foreign Affairs have evidently been ignored in the ministry of defence in Dublin. In 2009, the latter ministry awarded Elbit Systems a contract to install surveillance pods and masts into a new fleet of tanks being developed for the Irish army. That Elbit has supplied surveillance equipment to the massive West Bank wall does not appear to have perturbed Dublin officials fixated on getting the best gear for the best price.[55] The Irish defence ministry even boasts that the equipment from Elbit will help it minimise civilian casualties. A tender document relating to this equipment read: 'The [Irish] Defence Forces are cognisant of the requirement for increasing degrees of accuracy, which are required for effective target acquisition, thus avoiding collateral damage, particularly in robust peace support operations.'[56]

BUYING ISRAEL'S DEADLY WARES

Elbit is a prime example of how Israeli firms can first exploit the opportunities afforded by a military occupation close to home and then use the know-how they have amassed to penetrate prized markets abroad. By taking over many previous rivals, it controls 90 per cent of the defence sector in Israel that is not owned by the state. Incessant conflict in the Middle East and the 'war on terror' internationally have been a boon for the company, with the value of its backlog of orders rising from $3.8 billion in 2006 to over $5 billion at the end of 2008. Even more impressively, its profitability grew from $516 million in 2007 to $767 million the following year. And as well as racking up sales worth more than $1 billion in the United States, it has set up subsidiaries in Britain, Germany, Brazil, South Korea and Romania.[57]

In Romania, Elbit has been one of the main drivers behind the development of a military industry that many other governments envy. As a 2004 study on the arms industry in Central and Eastern Europe noted:

> It may come as a surprise that a country such as Romania, which is often portrayed as a Third World country, has a first-class defence industry. The hard facts support this. It is also important to emphasise a lesser-known fact, namely that the development of the Romanian defence industry has very little to do with subcontracting work for the former Soviet Union and more to do with its extensive work with France, as well as its extensive cooperation with Israel.[58]

As Romania tried to emerge from the long shadows cast by Nicoale Ceausescu's 24-year tyranny – brought to an end by his execution on Christmas Day 1989 – it made a conscious decision to edge closer to NATO and the European Union. Part of the requirement for this rapprochement was that it boosted its military expenditure. Too poor to buy new planes for its air force, Romania decided to upgrade its fleet of MiG-21s, the last warplanes it acquired under Ceausescu's rule. After a tender was issued for their modernisation in 1992, Elbit was awarded the contract to perform the work, which involved more than 100 planes.[59]

More than a decade later, the Bucharest government coveted state-of-the-art fighter jets, yet found it could not afford to buy new F16s from the United States. So instead it bought second-hand versions of the planes from Israel and hired Elbit to oversee their refurbishment as part of a deal with an estimated $150 million price tag. The transfer of the jets required special permission from the United States. Unlike Venezuela under Hugo Chavez, which also wanted to upgrade F16s, Romania had no problem obtaining the go-ahead from Washington.[60]

Elbit has become the largest formal partner to a number of Romanian defence companies, notably Aerostar, Avioane Craoia and IAR.[61] Through its work with IAR, for example, it has upgraded helicopters for the Romanian air force[62] and Bucharest has been willing to buy some of the latest and most pioneering technology from Elbit. In 2007, Elbit won a $15 million contract to supply unmanned turrets and electro-optic equipment to a new military vehicle project for the Romanian army. It is almost superfluous to add that such turrets, which are remotely controlled, have been tried and tested in Israeli tanks in occupied Palestine.[63] This technology is designed to allow tanks carry greater quantities of ammunition than they could before.[64] One of Elbit's vice-presidents Butzi Machlis summed up the significance of the deal with a mixture of clumsy corporate-speak and a slightly phallic hubris:

> The selection of our systems for the project attests to our ability to provide a completely integrated configuration for fighting/patrol/surveillance vehicles, including unmanned turrets equipped with missile fire control and threat detection systems. We are proud to be selected to take part in this important project. The selection of our unmanned turrets constitutes a breakthrough in an emerging international market emanating from a shift in the modern battlefield.[65]

Surely, it is not coincidental that another company linked to Elbit is investing heavily in Romania. In the 1990s Elbit Medical Imaging became independent of the defence company that spawned it. Elbit Imaging is focused on hotel developments and the healthcare industry but its roots in the arms trade make the quasi-evangelical tones of its 'vision' statement by chairman Motti Zisser hard to stomach:

> We build for people beautiful homes and a variety of beautiful entertainment and retail environments where they can spend special hours with their loved ones. We build for people beautiful hotels to encourage them to travel to see how wonderful life is. We develop innovative medical devices and medications to help people live a better and longer life.

Over the past few years Elbit Imaging has shown an interest in reshaping Bucharest's cityscape. In 2006, it bought 75 per cent of the Casa Radio complex from the Turkish company that owned it. Located on the shore of the Dambovita river, this is an unfinished 1980s building originally intended as a museum to the Romanian Communist Party and which hosts the balcony from where Ceausescu – in August 1989 – viewed his last parade marking Romania's national day. Elbit Imaging is involved in a partnership worth over $1 billion with the Bucharest government to turn the 360,000 square metre site into a luxury hotel, entertainment and business centre.[66] The project has not been without its hiccups; Austrian-born and British-based entrepreneur Bernard Schreier has started legal proceedings against Elbit Imaging because of allegations that he was muscled out of investing in the Casa Radio initiative. Schreier had previously teamed up with Motti Zisser to develop another holiday resort in the region: Hungary's Obuda Island.[67]

Israel's state-owned arms company Rafael has been similarly active in drumming up business in Europe. It would appear that no self-respecting European army can do without Rafael's Spike missiles, judging by their sales. Those journalists who sanitise the arms trade tell us that Spikes are precision-guided missiles and are practically guaranteed to minimise 'collateral damage'. Their mode of operation is 'fire-and-forget'. In military parlance, this means that they are not supposed to require further guidance once they have been launched. Less well known is that the 'seeker heads' that are integral to their much-vaunted precision contain parts manufactured by the Finnish company Insta DefSec. Insta provides infrared cameras used in the Spikes, too.[68]

The Polish prime minister Donald Tusk is reputed to have told Israeli politicians that the relationship between Rafael and his country is in some respects even more valuable than the assistance Poland receives from the United States, its chief ally. In

2004, Rafael signed a $250 million deal to equip the Polish army with Spike missiles. To assemble them, it has set up a plant near the city of Radom in central Poland. Rafael has also been hired to provide thicker armour for vehicles driven by Polish troops in Afghanistan.[69]

Rafael, meanwhile, clinched a deal worth over $400 million in 2006 to supply Spain with 2,600 Spike missiles.[70] Yet it was the Netherlands which was the first NATO country to view the Spikes as indispensable, agreeing to buy a batch of them worth $250 million from Rafael in 2000.[71] Other European customers of these weapons include the Czech Republic and Italy.[72]

MORAL BANKRUPTCY

Trading weapons with Israel is arguably the worst way that the European Union can support an economy built on military might and the occupation of another people's land. Yet it is by no means the only form of support that the European Union is offering to Israeli business. In November 2007, Israel became the first of the European Union's neighbouring countries to be integrated into its 'competitiveness and innovation programme'. Allocated €3.6 billion between 2007 and 2013, the programme allows Israel to take part in joint projects with European firms, as well as to join the Enterprise Europe Network, which helps companies access public funding.[73]

There has been some disquiet among EU officials about Israel's participation. European Commission sources have told me that they are under instructions from the institution's hierarchy to ensure that firms in Israeli settlements do not derive benefits from the programme. Yet officials in Brussels feel ill-equipped to distinguish firms working in settlements from those within Israel's recognised borders. 'How are we supposed to know if a firm is based in a settlement or not?' asked one, not unreasonably.

The European Commission's instructions evidently do not extend to companies that regularly do business in the occupied territories or make profits out of Palestinian suffering. Israel is represented in the network by several trade associations. One of these, the Manufacturers Association of Israel, numbers the aforementioned drone-maker Elbit among its members. Another participant in the network is Matimop, the Israeli industrial development centre, which zealously seeks out opportunities to export weapons tested on Palestinian towns and villages.

The professed concern about Israeli settlements by senior EU officials appears all the more hypocritical when you realise that the same officials have been giving valuable advice to Israel about how to milk the European Union for cash. I have obtained a copy of a letter sent by Eneko Landaburu, then head of the European Commission's External Relations Department, to Israel's EU ambassador Ran Curiel in November 2008. In it, Landaburu states that cooperation in the high-tech field 'has the potential for being of mutual benefit' for the European Union and Israel. (Needless to say, no concern is expressed about the umbilical link between Israel's technology sector and its arms industry.) He then recommends contacts in the European Investment Bank (EIB) that should be able to assist the ambassador in accessing finance for Israeli firms.

Located in Luxembourg, the low profile that the EIB has kept throughout its 50-year history belies its status as the world's largest lending institution. Its loan portfolio is twice as large as that commanded by the World Bank. Despite being an official EU body, it guards its autonomy from EU governments jealously, to the point that it appears to feel that rules on protecting the environment or respecting human rights do not apply to it. (In November 2008, the bank was scolded by the European Court of Justice, which ruled that its lending activities in poor countries must strive to attain the stated objectives of EU development aid policies, namely to combat poverty.[74])

After not providing any money to Israel for 11 years, the EIB ended that hiatus in December 2006. At a time when most EU representatives were still on their Christmas holidays, the bank's vice-president Philippe de Fontaine Vive was in Israel signing two agreements to release a combined total of €275 million. Some €75 million of this amount was to be funnelled through Bank Hapoalim over a decade, with the proviso that it be used to finance small and medium-sized enterprises.[75] The EIB press statement announcing the loans failed to inform us that Bank Hapoalim has branches in the Israeli settlements of Gilo and Pisgat Ze'ev in East Jerusalem, as well as in the Golan Heights, and has provided credit for building activities in these settlements. It has also supported Israeli firms operating in the West Bank industrial zones of Mishor Adumim and Barkan. And together with Leumi, another Israeli bank, it has been involved in providing over $500 million in loans to the City Pass consortium behind the light rail project in East Jerusalem.[76]

Israeli diplomats have been eager to acquire more EIB money. Oded Eran, Israel's former EU envoy, has had talks with senior figures in the bank about potential loans for energy, transport and telecommunications projects. He has also raised the possibility that Israel could formally join the bank, even though its membership is now restricted to EU governments. Eran has pointed out that Israel is a member of other financial institutions such as the Inter-American Development Bank and is represented on the board of the European Bank for Reconstruction and Development, a non-EU body based in London. 'Why should Israel not be able to participate in the activities of this bank [the EIB] as it does in regional banks in other areas of the world?' Eran has asked.[77]

Despite professing to deplore Israeli settlements, EU governments have generally kept mum as banks and companies based in their jurisdictions have done business with those settlements and striven to profit from the wider occupation. Dexia, the Franco-Belgian bank, offers an egregious case in point.

In 2001 Dexia, which specialises in providing loans to local authorities, bought the Israeli Municipality Treasury Bank, thereby forming Dexia Israel. Before long, this new kid on Israel's banking block was accused by members of the Knesset of paying insufficient heed to the development of Israeli settlements on Palestinian land. In response, Dexia assured parliamentarians in 2005 that it was actively providing long-term loans to Israeli municipalities in the occupied West Bank.[78] David Kapah, the chief executive of Dexia Israel, was asked at a hearing in the Knesset if the bank offered better terms to authorities within Israel's recognised borders than to those administering settlements. He replied that the location of the authorities made no difference to Dexia; in total, the bank has given loans to more than ten municipalities in the Israeli settlements, including Har Hebron, Ariel, Elkana, Kedumim and Giv'at Zeev.[79]

It took some time for news of this admission to make an impact in Europe. But when a number of Belgian peace and human rights activists became aware of it, they organised a campaign urging Dexia to divest from the settlements in 2008. Coincidentally, this mobilisation occurred at a time when Dexia took a severe bruising as a result of the international financial crisis. Alarmed by a rapid fall in value of its shares and convinced that it must not be allowed to fail, the governments of France, Luxembourg and Belgium jointly injected €6.4 billion of cash into the bank late that September.[80]

To oversee the recovery of the bank, one of Belgium's best-known politicians, Jean-Luc Dehaene (prime minister for most of the 1990s), was appointed its chairman. In May 2009, he took time out from running for the European Parliament (to which he had no trouble being elected) to attend Dexia's annual general meeting.

Dehaene told shareholders that the bank had not provided any money to the settlements since September 2008. He said:

> In the past Dexia Israel granted €5 million in loans to the settlements. This was only 1% of the total budget of Dexia Israel. The loans to the Jerusalem municipality are not included, as the Dexia Group feels that Jerusalem is not contested territory.[81]

A charitable interpretation of Dehaene's statement is that he was merely reciting a script prepared for him by the bank and that he was otherwise unfamiliar with the dossier. For it is hard to understand how someone of his political nous and experience could have convinced himself that Jerusalem is not contested territory. Just as seriously, Dexia has not been transparent or precise about its activities. After I had heard that it had approved a batch of new loans worth around €50 million to Israeli authorities in 2009, I asked the bank for a list of the authorities concerned. The loans followed a call by the Israeli Finance Ministry in March that year for credit to be provided to a range of authorities with cashflow problems, including five situated in settlements in the West Bank. A Dexia spokeswoman replied: 'We are sorry to tell you that, as a bank, the financial data of our clients are confidential and therefore not communicated.' And despite its claims that it is no longer offering loans to the settlements, Dexia has not said if it has stopped providing all services there such as hosting accounts for Israeli authorities on occupied land. My follow-up queries seeking clarification about whether such services are continuing have gone unanswered.

There are also inconsistencies between what Dexia has been telling its critics in Europe and what the bank has been saying in the Middle East. In July 2009, a Dexia source was quoted in the Israeli business publication *The Marker* saying that the bank 'continues to give loans to all Israeli authorities that respect Israeli law, without any other non-banking consideration'.[82]

Because Belgium's federal government, local and regional authorities hold around one-quarter of Dexia's shares, they have a duty to be vigilant in monitoring the bank's activities and vociferous in demanding that it does not acquiesce to illegality. Most of the country's authorities have not raised their voices. By the autumn of 2009, Namur in the French-speaking south was the only province to have passed a resolution urging Dexia to cease funding settlements. While some communes in the cities of Brussels and Liège had made similar calls, the country's larger and more powerful institutions have been afflicted by a disgraceful apathy.

THE RACIST RAILWAY

When Nicolas Sarkozy visited Israel in June 2008, he was accompanied by a well-heeled entourage. Around 100 members of the French corporate elite were in tow; many took advantage of the deepening Franco–Israeli political relationship to argue that it would be only logical to complement it with increased trade and investment. Speaking at a seminar of businesspeople in Jerusalem, Sarkozy said:

> The economic ties between France and Israel are not at a level that they should be. When you look at the trade and business figures, activity is lower than at the end of the 1990s. We have not been enough involved, pushed enough to be part of the economic developments and the wealth of R&D in this country. This situation needs to change. We need to do more to forge co-operation in the business realm, as well as with Israeli universities.[83]

There were two important exceptions to Sarkozy's gripe: Veolia and Alstom. Both firms, he acknowledged, had gone for a full immersion in Israel's economic waters.

Three years earlier Ariel Sharon fired the metaphorical starting pistol for the construction of a €500 million light rail project, involving these two companies, in East Jerusalem. Sharon was enthused by a scheme specifically designed to extend Israel's encroachment into the Arab parts of the city. Once completed, the gleaming modern trams would connect a number of Israeli settlements in East Jerusalem with the city centre, passing by the Damascus and Jaffa Gates in the Old City. Ammunition Hill, one of the key stations in the network, would also become a feeder centre to link the ever-growing Ma'ale Adumim in the West Bank and other settlements in the Jordan Valley with Jerusalem. 'Anything that can be done to strengthen Jerusalem, construct it, expand it and sustain it for eternity as the capital of the Jewish people and the united capital of the state of Israel, should be done,' Sharon declared at a signing ceremony.[84]

That French companies had entered into a public–private partnership with an explicit objective of consolidating Israel's stranglehold of Palestine did not appear to exercise Jacques Chirac, president at the time the deal was clinched, or Sarkozy, his successor. Fortunately, however, activists around the world were sufficiently incensed by the affair to mobilise against Veolia, the wealthiest company in City Pass (as the consortium awarded the contract for the railway is known). Veolia was a good target for an international campaign; because it was adept at winning municipal works contracts in several continents, its bottom line could be hurt if local authorities could be persuaded to jeopardise some of these deals. The mobilisation was effective and widespread:

- The City of Melbourne ripped up a contract awarded to Veolia subsidiary Connex for work on a suburban train network.[85]
- Stockholm Community Council announced that Veolia had lost a $4.5 billion chance to operate its subway.[86]
- A majority of politicians on Galway City Council in the Republic of Ireland supported a call for a water management contract to be taken away from Veolia.[87]
- London's mayor Boris Johnson has faced demands to block Veolia from running a bike-hire scheme.[88]
- Sandwell Borough Council, also in England, excluded Veolia from bidding for a $1 billion waste management contract.[89]

In June 2009, it was reported that Veolia was trying to sell its stake in City Pass to Egged or Dan, the Israeli bus operators.[90] It is understandable why Veolia would want to abandon the project, which has been plagued by delays, litigation (human rights activists in France have taken legal action against Veolia's involvement in the project) and controversy (the Dutch bank ASN withdrew its investments from Veolia in 2006, in response to pressure from Palestinian solidarity campaigners).[91] But it should be emphasised that – at the time of writing – Veolia has never officially confirmed that it wants out. On the contrary, it has gone to considerable lengths to indicate that it remains committed. For example, it has continued to advertise job vacancies in the Israeli press.[92] With Veolia displaying its allegiance to this deplorable scheme so publicly, it is only right that the campaign against it is being sustained.

VOLVO: A SUBCONTRACTOR FOR TORTURE

During 2009 Volvo unexpectedly found itself incurring the wrath of some Israelis. After the Swedish tabloid *Aftonbladet* published an article alleging that Israeli soldiers had stolen the internal organs of slain Palestinians, 10,000 irate Israelis signed an online petition in just two days calling for all Swedish goods to be boycotted.[93] Volvo may have been an obvious candidate for this knee-jerk reaction but it was also an ironic one. For the company that prides itself on its reputation as a maker of 'safe' vehicles has benefited from Israel's efforts to deprive Palestinians of safety and shelter.

Jane Smith, a member of the International Women's Peace Service, gave this graphic eyewitness account of how Israeli troops razed homes in the West Bank a few years ago:

> When we arrived in the village of Al Funduq, Salfeet, the aftermath of the first house demolition was already evident. A family stood on a pile of rubble, silenced and shocked. The second house demolition was just beginning, with the Caterpillar and Volvo bulldozers ripping into the top floor of the nearly completed house. The family, two of whom were handcuffed throughout the demolition, were powerless in this situation. Within an hour, years of labour and money were obliterated by the Israeli army. Caterpillar and Volvo are profiting from this family's grief.[94]

Faced with a bulky dossier of evidence about how its bulldozers had turned out to be a tool of Israeli aggression, a Volvo vice-president Mårten Wikforss said it was 'regrettable and sad if our products are used for destructive purposes'. He added:

> We do not condone such actions, but we do not have any control over the use of our products, other than to affirm in our business activities a code of conduct that decries unethical behaviour. However, just as a wheel loader can be used to clear the ground for a new house, it can be used to tear it down.[95]

It is true that Volvo is not as culpable as Caterpillar is. Whereas Caterpillar vehicles are exported directly to Israel as weaponry under the US foreign military sales programme, Volvo has sought to keep some distance between itself and the Israeli army, claiming that the latter simply buys its products. But this does not mean that executives in Volvo's Gothenburg headquarters can plead ignorance about how their products are being used. As a company which claims to adhere to principles of corporate social responsibility, it surely has an obligation to ensure that it does not facilitate violations of international law.

More fundamentally, Volvo's claims that ignorance equals innocence are devoid of credibility. Though synonymous with cars, Volvo has been bragging about how it is capturing an ever-increasing share of the market for new buses in Israel. High reliability and low fuel consumption are guaranteed by its models, the company says.[96] These ecologically virtuous buses can be regularly seen in illegal Israeli settlements. Together with Mayer Cars and Trucks, Volvo jointly owns the transport technology firm, Merkavim. It has produced an armoured version of Volvo's Mars Defender bus, which is used by Egged, the bus company, in the public transport services it provides for Israeli settlers. Videos on Merkavim's website trumpet how it is behind 'the world's most armoured bus yet the people inside never know the difference'. After images of Israeli troops are shown embarking on the bus – built on a Volvo chassis, the narrator says – the videos tell us that it can keep on rolling even after it has been ambushed.[97]

Merkavim also manufactures vehicles designed for transporting prisoners. Its Mars Prisoner Bus is 'the perfect solution for conveying prisoners under guard', according to the company, as its three separate high-security cabins, with a total of 44 'firmly fixed metal seats', allow 'close supervision' of detainees.[98] With ill-treatment rife in the jails where these buses often start and end their journeys, Volvo can legitimately be considered a subcontractor for torture.

Volvo's code of conduct says the company has resolved not to be complicit in the abuse of human rights. In its ruling on the 'security barrier' in the West Bank, the International Court of Justice found that it is illegal for an occupying power to transfer part of its own population to the territory that it occupies.[99] Volvo's buses are clearly helping such a transfer to occur on an indefinite basis. And through Merkavim, it is tailoring its services to the meet the perceived needs of the transferred population. Volvo's top managers in Gothenburg cannot shrug their shoulders and claim this has nothing to do with them.

Furthermore, the organisation War on Want has documented how vehicles manufactured by Volvo and machinery manufactured by the British firm JCB have been used in work relating to the construction of the 'apartheid wall' that snakes through the West Bank.[100] So too have bulldozers made by the French company Manitou;[101] cranes by the Dutch company Riwal;[102] and cement by the Irish company CRH (formerly Cement-Roadstone Holdings).[103] The involvement of these companies in the project contravenes

2003 UN guidelines on the human rights responsibilities of businesses. None of these companies can claim they are unaware of how their products are being used, yet rather than taking steps to ameliorate the situation some of them have become even more entangled in the occupation than they previously had. CRH, for example, decided during 2009 to buy the building company Hanson Israel, but the deal has subsequently run into trouble with Israel's finance and competition authorities.[104] That Hanson has been exploiting the natural resources of the Palestinian people through its quarrying activities in the West Bank did not appear to be an issue for CRH's Dublin headquarters, despite how, if one believes its website, it meets the 'highest standards of corporate social responsibility'.[105]

A TRADE IN DECEPTION

Yasser Arafat may have been a deeply flawed leader, yet he once cut through the flannel that often passes for international discourse on the Middle East when he said:

> Seventy per cent of the economy of Israel is with European countries and this card has not been used until now. Why not? You only have to wave this economic card and they will listen to you directly. At least wave it.[106]

Even though the European Union's association agreement with Israel stipulates that the latter's preferential terms of access to the former's markets are conditional on respect for human rights, no real action is taken when large-scale abuses of elementary rights occur. Threats to hit Israel's bottom line have in most cases been mere bluster.

Every year Europe takes in two-thirds of all Israeli exports, bringing a hugely valuable $18 billion to the Israeli economy. The association agreement, which came into force in 2000, exempted most Israeli goods from duties when entering the European Union. An accord to extend Israel's trade preferences for food and drinks even further was reached in 2008 and signed the following year. Applying to 80 per cent of all fresh produce and 95 per cent of all processed food, it removed tariffs and lifted levies and quotas on such products as concentrates for soft drinks, biscuits and marshmallows. As a result, Israeli agricultural exports to Europe were projected to double in the coming years.[107]

There is a snag: an estimated 20 per cent of all exports to the European Union with a 'made in Israel' label come wholly or partly from settlements in the occupied territories.[108] As most of these are food, cosmetics, wines, cut flowers or textiles, there is a high probability that nearly all of us have unwittingly bought products from illegal settlements in our local supermarket.

As the European Union does not consider the settlements as part of Israel, its governments agreed between themselves in 2001 that goods originating from them could not receive the same preferential treatment as goods from inside Israel's recognised borders.[109] In effect, the governments were simply confirming what article 83 of the EU–Israel association agreement says – that only goods from territory internationally recognised as part of Israel can benefit from trade preferences. Germany and the Netherlands had, however, staunchly opposed the enforcement of this provision. And though the problems had long been evident, it was not until 2005 that a 'technical arrangement' came into effect, whereby all goods exported from Israel to the European Union had to be marked with their postcode and place of origin. In 2004, Israel's Ministry of Industry and Trade estimated that $150 million of goods passed off as Israeli exports were in fact from the occupied territories. Losses stemming from the EU moves to prevent such exports from benefiting from trade preferences would amount to $8 million, the ministry calculated.[110]

Following a series of investigations by journalists and activists in Britain on how produce from the settlements was being sold in high street stores, the London government prepared a one-page 'non-paper' for EU foreign ministers in late 2008. (A 'non-paper', to use the sometimes arcane language of diplomacy, is a proposal put forward for informal discussion). The British document expressed concern that 'settlement goods may be entering the United Kingdom without paying sufficient duty, by illegally using the preferential trade arrangements under the association agreement between the EU and Israel'. It also said that British customs authorities were carrying out 'a range of targeted physical examinations' on imports purporting to be from Israel and would pass on the results of these to the European Commission.

The document was accorded a high importance by some journalists. In the United Kingdom, the *Independent* reported that 'Britain is taking the lead in pressing the European Union to curb imports from Israeli producers in the occupied West Bank as a practical step towards halting the steady increase in the construction of

Jewish settlements.'[111] *Haaretz* in Israel said that that country's civil servants were perturbed by the prospect of 'confrontation' with their British counterparts.[112] Britain's Foreign Office had confirmed, according to the *Jewish Chronicle*, that its document was 'merely the opening shot in a wider campaign it is waging against the settlements'.[113]

If that was true, then the campaign was extremely badly coordinated. Mindful of the promise that a report from the British customs authorities would soon be landing on the desks of EU officials, I contacted the customs authorities in the spring of 2009 to check on progress. 'I'm not aware that we're due to give any information to Europe,' their spokesman said.[114]

EU officials were similarly nonchalant. Although they had learned through the grapevine that the British authorities had discovered that two out of 26 companies based in Israeli settlements that they had investigated were benefitting illegally from EU trade preferences, Brussels officials said they could not do anything, until a dossier had been transmitted to them through formal channels. I'm no legal expert but that explanation struck me as lily-livered. The European Commission is constantly harping on how it is the guardian of EU law. In plenty of other instances, it has not had to wait for a report printed on a government's headed paper to act; the Commission's environment department, for example, regularly probes complaints from ordinary citizens, while its anti-trust wing can conduct dawn raids on companies suspected of price-fixing based on tip-offs from commercial sources. The failure to properly examine the abuse of the EU–Israel agreement appears symptomatic of a lack of political will, not a lack of information.

More shamefully still, the Commission has in effect accepted that Israeli settlers can legitimately run businesses on occupied Palestinian land.

During 2009, the European Court of Justice in Luxembourg considered a case referred to it by a finance court in Hamburg. It related to the activities of Brita, a German manufacturer of water filters, which buys accessories and syrups from Soda Club, a company based in the Israeli settlement Ma'ale Adumim. In 2002, the German customs office initially agreed to treat the goods provided by Soda Club as Israeli (and therefore eligible for EU trade preferences). But a year later, the customs office decided that the goods should be subject to duties, after the Israeli authorities failed to answer a request to clarify where they were produced.

Brita contested the decision of the customs office. And in an opinion issued by the European Court of Justice in October 2009, it was stated that the goods did not qualify for preferential treatment under the EU–Israel association agreement.[115] The opinion was confirmed through a formal ruling of the court at a later stage.

Like most deliberations of the Luxembourg court, the case has received very little press coverage. But Charles Shamas of the Mattin Group, the Ramallah-based human rights organisation, has followed the case closely. At a meeting of Palestinian solidarity activists shortly before the court's opinion was delivered, he expressed dismay at the position taken by the European Commission in the proceedings. Rather than using the opportunity to stress the illegal nature of Israeli settlements, the Commission suggested that the goods could have benefited from EU trade preferences if the Palestinian Authority had issued certificates for them, instead of the Israelis. 'This was a fallacious argument,' Shamas said. 'The Commission did not want to tell the court that these operators [in Israeli settlements] should be frozen out of any preferential treatment with the European Union.'

A related issue concerns the level of detail that should appear on produce from the settlements. In some British supermarkets, it is common to find fruit, vegetables or herbs, with 'West Bank' labelled as their place of origin. A customer could easily be misled, therefore, into thinking he or she is supporting hard-pressed Palestinian farmers by buying their dates or sage, when in fact the goods come from Israeli settlements on stolen land. The European Union's technical arrangements have not helped clarify this situation. 'We say that settlement products can't be labelled "made in Israel" but we don't say how exactly they should be labelled,' a senior EU diplomat confessed to me.

Britain's aforementioned 'non-paper' says that 'consumers should be empowered to make informed choices regarding goods from settlements'. Discussions have been held between retailers, human rights activists and the British government about resolving the surrounding conundrum and it is conceivable that labels stating that goods originated in Israeli settlements will be seen in some supermarkets before long. This would be a welcome step but it would be insufficient.

Israel's denial of Palestinian rights cannot be reduced to an issue of consumer choice. Deciding between a fruit from an Israeli settlement and one grown elsewhere is not the same as deciding between two different brands of baked beans or washing powder. Nobody should have to make a choice about whether or not to support an illegal activity when shopping for groceries. Goods from Israeli settlements should not be on sale in Europe, irrespective of how they are labelled.

There is another reason why it is impossible to take Britain's 'campaign' against Israeli settlements seriously. Barely a fortnight after Britain had presented its 'non-paper' to other EU governments, its then business secretary Peter Mandelson called for closer commercial relations with the country's 'firm friend' Israel. Jointly addressing 200 British business leaders with Shimon Peres, Mandelson voiced hopes that UK–Israeli trade would exceed £3 billion by 2012. In 2007, this trade was worth £2.3 billion, with Britain the third largest destination for Israeli exports.[116]

As Mandelson is a confidant of Tony Blair, it is no surprise that he sought to eulogise Peres, another warmonger, by claiming that the president had displayed 'tireless energy and bravery' in seeking peace. This duplicity is typical of British ministers who criticise Israeli settlements from one side of their mouths and woo Israeli firms (including many operating in the exact same settlements) with the other.

6

THE ISRAEL LOBBY COMES TO EUROPE

My first full-blown exposure to Israel's propaganda machine left me unsettled. Back in 2001, I was invited to meet some Israelis who had lost loved ones in suicide bombings and were then visiting Europe. Wide-eyed and with no other objective than gathering enough material for a 'human interest' story, I made my way to the Holiday Inn in Brussels. Within a minute of stepping into the conference room hired by the Israeli embassy, I felt that I was lost in a bewildering bazaar, where suffering and sorrow were the only commodities on offer. As reporters arrived, Israeli diplomats scanned the visitors they were hosting, before selecting one to recount their experience.

I was assigned a man whose daughter had been killed by Hamas when it attacked a pizzeria in Jerusalem during August of that year. He came across as a gentle and affable man, and spoke movingly about how his young girl had been taken away from him so cruelly. After jotting down those memories of her life and death that he agreed to share, I awkwardly asked him about the broader political situation. Did his own bereavement, I wondered, help him empathise with Palestinian parents who had also been robbed of children through violence? To my astonishment, the man answered as if such violence did not exist. Israeli soldiers, he insisted, went to enormous lengths to avoid causing harm to civilians. Although I took issue with him by saying there was plenty of evidence to the contrary, he kept on stressing his confidence in his nation's army.

Angered by how Israeli officialdom was using a grieving father as a pawn in a sordid public relations battle, I decided against writing a story based on this interview. I didn't make a big fuss about my decision but when the next issue of the newspaper I was then working for appeared, the Israeli embassy called me to enquire about the omission. Politely but firmly, I told the diplomat that the meeting to which he had invited me smacked of a propaganda exercise and I was not prepared to play along with it.

In 15 years of writing about European and international politics, I have had several unedifying encounters with diplomats. A Russian source even offered to pay me if I could give him information about what US correspondents in Europe talked about over coffee and beer. And I could give numerous examples of the guff I have heard spouted as envoys from many different countries sought to justify injustice or deny the undeniable.

The Israeli embassy (or 'mission', to use its formal title) is, however, in a class of its own. Whereas every other non-European embassy in Brussels has to make do with its own staff and perhaps a business association to defend its interests, Israel has a burgeoning network of advocacy groups and 'think-tanks' dedicated solely to its promotion. Israel's only competitor in this regard is its patron-in-chief, the United States, which also has many nominally independent organisations staffed with defenders of its foreign and economic policies.

Across the Atlantic, some pundits believe that pro-Israel advocates are second only to the National Rifle Association in terms of the influence they have wielded over law-makers since the 1970s.[1] The power of the lobby has been the subject of considerable debate in recent times, thanks in large part to the thought-provoking book *The Israel Lobby and US Foreign Policy* by John Mearsheimer and Stephen Walt. Although its publication in 2007 engendered much controversy, the subsequent presidential campaign appeared to support their thesis that US politicians feel they are under immense pressure to placate the Israel lobby. One of Barack Obama's key foreign policy statements as a candidate was delivered to a June 2008 conference hosted by the American Israel Public Affairs Committee (AIPAC), where he received a standing ovation for declaring that 'Jerusalem will remain the capital of Israel and it must remain undivided'.[2]

In Europe, the pro-Israel lobby is in no way as well organised or resourced as that in the United States. But over the past few years, it has grown in both size and strength, a phenomenon that has gone unnoticed by most of the mainstream press.

I am fully aware that some of Israel's more inveterate supporters try to smear everyone who talks about an 'Israel lobby' as a Jew-hater or as a conspiracy theorist. Some even insinuate that uttering the word 'lobby' betokens hostility to Jews; Denis MacShane, a British Labour MP and former government minister, wrote in his book

Globalising Hatred: The New Anti-Semitism: 'Across Europe, the term "lobby" is becoming a new scattergun device for accusing Jews anywhere of exercising secret and sinister power.'[3]

So let me be clear: I despise anti-Semitism (including antipathy towards Palestinians, who are also Semites), just as I despise every other prejudice based solely on race, religion, gender or sexual orientation. But I disagree passionately with the notion that it is anti-Semitic to draw attention to how the Israeli state has become consumed by aggression and xenophobia, both of which are highly destructive for the Palestinians, for Israel's neighbouring countries and ultimately, I believe, for Israel itself. Equally, I cannot accept that it is anti-Semitic to shed light on how the Israel lobby operates. For starters, only a fraction of the world's Jews are active in the Israel lobby. Nor is this lobby exclusively Jewish; its adherents include more than a few Christians, and difficult though it may be to believe, even some Muslims (as I shall discuss later).

My intention here is not to claim that the pro-Israel lobby is the only, or even the most important, factor behind Israel's deepening relations with the European Union. But I do believe that its activities should be carefully monitored. This is not because I suspect the lobby has a hidden agenda. Rather, it is because the lobby (although not transparent about all its affairs) has a transparent agenda of winning support for Israeli aggression from foreign governments and institutions.

EUROPEAN FRIENDS OF ISRAEL: ENEMIES OF TRUTH

Although only established in 2006, the European Friends of Israel (EFI) has emerged as the pro-Israel group with the highest profile in Brussels. Based around a cross-party alliance of members of the European Parliament (MEPs), it is the closest thing that the European Union has to AIPAC, which is widely considered the most powerful group working on international relations in Washington.

Officially, the EFI says that it is not trying to replicate AIPAC's *modus operandi*. Nonetheless, it enjoys close contacts with AIPAC and its key personnel have clearly studied how the pro-Israel lobby has harried members of Congress so successfully. Dimitri Dombret, EFI's first director, has confirmed to me that he has attended AIPAC events in the United States. The EFI's core activities also differ little from those of its sister organisations in the United States. It throws sumptuous dinners for politicians and officials, brings them on expenses-paid trips and supplies them with briefing notes that sometimes have a tenuous relationship with the truth and on other occasions contain bare-faced lies.

British Conservative MEP Charles Tannock, one of its founding members, has presented EFI as a necessary counterbalance to the Palestinian solidarity movement:

> There is a clear need to reverse some of the demonising of Israel and the black propaganda peddled by its enemies both within and outside of the EU. Israel is at the front line in fighting international terrorism, which threatens us all, and therefore deserves our strong support.[4]

Such talk of 'black propaganda' is hard to stomach coming from an organisation that – despite its short history – appears to have mastered the dark and dishonest arts of spin. When Israel bombed the area surrounding a UN school in Gaza in the first week of 2009, the UN's Relief and Works Agency for Palestinian refugees (UNRWA) said it was '99.9 per cent certain' that there were no Hamas militants in the school at the time.[5] Insinuating that it knows better than humanitarian aid workers with no political axe to grind, the EFI circulated a 'fact-sheet' later that January stating that Hamas had used civilians as 'human shields' by launching attacks from the grounds of UN schools in Gaza. The 'fact-sheet' recycled a series of other suppositions and groundless allegations, and fallaciously presented Hamas as the cause of the suffering inflicted on the people of Gaza by the Israeli state:

> Hamas returned fire on civilian areas by launching attacks from densely populated areas and, specifically, from inside and the vicinity of private homes, schools, mosques and hospitals. In a report to the Israeli cabinet, Israeli intelligence chief Yuval Diskin, indicated that the Gaza-based leadership of Hamas was hiding in an underground bunker beneath Shifa Hospital, the largest in the Gaza Strip. Hamas also endangered civilians by ordering its forces to discard uniforms and dress in regular clothes that made them indistinguishable from the civilian population.[6]

The propensity of the EFI to lie has not stopped some EU top-level representatives from giving it their seal of approval. Benita Ferrero-Waldner, then the EU commissioner for external relations, attended the group's inaugural dinner, along with Elmar Brok, then chairman of the European Parliament's foreign affairs committee. Nicolas Sarkozy also gave it a boost when France held the EU presidency in 2008. Shortly before Dalia Itzik, then the Knesset's speaker, addressed 1,000 parliamentarians at an EFI conference in Paris, she met Sarkozy and his foreign minister Bernard Kouchner for a bout of sabre-rattling towards Iran. Enthused by the warm reception granted to her by the Parisian elite, she told the gathering that Iran 'endangers not only Israel, but the entire world', adding: 'If terror groups are able to lay their hands on nuclear weapons provided by Iran, they will be able to target Paris, London and New York as well.'[7]

This was one of several instances in which the EFI has presented Iran as the number one bogeyman for the West, conveniently ignoring how Israel was the country that introduced nuclear weapons to the Middle East. As well as working for EFI, Dimitri Dombret has written several pamphlets for the European Strategic Intelligence and Security Centre (ESISC), which bears the dubious distinction of being the most hawkish think-tank in Brussels. In a joint recent paper, Dombret and ESISC president Claude Moniquet alleged that Iran is training violent extremists intent on attacking Europe. The threadbare nature of their argument is highlighted by how the only source from the past decade they cite to back up this claim was a report in the UK's *Daily Telegraph* that a man who carried out a bombing in Istanbul in 2003 had travelled to Iran, where he allegedly learned how to use explosives.[8]

The EFI has two steering committees; one in the European Parliament, the other comprising members of national parliaments from EU member states. Cleverly, the events that they organise imply that they relish healthy debates about Israel. Yet while they have invited speakers from diverse backgrounds, their guests have been united by supporting Israel unequivocally. In 2009, they even hosted a visit to Europe by two Arabs who were among the most gung-ho supporters of Israeli militarism I have heard. Nonie Darwish, an Egyptian woman now living in the United States, experienced the reality of Israeli state violence when she was eight years old. Her father, Mustafa Hafez, was killed by an Israeli mail bomb in 1956, after a few years service as head of Egyptian army intelligence in Gaza; he has been described as the first victim of Israel's targeted assassination policy. Despite that traumatic history, her group, Arabs for Israel, vigorously defends Israeli actions. When I put it to her that many would regard her as a 'puppet' for Israel she retorted, 'If you think that I'm a puppet, that's your problem.' My question was prompted by what I considered to be her heartless – and frankly racist – dismissal of Palestinian anguish. 'Palestinian people are trained to just marvel at their own misery,' she said. 'Israelis are not as dramatic as Palestinians. They don't stand and pose for the cameras as much.'

Darwish was joined on her European jaunt by fellow Egyptian Tawfik Hamid. Once a member of the militant group Jemaah Islamiyyah, Hamid is reputed to have prayed alongside Ayman al-Zawahiri, who went on to become a top figure in al Qaeda, in his youth. Nowadays, he spends his time as a 'terrorism expert'. As well as contributing to CNN, FoxNews and the *Wall Street Journal*, he has written a book *Inside Jihad: Understanding and Confronting Radical Islam*. While he would appear well qualified to address this topic, he displays a fickle understanding of how the violence of some militant organisations is a direct consequence of oppression and dispossession, principally in Palestine. I was gobsmacked when he, a trained medical doctor, likened Israel's war against Gaza to a prescription for strong medicine. 'If you have an infection and I give you a half-dose of antibiotics, that aggravates the problem,' he said, arguing that all-out warfare was needed to turn Gazans away from Hamas.

The EFI has also organised visits to EU institutions for several prominent Israeli politicians. Colette Avital, whose CV includes a stint as speaker of the Knesset and a candidacy for the country's presidency, has attended several of the lobby group's events. It is easy to see why she would be regarded as a good ambassador for Israel in Europe, and not just because she was born in Romania and is a skilled communicator in French and English. Avital belongs to what is known (often inaccurately) as the 'peace camp' in Israel. When she was Israel's consul-general in New York during the mid-1990s, she urged major pro-Israel groups in the United States to speak out in favour of the Oslo Accords.[9]

In reality, Avital is an embodiment of how there is no substantial difference between Israel's three largest parties – Likud, Labour and Kadima – on the occupation. True, she was critical of aspects of Israel's policy towards Gaza – like its denial of basic goods to the Strip's population.[10] But given that she broadly favours Israel's military excesses, including its attack on Gaza, her stance on such issues amounts to no more than quibbling. For someone who expresses pride in being a socialist, Avital seems to have a blinkered outlook. When I met her for coffee in one of Brussels' most luxurious hotels, she spoke eloquently about the inequalities in Israeli society and how 'children come to school without having a decent meal'. I put it to her that such poverty could be reduced if Israel allocated less resources to fighting wars and more to social programmes. 'This is not connected at all to the military budget,' she insisted.

The EFI is evidently not short of cash, judging by the events it organises. But when I asked Dombret about where it gets its money, all he would say was: 'EFI is funded by private donors from Europe. I'm sure you would understand that I cannot give any figures about our budget.' Well, I don't understand. If organisations are striving to influence decision makers, the least that can be expected is a modicum of openness about how they are funded.

Unlike their counterparts in the United States, EU institutions do not require that lobbyists who seek to influence lawmakers sign up to a mandatory register. While the European Commission has introduced a register for 'interest representatives' in the recent past, it has left it to lobbyists themselves to decide whether they wish to be included in it. The Commission's puny efforts to boost transparency have meant that by October 2009, just over 750 Brussels-based lobby firms or individuals had entered details (often skimpy) of their activities in the register, even though the number of such firms in Brussels probably exceeds 2,600 and the number of individual lobbyists 15,000.[11] Among the lobby groups that cannot be found in the register at the time of writing are the European Friends of Israel.

TRANSATLANTIC INSTITUTE: STIFLING DEBATE WITH SMEARS

Search the archives for speeches given by Javier Solana in February 2004 on his website and you will find just two entries. One of them was delivered at the launch of the Transatlantic Institute, a Brussels-based 'think-tank' set up by the American Jewish Committee (AJC). Most of Solana's remarks, particularly his calls for greater contacts between Jews and Muslims, appear sensible. Yet the lavish praise he heaped on the AJC (he described it as an organisation based on 'openness, dialogue and respect for the views of others') was surely misplaced.[12]

Far from advocating respect for the views of others, the AJC has readily deployed the most illiberal tactic favoured by pro-Israel zealots: automatically branding critics of Israeli aggression as anti-Semitic. It has been well documented that the establishment of Israel involved what Israeli historian Ilan Pappe called the ethnic cleansing of Palestinians from land they had lived on for many generations. There are sound reasons for anyone concerned with justice to criticise the way in which Israel came into being through acts of patent injustice. Those acts were wrong, regardless of the religious faith followed by their perpetrators. Yet in 2006, AJC director David Harris contended that Jewish political activists have no right to criticise the Zionist foundations on which the state of Israel were built. Such Jews, he suggested, are guilty of a new form of anti-Semitism. 'There can be healthy disagreement and debate within a family or a country as to what the right course of action is – but never of the fundamental rightness of its being,' he wrote.[13]

AJC offshoot UN Watch – a group in Geneva that monitors criticism of Israel – has gone even further with its barrage of attacks on the Jewish writer Naomi Klein. Hillel Neuer, director of UN Watch, has accused Klein of harbouring a 'Goebbels-like venom' towards Israel. The only evidence that Neuer cited in comparing the courageous Canadian to the infamous Nazi propagandist was that Klein had authored a strongly worded missive arguing that racism and misogyny are rampant in Israel.[14]

In contrast to his colleagues' fulminations, Emanuele Ottolenghi, the Transatlantic Institute's chief from 2006 to 2010, came across as a calm and personable character when I interviewed him in his spacious Brussels headquarters, a short stroll from the European Parliament. The Bologna-born academic wore his impressive knowledge lightly as he reeled off a list of reasons why he felt it was in the mutual interests of Europe and Israel to forge ever-closer links.

Ottolenghi was adamant that the AJC doesn't expect the pro-Israel lobby to become as important a player in European politics as it is in the United States. He said:

> The whole point of our activities in Europe is of engaging thoughtfully in the battle of ideas. It is not about convincing politicians to undertake this or that course of action because you have a lot of pro-Israel votes in your constituency or because you can get pro-Israel contributions for your election campaign. It is about adding a voice to the debate. In America, the lobby is a lot more entrenched.

Even if his analysis is slightly more nuanced than that sometimes offered by the AJC, Ottolenghi is nonetheless quick to wave the anti-Semitism card at Israel's critics. I don't agree with the banners that appeared at some marches against the war in Gaza in 2008 and 2009 that sought to equate Israel's actions with those of the Nazis. But while such comparisons may be disproportionate, I cannot accept that they are inherently anti-Semitic. Away from the passions that street protests can stir up, more sober commentators have explained how some of the comparisons are not undeserved. For example, collective punishment – as practiced by Israel against the civilians of Gaza – was recognised as an affront to humanity in 1949 in response to Hitler's efforts to annihilate the world's Jews.[15] Surely it is not anti-Semitic to draw attention to such a fact.

And surely the British Jewish politician Gerald Kaufman did not express a bias against his own co-religionists when he told the House of Commons in December 2008 that his grandmother, slaughtered by the Nazis in her sickbed, did not die to 'provide cover for Israeli soldiers murdering Palestinian grandmothers in Gaza'. Kaufman may have used injudicious language by describing the Israeli tactic of claiming that a high proportion of those killed by its soldiers are Palestinian militants as the 'reply of the Nazi' and by saying that 'I suppose the Jews fighting for their lives in the Warsaw ghetto could have been dismissed as militants.'[16] But as the bombs fell on Gaza, was it not only proper for Kaufman to underscore his revulsion – a revulsion shared by many other Jews?

Ottolenghi, however, insisted that such analyses are an effort to demonise all Jews. He told me:

> Kaufman thinks he can comment on World War II and the Holocaust just by being Jewish. But when you call someone a Nazi, the game is over. To suggest what Israel did in Gaza was like what the Germans did in the Warsaw Ghetto is an attempt to shut out all debate.

As well as seeking to lend credence to the canard that Jews who criticise Israel are 'self-hating' Jews or leading subscribers to the 'new anti-Semitism', the Transatlantic Institute has been pounding the drums of war against Iran. The shelves in its headquarters are laden down with copies of Ottolenghi's book *Under a Mushroom Cloud: Europe, Iran and the Bomb*. It's an accessible tome but a deeply flawed one. Iran's execrable human rights record is rightly condemned – much is made of how the Iranian authorities consider it acceptable to use torture in interrogations. But there is no recognition that the same criticism can be levelled at Israel and the United States. And despite dealing meticulously with Iran's nuclear ambitions, he makes the ludicrous case that Israel's own nuclear programme is basically benevolent and that war-addicted Israel poses no threat to stability in the Middle East. He wrote:

> Arab leaders sleep soundly under the shadow of Israel's nuclear umbrella; it is Iran's nuclear quest which gives them nightmares. They know – they have always known – that Israel's military prowess serves its survival and does not seek to impose a political diktat on its neighbours. The same cannot be said of Iran, with its hegemonic ambitions, and its desire to refashion the region.[17]

Like EFI, the Transatlantic Institute cannot be found in the EU register of lobbyists at the time of writing. According to Ottolenghi, it has an annual budget of around €500,000. After I expressed scepticism at that figure, he said its budget did not need to be higher as it is focused more on research than on hectoring policy makers. He also hinted that he would like to have the think-tank scene in Brussels spiced up so that it has credible institutes representing all shades of political opinion. 'The debate would become richer if pro-Israel advocacy is a legitimate and relevant part of the debate,' he said. 'My aim and aspiration is to ensure the spectrum of voices heard is increased.'

This may sound admirable, even noble. Yet the reality is that the Transatlantic Institute is not bringing any balance to the political debate. Most think-tanks in Brussels are right of centre in their political leaning and are heavily dependent on large corporations for funding.[18] The only way in which the Transatlantic Institute is different is that it is a bit more strident and extreme than many of its peers. It is nonetheless careful enough to present its myopic and one-sided views, particularly on the Iran dossier, as reasonable in order to ensure that it has influence.

B'NAI B'RITH: A MAKER OF MYTHS

One of the world's oldest Zionist organisations, B'nai B'rith was founded in New York in 1843. It might seem surprising, then, that it took it until 2007 to set up an office specifically dedicated to relations with EU institutions.

Located in the shadow of the Berlaymont, the European Commission's sprawling headquarters in Brussels, the office has certainly helped bring B'nai B'rith closer to the corridors of power. But the organisation's absence from Brussels' European quarter until then (it also has an office in another part of the city – beside the chic Avenue

Louise) did not mean that it lacked clout. On the contrary, it has a long established network throughout this continent – with 150 branches (or 'lodges' as they are known to insiders) in 29 countries, according to its own data.

Arguably more importantly, B'nai B'rith is the parent organisation of the Anti-Defamation League (ADL). Set up in 1913, the New York-based ADL is the self-anointed leading civil rights organisation in the United States. Many EU policy-makers have accepted its bona fides, too, and it has acquired a reputation – in my view, unmerited – as the definitive international authority on anti-Semitism.

Official EU efforts to gauge whether anti-Semitism is prevalent are led by its Fundamental Rights Agency (FRA) in Vienna. In early 2009, the FRA published a 29-page report, which purported to give a snapshot of opinions towards Jews in the European Union from 2001 to 2008. The main source for EU-wide attitudes (as opposed to those in individual countries) cited by the agency was a telephone survey conducted by the ADL in December 2008 and January 2009. The FRA document briefly mentions that this period coincided with Israel's attacks on Gaza but only says that this 'might have influenced the results' of the survey. It then tells us that the ADL concluded that 'significant percentages of European respondents continue to believe in some of the most pernicious anti-Semitic stereotypes'.

It is clear from the questions asked by the ADL that it views criticism of Israeli militarism as tantamount to anti-Semitism. The first question it asked the 3,500 people in its survey sample was whether they agreed with the statement 'Jews are more loyal to Israel than to their country', to which the proportion of respondents who said that they felt this statement was 'probably true' ranged from 37 per cent in Britain to 64 per cent in Spain.

Could someone please explain to me why the responses to this statement indicate that 'some of the most pernicious anti-Semitic stereotypes' are alive and well? Israel styles itself as a Jewish state and ever since its inception it has demanded the loyalty of Jews throughout the world. Perceiving that Jews are more loyal to Israel than the country in which they live does not, in my view, suggest that the respondents have an innate dislike of Jews. I can accept that some of the other statements put to participants in the survey – that 'Jews have too much power in the business world' and that 'Jews still talk too much about what happened to them in the Holocaust' – might help give a more accurate reflection of attitudes. But does quizzing a sample of 3,500 Europeans give you enough information to conclude, as the ADL did, that 'millions continue to believe the classical anti-Semitic canards that have persistently pursued Jews through the centuries'?[19] As the evils of the Holocaust were being carried out less than 70 years ago, how can a statement about it yield enough scientific evidence to detect trends that span several centuries?

The flaws in the ADL's methodology might be apparent to anyone with a rudimentary grasp of history or current affairs, yet an official EU agency regarded its findings as sufficiently credible to cite it as one of only two sources for EU-wide attitudes towards Jews. Furthermore, it is instructive that the only finding from the ADL survey that the agency highlighted was the one on loyalty to Israel.[20] For several years the agency has been happily conflating criticism of Israel with hatred of Jews. Indeed, the working definition of anti-Semitism drawn up by the European Monitoring Centre on Racism and Xenophobia, as the FRA was formerly known, is a prime example of muddling two distinct phenomena. It reads:

> Anti-Semitism is a certain perception of Jews, which may be expressed as hatred towards Jews. Rhetorical and physical manifestations of anti-Semitism are directed toward Jewish or non-Jewish and/or their property, toward Jewish community institutions and religious facilities. In addition, such manifestations could also target the state of Israel, conceived as a Jewish entity.

The same succinct paper from the monitoring centre lists several examples of behaviour that it regards as anti-Semitic. They include 'denying the Jewish people their right to self-determination, e.g. by claiming that the existence of the state of Israel is a racist endeavour' and 'drawing comparisons of contemporary Israeli policy to that of the Nazis'. It is true that the paper says that 'criticism of Israel similar to that levelled against any other country cannot be regarded as anti-Semitic'. But this misses – maybe deliberately – a vital point; Israel does not behave like 'any other country'. There are only a handful of other states in the world that occupy the land of another people or defy international law as brazenly as Israel does. By the FRA's reckoning, then, anything that highlights Israel's exceptional conduct can be construed as anti-Semitism.

The FRA has acknowledged that it drew up that definition after consulting several pro-Israel lobby groups, including the aforementioned American Jewish Committee and the European Jewish

Congress (EJC).[21] Why was the agency unperturbed by the breadth of the definition and how it is clearly designed to muzzle criticism of Israeli aggression? That the state of Israel is largely, in the words of this definition, a 'racist endeavour' is a statement of fact. That narrowly focused lobby groups might want to brand anyone who speaks an inconvenient truth as anti-Semitic is one matter. But when an official – and ostensibly objective – EU body accepts the bogus rationale of partisan organisations, how can any of its work be taken seriously?

EUROPEAN JEWISH CONGRESS: APOLOGISTS FOR APARTHEID

Like B'nai B'rith, the European Jewish Congress (EJC) has taken its time in opening an EU affairs office in Brussels. Although formed in Paris in 1986, the 'sole representative body of democratically-elected European Jewish communities', as the EJC describes itself, only set up its EU 'embassy' in October 2009. Its inauguration was attended by two presidents of the main institutions of the EU: José Manuel Barroso from the European Commission and Jerzy Buzek (a former Polish prime minister) from the European Parliament.

Barroso used the occasion to praise the EJC for 'being fully committed to the resumption of the peace process' in the Middle East.[22] These vacuous words glossed over how the EJC is even more committed to supporting Israeli wars. That much was exemplified earlier in 2009, when the EJC boasted of how it had successfully lobbied MEPs to water down a resolution on Operation Cast Lead. In January that year, the EJC took credit for how a majority of MEPs agreed to denounce what it labelled 'Hamas' provocations', ignoring evidence that rockets fired by Hamas were a response to Israeli attacks that began the previous November (as discussed in Chapter 1).[23]

This was one of several instances in which the EJC has had a decisive role in shaping EU policy. In 2004, its leading role in convincing EU policy makers that many criticisms of Israel could be equated with anti-Semitism was confirmed, when it jointly hosted a conference in Brussels with the European Commission. That event was in response to a survey conducted by the EU in-house polling agency Eurobarometer, which found that when 7,500 people were asked which country they regarded as the biggest threat to world peace, 59 per cent chose Israel. The finding was feverishly denounced by pro-Israel lobby groups, with the Simon Wiesenthal

Centre demanding that the European Union be excluded from the so-called peace process and contending that it was a 'racist flight of fancy' to deem nuclear-armed Israel to be more dangerous than Iran or North Korea, both of which had less advanced nuclear programmes.[24]

Rather than properly analysing why the ordinary Europeans they purport to serve were exercised by the brutality of Ariel Sharon's then government, EU representatives have gone to considerable lengths to temper the passions of pro-Israel lobbyists. That the EJC and similar organisations exert a great deal of influence over these representatives was demonstrated in March 2009 when Jacques Barrot, then the EU justice commissioner, addressed an EJC conference in Brussels. Barrot's script resembled EJC policies so closely that the EJC might as well have written it. This was particularly so regarding preparations for the UN conference on racism in Geneva the following month. Pro-Israel lobbyists were adamant that this event (known as Durban II as it was a follow-up to a 2001 conference in South Africa) must not facilitate any censure of Israeli apartheid. Echoing this demand, Barrot pledged that no censure of that nature would be tolerated by the European Union. He would recommend 'strong action' – including that EU governments withdraw from the conference – if 'unacceptable texts' were proposed for its final *communiqué*.[25]

When the anti-racism conference took place a few weeks later, EU participants did not have to worry about 'unacceptable texts'. There was no reference to Israel in the final statement approved by the conference. Nonetheless, European governments walked out of the conference during a speech given by Iranian president Mahmoud Ahmadinejad. The protest was not prompted by a despicable inference made in a prepared version of his speech that proof the Holocaust occurred was 'ambiguous and dubious' (this claim was omitted from his eventual address). It was in response to his assertion that Israel was a 'totally racist regime', established by the Western powers who had left 'an entire nation homeless under the pretext of Jewish suffering'.[26]

Yes, Ahmadinejad has displayed a crass insensitivity to the world's Jews and their suffering at the hands of the Nazis. But the essence of his criticisms of Israeli racism is rooted in fact, and the horrors of the Holocaust cannot exonerate Israel for its callous treatment of the Palestinians. Efforts by EU representatives to prevent such racism from being exposed illustrate that they are insincere in claiming to abhor all forms of discrimination.

A FRENCH TABOO

So far I have concentrated on lobby groups with a presence in Brussels. However, it is important to note that the pro-Israel lobby has cultivated strong links at national level with the ruling elites of the largest EU member states, especially France and Britain.

These links have received scant attention from the mainstream media, largely because journalists and editors work within a culture of censorship. Most of this censorship is self-censorship motivated by fear that newspapers which criticise the pro-Israel lobby will be branded anti-Semitic. The ADL has been particularly adept at instilling such fear; it has contacted the editors of numerous publications telling them that it is monitoring their content to ensure that it was not offensive to Jews. I have even heard of obscure publications that rarely cover the Middle East being intimidated in this way.

The historian Paul-Éric Blanrue has both helped expose and been prevented from exposing how the lobby's reach is a taboo subject in France. His book *Sarkozy, Israël et les juifs* (its title alludes to Raymond Aron's 1968 work *De Gaulle, Israel and the Jews*) is a scholarly and concise analysis of French policy on the Middle East. Yet it was turned down by every French publisher that Blanrue approached – some, he said, fobbed him off by claiming that their calendar for new releases was saturated until 2012; others admitted that its contents were too sensitive. Fortunately, the Belgian company Oser Dire was braver; yet while it has made the book available via Internet sales, its normal French distributer refused to circulate the book in France. Fortunately, too, Blanrue has been able to turn the attempts to muzzle him to his advantage; the effective ban on the book in France stirred up so much interest that it is being translated into several languages.[27]

Blanrue emphasises that the pro-Israel lobby represents a minority of French Jews. Just one-sixth of the country's 600,000 Jews belong to organisations that have styled themselves as the Jewish community, he notes. Yet this lobby and its sister organisations in the United States have had a marked impact on Sarkozy. For four years before he could ensconce himself in the Élysée, Sarkozy was in contact with the American Jewish Committee. While Jacques Chirac rebutted accusations made by the AJC in 2003 that Europe – and in particular France – was plagued by a 'new anti-Semitism', Sarkozy was far more receptive to the lobbyists.

As France's interior minister, Sarkozy visited the United States in 2006, where he held discussions on foreign policy with representatives of several Zionist groups. David Twersky from the American Jewish Congress (nominally separate from its near-namesake, the American Jewish Committee) celebrated how this was 'the first time that one of the main candidates for the Élysée has publicly maintained such relations with the American Jewish community'.

Blanrue's book does not contain explosive revelations. But he does show how the pro-Israel lobby has allies holding many different positions in the political system. Patrick Devedjian, who Sarkozy appointed as a minister in charge of economic recovery in 2008, is a member of the France–Israel Association and has previously brokered military cooperation deals between the two countries. Foreign minister Bernard Kouchner is reputed to have told a New York meeting of the American Jewish Committee in 2007 that 'we have the duty to inculcate Israel in our children and grandchildren'. And Claude Goasguen, a leading figure in Sarkozy's UMP party, made statements that smacked of racism in 2008 when he described an attack on a *yeshiva* (a Jewish religious school) in Jerusalem as the work of 'a wild people of dreadful terrorists'. Goasguen later said he did not hate all Palestinians and was only condemning those who resorted to violence. But, as Blanrue notes, not everyone was reassured by that clarification. Goasguen has also been active in a 'friends of Israel' parliamentary group, to which over 100 of the 577 deputies in the National Assembly have signed up, making it one of the largest such pressure groups in French politics.[28]

Blanrue's book has proven to be prescient. Since its publication the influence of the pro-Israel lobby over France's Middle East policy has grown. In the autumn of 2009, Sarkozy tried to inject fresh momentum into an industrial development project that France is financing in Bethlehem. Paris councillor Valérie Hoffenberg was tasked with negotiating with Israel to obtain the permits needed for this scheme. Hoffenberg, as it happens, is the AJC's chief representative in France.[29] The AJC, it should be recalled, supports Israeli policies without equivocation, policies that have suffocated Bethlehem. According to the UN's Office for the Coordination of Humanitarian Affairs, the construction of Israeli settlements, the road network supporting them and the massive West Bank wall that encroaches into the heart of this historic city and a few other factors have combined to leave just 13 per cent of the Bethlehem governorate (with its total surface area of 660 sq km) open to Palestinian use.[30] Trusting a pro-Israel lobbyist to improve the lot of Bethlehem's Palestinians has to be one of the most misguided decisions that Sarkozy has taken in a career riddled with them.

ACCESS ALL AREAS: THE LOBBY IN LONDON

In January 2009, the BBC found itself the target of protests after it refused to broadcast an emergency aid appeal for Gaza. Mark Thompson, the corporation's director-general, declared that he had blocked the appeal from being shown 'to avoid any risk of compromising public confidence in the BBC's impartiality in the context of an ongoing news story'.[31]

Thompson's explanation was feeble. The BBC has had no problem in the past airing similar appeals for civilians affected by wars and civil strife in Rwanda and Congo. Then it did not worry about its impartiality being called into question by siding with the victims of violence and implicitly denouncing its perpetrators. Similarly, the BBC was willing to air an appeal for civilian victims of Israel's invasion of Lebanon in 1982.

Its cowardly stance more recently can only be explained by fear of Zionist zealots who comb through every utterance of BBC reporters to try to unearth an anti-Israel bias. It is no accident that the corporation's refusal to show the appeal followed intense and prolonged scrutiny of reports by its correspondents Orla Guerin and Jeremy Bowen. The latter even found himself the subject of an investigation by the BBC's editorial standards committee, after the Zionist Federation of Great Britain and Ireland and the Committee for Accuracy in Middle East Reporting in America lodged a complaint about some of his dispatches from Jerusalem. Bowen's critics were incensed by a blog he wrote for the BBC website in 2007 and a related article for the *Jewish Chronicle* concerning the 1967 war (on which he has authored a book). All Bowen had done was to make the entirely reasonable observation that Israel's occupation of the West Bank was 'in defiance of everyone's interpretation of international law except its own' and that 'most of the shameful, brutal and tragic events' he had witnessed as a reporter in the region were a consequence of the occupation.[32]

Far from being concerned about 'compromising public confidence in the BBC's impartiality', Thompson was almost certainly worried about incurring the wrath of a small but well-connected clique that is dedicated to supporting Israel no matter what heinous crimes it commits. It is no exaggeration to say that this clique has ingratiated itself with the most powerful people in Britain.

One day after Gordon Brown became prime minister in June 2007, the president of the Jewish National Fund's British branch, Gail Seal, invited him to become its patron, an offer that Brown promptly accepted. His predecessor Tony Blair and the Conservative Party leader David Cameron have also agreed to endorse the JNF in this way.[33] Although the fund has the status of a charity in most of Europe and brags that its work is of a 'humanitarian' nature, it is in fact a linchpin in Israel's apartheid system.

Around the same time the JNF was courting Brown, its status as a racist organisation which is heavily involved in Palestinian dispossession was being strengthened. In July 2007, a law was passed by the Knesset which made it illegal for any land held by the JNF to be sold to Palestinians. This patently discriminatory bill was designed to negate a 2004 ruling from the Israeli high court and subsequent advice from the country's attorney-general that refusing to sell such land to Palestinians was illegal.[34]

The JNF now 'owns' 13 per cent of the land of Israel. This land was acquired by driving Palestinians from their homes in a campaign of ethnic cleansing that the fund had been exhorting years before the state of Israel was established. Joseph Weitz, a leading member of the JNF for several decades, was an important contributor to Zionist ideological debates. In 1937, he argued that Arabs should be driven from their farms and villages so that these could be released for Jewish use. After his wish was granted around ten years later, the JNF was central to a plan ordered by David Ben-Gurion to erase the names that Arabs had given to their lands and replace them with Hebrew names. Some 200 new names were given by the JNF to land stolen from the Palestinians between 1948 and 1951.[35] This large-scale larceny has led to about half of all land held by Arabs in British Mandate Palestine being confiscated by the state and transferred to the JNF's authority.[36]

That the pro-Israel lobby has many British MPs in its pocket is not supposition; it is fact. All three of the main political parties have 'friends of Israel' groups within them. And it cannot be a coincidence that some of Britain's most ardent Zionists are also some of the most lavish donors to its political parties.

When a callow Tony Blair was first elected to the House of Commons in 1983, he wasted no time in signing up to the Labour Friends of Israel (LFI). While it was only a bit player in British politics during the Thatcher years, the LFI cleverly nailed its colours to the New Labour mast over the next decade. As Labour prepared itself for victory in the 1997 general election, some of the largest contributors to its war chest came from men who also belonged to the LFI. David Sainsbury – a billionaire thanks to his involvement with the supermarket chain bearing his family's name – became one of the largest donors to a political party in British history; he is reported to have given £16 million between Blair's election as Labour leader in 1994 and the eruption of a 'cash for honours' controversy in 2006. Sainsbury is a life peer in the House of Lords and served as a science minister in the British government from 1998 to 2006.[37]

Michael Levy, another Labour lord embroiled in the same controversy, was the party's most important fundraiser, reaping about £12 million for it ahead of its 1997 landslide victory. An unapologetic Zionist who has also raised money for one-time Israeli premier Ehud Barak, Levy has been described by the *Jerusalem Post* as 'undoubtedly the notional leader of British Jewry'.[38] Despite lacking the requisite impartiality to mediate in the Israeli–Palestinian conflict, Levy was appointed as Blair's special envoy to the Middle East.

SpinWatch, an organisation that monitors the public relations and lobbying industries, has documented how most recent British ministers with responsibility for the Middle East have also been affiliated to LFI. It is not surprising, then, that some of these ministers have been evasive when quizzed about the more contentious aspects of Anglo–Israeli relations. When he was a Foreign Office minister from 2001 to 2002, Ben Bradshaw insisted there was no evidence that British arms and equipment were being used against the Palestinians, even though Amnesty International had illustrated how key instruments of death in the Israeli arsenal (Apache helicopters, F16s, Merkava tanks) contained parts supplied by British firms and British-made Land Rovers were routinely used by Israeli troops in the occupied territories.[39]

Being active in the LFI is a shrewd career move, it would appear. One of the many Labour MPs who enjoyed the free trips to Israel that the LFI provided was Lorna Fitzsimons. Although she lost her seat in the 2005 general election, Fitzsimons did not have much trouble finding work. The following year, she became chief executive of the British Israel Communication and Research Centre (known by the acronym BICOM). In its short history – BICOM was only set up in 2001 – this centre has worked tirelessly and effectively to skew media coverage more in favour of the Israeli aggressor than the Palestinian underdog. When Israel went to war in Gaza in late 2008, BICOM assumed the role that an embassy would normally have of organising press briefings with Israeli spokespeople.

The *Observer* has revealed that BICOM is bankrolled by the billionaire Paju Zabludowicz, who provided it with almost £1 million in 2007, half its total income that year, and about £400,000 in 2006. Zabludowicz's enormous wealth – he is one of the 40 richest people in Britain, according to the *Sunday Times* – has been amassed through the arms business. His father Shlomo was the founder of Soltam, the Israeli arms company, and worked closely with Shimon Peres when he was director general of the Israeli defence ministry.[40] Paju Zabludowicz is known to have invested in business activities in Israeli settlements, including in a shopping centre serving the Ma'ale Adumim settlement in the West Bank.[41]

Given the cruel treatment that Israel metes out to Palestinians on a daily basis, it is deeply ironic that Fitzsimons says she entered politics in order to fight bullying and harassment. Like many pro-Israel lobbyists, she has been quick to accuse Israel's critics of anti-Semitism on spurious grounds. A former student union leader, she has misconstrued the campaign for an academic boycott of Israel as motivated by racism. 'The idea that a lecturer, student or institution should be assessed according to nationality, not academic merit, is one that should frighten all of us who value an open, democratic society,' she wrote in the *Independent*, at a time when Britain's University and College Union was debating a 'boycott Israel' motion.[42] Her argument missed the point, probably deliberately. Calls for an academic boycott are driven primarily by the extensive links between Israeli universities and the country's military-industrial complex, not the nationality of their professors.

Following the May 2010 general election, a coalition government was formed by the Conservatives and the Liberal Democrats. It is most unlikely that William Hague, the new foreign secretary, will usher in any major changes in terms of Britain's relationship with Israel. While it is true that William Hague, then shadow foreign secretary, described Israel's bombardment of Lebanon in 2006 as 'disproportionate', this position can be ascribed more to his status as a prominent member of the opposition at the time than to any principled opposition to warfare. It is significant that Hague's stance encountered heavy criticism from within the Tories' ranks; Stanley Kalms, a Conservative lord and a frequent donor to the party, complained that Hague's 'usual good sense has deserted him', adding: 'Criticising Israel for being disproportionate without serious consideration of the alternatives merely mouths the buzzwords of the ignorant armchair critic.'[43]

The most persuasive internal grouping within the Tories on foreign policy issues is the Conservative Friends of Israel (CFI). Some 80 per cent of the party's MPs belong to the CFI. Just as its Labour equivalent has attracted the party's luminaries, the CFI has no difficulty persuading front bench figures to attend its events or participate in its trips to Israel; visit its website and you will be greeted by photos of Boris Johnson, the bouffant London mayor, in Jerusalem. David Cameron, Conservative leader and then aspiring prime minister, addressed its annual business lunch in June 2009, during which he made the ridiculous assertion that 'Israel strives to protect innocent life' and argued that a tougher European position on Iran is necessary to complement Obama's stated willingness to talk with Tehran. He said:

> We in Europe must use this time to develop a stick to go with the American carrots. Today, America maintains its sanctions and stands ready to talk. But contrast that with the approach in Europe, where in the past, we have preferred endless carrots, lots of talks but no sticks, no hard decisions about sanctions.[44]

ISRAELI AGGRESSION HARMS JEWS, TOO

Mohammed El Baradei, former director-general of the International Atomic Energy Agency, has observed that the language of carrots and sticks is 'suitable for a donkey but not for a proud nation' like Iran.[45] And Noam Chomsky has offered a calm counterpoint to the shrill and paranoid tone of much Western discourse about Iran's nuclear programme. It is instructive that many of the same commentators who depict Iran as lusting for Armageddon have been largely silent about India and Pakistan's nuclear capabilities, which were developed with US assistance. As Chomsky noted:

> Iran has not invaded another country for hundreds of years, unlike the United States, Israel and India (which occupies Kashmir, brutally). The threat from Iran is miniscule. If Iran had nuclear weapons and delivery systems and was prepared to use them, the country would be vaporised.[46]

And yet the pro-Israel lobby keeps on churning out scare stories that have a tenuous relation with the truth. Just as its sister organisations in the United States were generally unflinching in their support for the disastrous war in Iraq, the lobby in Europe appears determined to convince policy-makers that a war is needed against Iran. This would not be a cause for concern if lobbyists were treated as extremists, who are given the freedom to express their opinions and then ignored by the political mainstream. But the tragic reality is that they have been granted access to the highest levels of power on this continent, and that almost everything they say is taken seriously.

I was baptised a Catholic but nowadays only enter churches for weddings, funerals and to admire stained-glass windows. Although I feel uncomfortable offering advice to followers of any religion, it seems vital to me that as many Jews as possible emphasise that the pro-Israel lobby does not speak in their name.

By the end of May 2010, more than 6,000 European Jews had signed a new appeal urging the European Union and United States to put pressure on both Israeli and Palestinian political figures 'and help them to find a reasonable and rapid solution' to the conflict. 'Systematic support of Israeli government policy is dangerous and does not serve the true interest of the state of Israel,' the declaration – known as JCall after a similar initiative in the United States called J Street – noted.[47] Supported by such illustrious individuals as MEP and one-time leader of the 1968 student revolt in Paris Daniel Cohn Bendit and the French philosopher Bernard-Henri Lévy, the effort was derided by the conventional pro-Israel lobby. According to Emanuele Ottolenghi, the JCallers were 'self-important sofa intellectuals'.[48]

It is too early to say whether JCall will develop into an alternative to the pro-Israel lobby in Europe or whether it will offer anything more than mild criticism of the Israeli state. But the willingness of its signatories to underscore that the mainstream lobby does not represent all Jews is certainly something that should be welcomed.

For the most part, the mainstream lobby does not appear interested in tackling genuine anti-Semitism. If it was, it would be campaigning for Israel to cease its war-mongering, for that is surely the greatest catalyst for attacks against Europe's Jews. It is no accident that anti-Semitic incidents in some parts of Europe were twice as high for the first six months of 2009, a year kicked off by the war in Gaza, than they were in the corresponding period in 2008.[49] This does not in any way condone any incident, but it does help to explain the increase. Jean Bricmont, a Belgian academic, put it succinctly:

> As for anti-Semitism, it must not be forgotten that Israeli policy is carried out by a state that calls itself Jewish, and is strongly supported by organisations that claim to represent Jews (correctly or incorrectly). It is unavoidable in such a context that some people who have nothing to do with historic anti-Semitism will identify Jews with Israel and express hostility towards Jews. That

> is regrettable but no more surprising than the fact that partisans of Israel speak in derogatory terms of 'Arabs'.[50]

When will the 'friends of Israel' realise that Israel does not act in the interest of Europe's Jews?

CONCLUSION: CONFRONTING EUROPE'S COWARDICE

For all his tough-guy posturing, Binyamin Netanyahu seems to be afraid of words. Two particular words, pundits would have us believe, have terrified him throughout his political career: Palestinian state.

In June 2009, the prime minister 'crossed a personal Rubicon', according to his policy adviser Ron Dermer. Addressing an audience in Bar-Ilan University near Tel Aviv, Netanyahu said: 'We will be ready in a future peace agreement to reach a solution, where a demilitarised Palestinian state exists alongside the Jewish state.'[1]

Predictably, the European Union welcomed these comments. Javier Solana, then EU foreign policy chief, claimed that Netanyahu had 'finally generated an Israeli consensus' on how the Israeli–Palestinian conflict should be solved by setting up two states.[2] Solana, it should be said, is a cheerleader for the two-state solution. One month after Netanyahu delivered his Bar-Ilan speech, Solana called on the UN Security Council to recognise a Palestinian state, even if an agreement on forming one could not be reached between Israeli and Palestinian representatives.[3]

A superficial reading of statements by Solana and his ilk might leave one with the impression that the European Union is doing what it can to promote a just and viable solution to the conflict. The reality is very different.

By inching ever closer to Israel and its military-driven economy, the European Union is helping to guarantee that the Middle East will be blighted by violence and injustice for some time yet. So long as this violence and the threat of more persists, any talk of a Palestinian state by Israeli leaders will be a tasteless joke. That is because these same leaders are approving policies that make the emergence of a Palestinian state worthy of the name virtually impossible.

Netanyahu did not spell out what the contours of the state he envisaged would be, yet it is difficult to see how he is talking about any more than a tiny sliver of the West Bank. In this respect, his vision is no different from that offered by the late David Bar-Illan, who as Netanyahu's chief spin doctor during his earlier premiership in the 1990s, indicated that Palestinians will only ever be granted control of a fraction of historic Palestine. The Palestinians could call the fragments that escape full-scale Israeli colonisation whatever they wished (including a state), Bar-Illan indicated. 'Semantics don't matter,' he said. 'If Palestinian sovereignty is limited enough so that we feel safe, call it fried chicken.'[4]

Their deep flaws notwithstanding, the Oslo Accords did at least oblige Israel to treat the West Bank and Gaza as 'one territorial unit'. Not only has Israel failed to respect this obligation, it has gone out of its way to keep the two parts of this nominally single unit divided from each other in almost every conceivable way. Face-to-face contact between Gazans and West Bankers has been minimal in recent years. Between the eruption of the *intifada* in 2000 and the execution of Ariel Sharon's Gaza 'disengagement' plan in 2005, travel from Gaza to the West Bank declined by 98 per cent, the Israeli human rights group HaMoked has calculated.[5]

Operation Cast Lead even severed some of the virtual links between the two. It was surely a calculated move that the Palestinian Legislative Council was one of the first buildings Israel struck during the offensive. The effect of this attack was to deprive elected representatives from Gaza with the opportunity to communicate with their colleagues from Gaza through video conferencing. How can Israeli leaders talking of a Palestinian state be taken seriously, when they have ordered the destruction of the closest thing that the Palestinians have to a parliament?

STOP THE SUFFOCATION OF PALESTINE

In 2000, the peace activist and anthropologist Jeff Halper coined the term 'matrix of control' to describe how an elaborate Israeli network of settlements and restrictions of movement was leaving Palestinians hemmed in to small pieces of their native land. Unless this matrix was dismantled, a two-state solution could not be realised, he argued. A decade later, the occupation and all its appurtenances have 'grown immeasurably stronger and more entrenched', Halper recently observed.[6]

In official statements, the European Union has opposed the suffocation of Palestine. Yet, as I have tried to demonstrate in this book, EU statements cannot be taken at face value. That is because the European Union and its governments have allowed themselves to be seduced by Israeli politicians and have happily embraced Israeli firms that are intimately involved in and profiting from the occupation. Rather than contributing to a solution, the European Union has allowed itself to become part of the problem.

The most serious alternative to a two-state solution that is being debated by analysts of Middle East politics, as far as I can see, is a one-state solution. The most persuasive case I have seen for this approach is that put forward by Ali Abunimah, author of *One Country: A Bold Proposal to End the Israeli–Palestinian Impasse*. He recommends that a unitary Israeli–Palestinian state should be set up, with full respect for the rights of both peoples. South Africa's transition from minority white rule to a more inclusive democracy or Northern Ireland's experiment in sharing power between Catholics and Protestants could serve as models, in Abunimah's view.[7] While both South Africa and Northern Ireland remain plagued by inequality and racism or sectarianism, and while there are many lessons that could be learned from their transformations, major efforts have at least been made in both cases to address their core injustices.

I would generally be sympathetic to the ideas that Abunimah espouses (for the record, I was an admirer of Abunimah's work before I became an occasional contributor to *The Electronic Intifada*, which he founded). Although some might regard his vision as utopian, I feel that it might also be more realistic than a two-state formula in the long-term, now that Israel has effectively strangled the prospects of an independent Palestine.

Tragically, however, the European Union and other important players in international diplomacy are not doing anything that would help the attainment of a unitary state either. For this solution to work, Israel would have to relinquish its claim that it cannot be anything other than a Jewish state. Rather than being the state of just one religion, the new unitary state would have to be pluralistic and treat Jews, Muslims, Christians and non-believers as equal citizens with equal rights.

The European Union ought to be open to supporting such a solution. After all, the European Union prides itself in being 'united in diversity', to use the slogan chosen to mark the fiftieth anniversary of its inception in 2007. Yet this solution could only prove durable if all of the main parties to the conflict have a stake in it. By shunning Hamas, the European Union and the United States are also slamming the door to a comprehensive peace. By insisting that Hamas recognises Israel as it stands today, the European Union is implicitly backing the agenda of the Israeli establishment of maintaining Israel as a purely Jewish state and not the state of all its citizens (including a large Arab minority). Whether EU representatives realise it or not, they are defending a status quo accurately defined by the Israeli journalist Amira Hass as 'a special blend of military occupation, colonialism, apartheid, Palestinian limited self-rule in enclaves and a democracy for Jews'.[8]

Every European concerned about human rights has good reason to be angry at how their government has cosied up to Israel. But this anger does not have to lead to despair; on the contrary, it should be harnessed for positive ends. Because it is Israel's main trading partner, the European Union is far from powerless in the Middle East. Its association agreement with Israel, as I have noted repeatedly in this book, makes the furtherance of economic and political links between the two sides conditional on respect for human rights. This means that the European Union has a legal instrument with which it can withhold trade preferences that are hugely important to an open economy like Israel's until Israel ceases treating Palestinians as sub-human.

Yes, there are powerful forces that prevent the European Union from closing the immense gap between its fine rhetoric on human rights and the reality that it usually avoids taking action when an abuser of human rights is deemed too strong. This cowardice is a major obstacle to having the European Union contribute towards achieving a genuine peace in the Middle East. But the obstacle does not have to be insurmountable.

Hard though it may be to believe, EU representatives are not impervious to public opinion. There have been many issues that EU institutions have started taking seriously as a direct result of campaigning from ordinary individuals. Efforts to increase EU development aid and to reduce EU emission of greenhouse gases are largely the result of public campaigning against global poverty and environmental destruction. And Brussels officials have confirmed to me that some of their initiatives on animal welfare have been taken because they were inundated with letters from people troubled by the cruelty that has become integral to the modern food industry.

If the animal welfare lobby can effect change, why should advocates of human rights not be able to, even on a dossier so replete with historical baggage and intense emotion as the Israeli–Palestinian conflict? Convincing the European Union to hold Israel to account will not be easy, but I am convinced that it can be done. I do not have an elaborate blueprint for bringing about the fundamental shift that would be needed in the policy of its governments but here are a few thoughts on how this process could be started.

The most obvious ingredient for the success of this work, it seems to me, is having a critical mass of Europeans (with support from outside this continent) telling their leaders and representatives that they cannot continue acting as an alibi for Israel. Building this critical mass requires a coalition of organisations working on human rights (in the broadest sense of that term, including the rights to live free of war and poverty) to come together and holler in harmony.

Researching for this book, I have seen that such a coalition exists in an embryonic form. I have been lucky enough to meet many dedicated and knowledgeable activists, from a multiplicity of backgrounds, who are in regular contact with each other. Yet while their networking nous is impressive, one factor that prevents these activists from having a greater impact is the lack of consensus on what tactics they should employ. The crucial question on which organisations concerned about the Palestinians plight cannot agree is whether or not Israel should be boycotted.

BOYCOTTING ISRAEL: A TACTIC, NOT A STRATEGY

My view is that Israel should be boycotted, for two simple reasons. First, a campaign of boycott, divestment and sanctions helped end white minority rule in South Africa. Second, a cross-section of Palestinian society has united to call for a boycott of Israel. The organisations that have signed up to the appeal, launched in 2005, represent farmers, trade unionists, women, youth, health workers, teachers and engineers. They also represent Palestinian refugees outside the occupied territories and Palestinians living in Israel. And it should not be forgotten that organisations like the Alternative Information Centre that are staffed by both Israelis and Palestinians have endorsed the call. (A list of the appeal's signatories can be found on the www.bdsmovement.net website.)

It should be emphasised, then, that the boycott plan was not hatched by bleeding-heart liberals in the West. It was initiated by the very people who have to bear the brunt of apartheid Israeli-style.

Supporting this boycott is a practical act of international solidarity. And it is an excellent way of involving people from all walks of life in the quest for justice in the Middle East. The actions that can be taken as part of the campaign are ones that almost everyone can relate to; they range from refusing to put Israeli goods in your basket when you do your grocery shopping to demanding that your local or national authority cancels contracts with firms linked to the occupation. The experience of the anti-apartheid campaign in the 1980s showed how such campaigning raised enormous awareness about the cancer of racism in South Africa, and today the Apartheid Museum in Johannesburg has many exhibits devoted to the importance of this international movement. A similar awareness-raising exercise could be achieved in relation to Israel and Palestine, provided there is enough dedication and coordination on the part of campaigners.

The reluctance of some organisations to support a boycott of Israel is understandable. Some human rights activists argue that a boycott can be a form of collective punishment, the very thing that we criticise Israel for inflicting on Gaza. Yet, in my view, the blockade of Gaza cannot be equated with a boycott of Israeli goods. The fact that many Israeli firms who export goods are interlinked with the occupation makes them legitimate targets for a boycott that is clearly designed to hurt the profits of Israeli executives, not the well-being of ordinary Israelis. Indeed, contacts with ordinary Israelis should not only be maintained but strengthened, especially with those critical of the occupation.

Some activists even fear that refusing to buy Israeli goods could be redolent of 1930s Germany, where Joseph Goebbels ordered his compatriots to stay out of Jewish shops. Yet while the pro-Israel lobby will inevitably seek to draw such parallels once the boycott campaign gains greater momentum, the comparison is bogus.

The 'boycott Israel' campaign is in no way motivated by anti-Semitism. Rather, it is motivated by an abhorrence of Israeli state violence and of Israel's denial of Palestinian rights. It is true, of course, that some anti-Semites criticise Israel, but these people almost invariably have nothing to do with the Palestinian solidarity movement. Michael Neumann, the philosopher and son of German–Jewish political activist Franz Leopold Neumann, has noted correctly that 'concern for the agonies of Palestinians' is not a priority for anti-Semites; 'it is an afterthought'. As he noted, too: 'The more-than-overwhelming majority of those who criticise Israel are genuine humanitarians, genuine enemies of oppression and ethnic nationalism, genuine fighters for justice.'[9]

It should be emphasised that a boycott is a tactic, not a strategy. Therefore, it is vital that a boycott is combined with other political activities. In Europe, public pressure needs to be ratcheted up on our governments so that they cease rewarding Israel for its appalling behaviour towards the Palestinians. The most tangible steps they could take in this respect would be to suspend the EU association agreement with Israel and the trade preferences that are central to it. They must cancel plans to 'upgrade' their relations with Israel, not merely delay the process of making Israel a de facto EU member (a process which is still under way, despite Israel's repeated war-making of recent years and despite its worsening violations of human rights). And Israel should be expelled from scientific cooperation programmes with Europe, particularly because the country's arms industry is heavily involved in these programmes and stands to benefit considerably from them. Finally, the European Union must cease allowing the United States to dictate its Middle East policy and have the gumption to match its rhetoric on human rights with principled action.

These steps would not end the occupation in themselves, but they would hurt Israel, where exports account for about 40 per cent of gross domestic product, economically and diplomatically.[10] Israel clearly recognises that access to EU markets is important for its exporters, and there is a growing understanding in Israeli political circles that it would be foolhardy to depend only on the United States for diplomatic and economic support. Restricting Israel's access to EU markets would be the strongest action that the European Union could take to demand respect for the rights of Palestinians.

None of this is going to happen as a result of EU representatives suddenly feeling ashamed of how their courtship of Israel has been a squalid example of ethics being sacrificed to *realpolitik*. It will only happen if enough ordinary Europeans insist on it. Now that you have read this far, please do not simply put the book on your shelf and forget about its contents. Contact your local and national politicians and members of the European Parliament, telling them that the mollycoddling of Israel must stop. Inform yourself as well as you can about the surrounding issues. And take part in activities organised by the Palestinian solidarity group closest to where you live; if there is not one, how about setting one up yourself?

Israel's treatment of the Palestinians is cruel, vindictive and illegal. But there is no reason why this dreadful state of affairs has to continue indefinitely. No matter how bleak things look at the moment, I genuinely believe that peace and justice can prevail in the Middle East. There is no magic recipe for achieving this goal; it will have to be brought about by sustained international campaigning. By all of us.

www.ICAHD.org.

160,000.

→ T. Aviv

We never finish 1948 (exhibition)

Stephen Sizer: bought into Nothing less than a heresy.

Land theologically is on load

Liticus 11 are ... & tenants

If you obey u can stay

The land may b stewarded – not the reward of conquest.

J. is 2b ......

faith not race...

"Christians of Zion?"

Strategy

1. Intimidate
2. Isolate
3. Incriminate (assoc. with illeg. actives)
4. Incarcerate.

~~IMRI~~ –

Sabeel.org

christianzionism.org

withgodonourside.com

NOTES

INTRODUCTION

1 Donald Boström, 'Our sons are plundered for their organs', *Aftonbladet*, 26 August 2009.
2 Jonathan Cook, 'The missing link in Israeli organ theft? The autopsy surgeon *Aftonbladet* forgot', *Counterpunch*, 4–6 September 2009, <www.counterpunch.org>.
3 Roni Sofer, 'Lieberman: Sweden acting like in WWII', *Ynetnews*, 20 August 2009, <www.ynet.co.il>.
4 Raphael Ahren, 'Solana: EU has closer ties to Israel than potential member Croatia', *Haaretz*, 21 October 2009.
5 United Nations Human Rights Council, *Report of the United Nations Fact-Finding Mission on the Gaza Conflict*, advance edited version, 15 September 2009, <www2.ohchr.org>.
6 'UN vote on Goldstone report a defining step for accountability, says Amnesty International', press release, Amnesty International, 5 November 2009, <www.amnesty.org>.
7 *EU's Position on the Middle East Peace Process: Key Inconsistencies*, report by Amnesty International, Oxfam, War Child and several other organisations, September 2009, p. 2.
8 Robert Fisk, 'Obama, man of peace? No, just a Nobel prize of a mistake', *Independent*, 11 October 2009.
9 Ilan Pappe, *The Ethnic Cleansing of Palestine*, Oxford: Oneworld, paperback edn, 2007, p. 40.
10 Avraham Burg, *The Holocaust is Over; We Must Rise from its Ashes*, New York: Palgrave Macmillan, English edn, 2008, p. 207.
11 Steven Erlanger, 'Doubts about Obama', *New York Times* (international weekly section published in *Le Monde*), 7 November 2009.
12 International Atomic Energy Agency, 'Israeli nuclear capabilities, Resolution adopted on 18 September 2009 during the tenth plenary meeting', <www.iaea.org>.
13 'IAEA urges Israel to allow nuclear inspection', *Ynetnews*, 18 September 2009, <www.ynetnews.co.il>.
14 Naomi Klein, 'The Tel Aviv party stops here', *The Nation*, 9 September 2009.
15 Harry Bellet, 'Tel-Aviv s'expose à Paris le temps d'une nuit blanche', *Le Monde,* 2 October 2009.

16 Rory McCarthy, 'Israel annexing East Jerusalem, says EU', *Guardian*, 7 March 2009.
17 European Commission, *Jerusalem and Ramallah Heads of Mission Report of East Jerusalem*, unpublished, undated, p. 1.
18 Susan Rockwell, 'Euro–Israeli and Euro–Palestinian relations: an asymmetric European commitment?', presentation to seminar organised by Catholic anti-poverty group CIDSE, Brussels, 7 November 2008, <www.cidse.org>.
19 Jonathan Cook, 'Archaeology used politically to push out Silwan residents', *Electronic Intifada*, 26 September 2008, <www.electronicintifada.net>.
20 'PA demands Canada cancels scroll exhibition', Al Arabiya, 11 April 2009, <www.alarabiya.net>.
21 Anna-Lena Svensson McCarthy, *Israel and the Occupied Palestinian Territories: A Study on the Implementation of the EU Guidelines on Torture and other Cruel, Inhuman or Degrading Treatment or Punishment*, United Against Torture Coalition, December 2007, p. 30, <www.unitedagainsttorture.org>.
22 Amnesty International, *Amnesty International Report 2008: The State of the World's Human Rights*, p.168, <www.amnesty.org>.
23 Israel Ministry of Foreign Affairs, 'Israel's Comments on the 1992 Amnesty International Annual Report', 7 July 1993, <www.mfa.gov.il>.
24 Ben White, *Israeli Apartheid: A Beginner's Guide,* London: Pluto, 2009, pp. 79–80.
25 Human Rights Watch, 'Torture worldwide', 27 April 2005, <www.hrw.org>.
26 Public Committee Against Torture in Israel and World Organisation Against Torture, *Implementation of the UN Convention Against Torture and Other Cruel, Inhuman or Degrading Treatment or Punishment by Israel,* June 2009, p. 37, <www.stoptorture.org.il>.
27 David Cronin, 'Police cooperation with Israel challenged', Inter Press Service, 5 February 2009.
28 'Britain expels Israeli diplomat over Dubai passport row', *BBC News*, 23 March 2010, <www.bbc.co.uk>.
29 Ian Black and Ian Cobain, 'British court issued Gaza arrest warrant for former Israeli minister Tzipi Livni', *Guardian*, 14 December 2009.
30 Gordon Brown, 'Britain must protect foreign leaders from private arrest warrants', *Daily Telegraph*, 3 March 2010.
31 Tobias Buck, 'Israel becomes OECD member', *Financial Times*, 10 May 2010.

CHAPTER 1

1 David Cronin, 'Cornering of civilians unprecedented, says UN official,' Inter Press Service, 22 January 2009.
2 'EU presidency says Israeli action is defensive', Reuters, 3 January 2009.
3 'Official EU presidency statement concerning the situation in the Middle East', 4 January 2009, <www.eu2009.cz>.

4 Noam Chomsky, *Hegemony or Survival: America's Quest for Global Dominance*, London: Hamish Hamilton, 2003, p. 190.
5 Jimmy Carter, 'An unnecessary war', *Washington Post*, 8 January 2009.
6 Donald Macintyre, 'Chronic malnutrition in Gaza blamed on Israel', *Independent*, 15 November 2008.
7 John Vinocur, 'In a German comfort zone, going nowhere fast', *New York Times*, 5 January 2009.
8 Leigh Phillips, 'Member states divided over condemning Israeli attacks', *EUobserver*, 22 January 2009, <www.euobserver.com>.
9 Dan Lieberman, 'World leaders respond timidly to Gaza massacre', *Palestine Chronicle*, 28 December 2008, <www.palestinechronicle.com>.
10 'Confirmed figures reveal the true extent of the destruction inflicted upon the Gaza Strip', press release from the Palestinian Centre for Human Rights, 12 March 2009, <www.pchrgaza.org>.
11 Etgar Lefkovits, 'Leaders pledge to end arms smuggling', *Jerusalem Post*, 19 January 2009.
12 Michel Bôle-Richard, 'A Jabaliya, parmi les décombres, le récit terrible d'une famille palestinienne', *Le Monde*, 28 January 2009.
13 Ian Traynor, 'Europe stalls on closer Israel links in Gaza protest', *Guardian*, 14 January 2009.
14 European Parliament debate on the situation in the Middle East/Gaza Strip, 14 January 2009, <www.europarl.europa.eu>.
15 'Minister Rupel heads the EU-Israel Association Council', press release, Slovenian presidency of the European Union, 16 June 2008, <www.eu2008.si>.
16 Ian Traynor, 'Europe stalls on closer Israel links in Gaza protest', *Guardian*, 14 January 2009.
17 David Cronin, 'Thousand deaths do not put off EU', Inter Press Service, 14 January 2009.
18 Antonio Tajani, 'The use of space – the European point of view', speech, Tel Aviv, 28 January 2009, <www.ec.europa.eu>.
19 Rory Miller, 'Troubled neighbours: the EU and Israel', in Efraim Inbar (ed.), *Israel's Strategic Agenda*, New York: Routledge, 2007.
20 Michael Prior, 'Zionism and the challenge of historical truth and morality', in Michael Prior (ed.), *Speaking the Truth*, Northampton: Olive Branch Press, 2005, p. 28.
21 Alfred Tovias, 'Why should Israel become a member of the European Union?', speech to conference, Brussels, 4–6 March 2002, <www.radicalparty.org>.
22 Martin Walker, 'Israel weighing EU membership', *United Press International*, 21 May 2003.
23 Inbar (ed.), *Israel's Strategic Agenda*, p. 29.
24 Leon Hadar, *Sandstorm: Policy Failure in the Middle East*, Basingstoke: Palgrave Macmillan, 2005, p. 164.
25 Herb Keinon, 'Israel wins significant EU upgrade', *Jerusalem Post*, 16 June 2008.

26 Barak Ravid, 'EU votes to upgrade Israel relations despite Arab lobbying', *Haaretz,* 9 December 2008.
27 European Commission, *Progress Report: Israel,* 3 April 2008, <www.ec.europa.eu>.
28 David Cronin, 'EU "closer than ever" to Israel', Inter Press Service, 4 April 2008.
29 'EU looks to day after Annapolis', Associated Press, 26 November 2007.
30 Tobias Buck, 'Palestinians protest over Israeli settlement plan', *Financial Times*, 4 December 2007.
31 Hagit Ofran, 'The death of the settlement freeze', <www.peacenow.org.il>, March 2008.
32 'Peace now: settlement freeze is dead', *Jerusalem Post*, 31 March 2008.
33 'High Commissioner for Human Rights and Special Rapporteur on Situation in Occupied Palestinian Territories address Council', press release, United Nations, 16 June 2008, <www.unhchr.ch>.
34 Robert Cooper, *The Breaking of Nations: Order and Chaos in the Twenty-First Century*, New York: Atlantic Monthly Press, 2003, p. 118.
35 Kevin Peraino, 'Olmert's lament', *Newsweek*, 22 June 2009.
36 'Livni says doesn't want intervention in peace talks', Reuters, 2 December 2008.
37 'EU deplores Israel's plans to expand settlement', Associated Press, 10 March 2008.
38 'Summary of remarks by EUHR Solana at the 19th Arab League Summit', 28 March 2007, <www.europa-eu-un.org>.
39 'Palestinian PM: Israel breaks its commitments to EU', Palestine Media Centre, 4 June 2008, <www.palestine-pmc.com>.
40 'Salam Fayyad – Re. potential upgrade of EU–Israel relations', *Palestine Think Tank,* 13 June 2008, <www.palestinethinktank.com>.
41 'Dr Barghouti: upgrading relations with Israel would serve to condone its policies', Palestine News Network, 3 December 2008, <www.english.pnn.ps>.
42 Jonathan Cook, *Disappearing Palestine: Israel's Experiments in Human Despair,* London: Zed, 2008, p. 132.
43 David Cronin, 'Double standards on trade', Inter Press Service, 22 December 2008.
44 Joel Kovel, *Overcoming Zionism: Creating a Single Democratic State in Israel/Palestine*, London: Pluto, 2007, p. 212.
45 White, *Israeli Apartheid*, p. 9.
46 Gabriel Piterberg, *The Returns of Zionism: Myths, Politics and Scholarship in Israel,* London: Verso, 2008, p. 77.
47 Kovel, *Overcoming Zionism*, p. 211.
48 'Tutu condemns Israeli "apartheid"', *BBC News,* 29 April 2002.
49 Memo from Nelson Mandela to Thomas Friedman, 28 March 2001, <www.jeffersoncorner.com>.
50 Tanya Reinhart, *Israel/Palestine*, 2nd edn, New York: Seven Stories, 2005, p. 175.

51 Michel Bôle-Richard, 'Des militants anti-apartheid juifs sud-africains "choqués" par leur visite en Cisjordanie occupée', *Le Monde*, 20–21 July 2008.

52 Sharon Roffe-Offir: 'Olmert: discrimination against Arabs deliberate', *Ynetnews*, 12 November 2008, <www.ynet.co.il>.

53 'Supreme Court to decide soon on whether the citizenship law, which discriminates on the basis of nationality and violates the right to family life, is compatible with Israel's basic laws', press release, Adalah (legal centre for Arab rights in Israel), 16 March 2009, <www.adalah.org>.

54 Arab Association for Human Rights, *The Right to Health of the Palestinian Arab Minority in Israel*, February 2009, <www.arabhra.org>.

55 Norman Finkelstein, *Beyond Chutzpah: On the Misuse of Anti-Semitism and the Abuse of History*, updated edn, London: Verso, 2008, p. 169.

CHAPTER 2

1 Avi Shlaim, *The Iron Wall: Israel and the Arab World*, London: Penguin, 2000, p. 309.

2 Rashid Khalidi, *Resurrecting Empire: Western Footprints and America's Perilous Path in the Middle East*, (2nd edn), Boston, Mass.: Beacon, 2005, p. 53.

3 Amir Mizroch, 'Israel begins overhaul of EU relations', *Jerusalem Post*, 24 February 2008.

4 European Parliament, *Report on the Alleged Use of European Countries by the CIA for the Transportation and Illegal Detention of Prisoners*, 30 January 2007, <www.europarl.europa.eu>.

5 Ben Hall, 'The volte-face', *Financial Times*, 27 March 2009.

6 Rosemary Hollis, 'Europe and the Middle East: power by stealth?' in Wyn Rees and Michael Smith (eds), *International Relations of the European Union, Vol. IV*, London: Sage, 2008, p. 229.

7 Helene Fouquet, 'Sarkozy says Palestinian state would secure Israel', Bloomberg, 23 June 2008.

8 'Sarkozy attacks Iran for its stance on Israel', Reuters, 14 February 2008.

9 'Text of Mahmoud Ahmadinejad's speech', *New York Times*, 30 October 2005.

10 Rory McCarthy, 'Sarkozy urges Israel to share sovereignty over Jerusalem', *Guardian*, 23 June 2008.

11 Speech by Nicholas Sarkozy to the Knesset, 23 June 2008, <www.ambafrance-il.org>.

12 Raymond Deane, 'Scapegoat upon scapegoat: Angela Merkel addresses the Knesset', *Electronic Intifada*, 20 March 2008, <www.electronicintifada.net>.

13 Speech by Federal Chancellor Angela Merkel to the Knesset in Jerusalem, 18 March 2008, <www.bundesregierung.de>.

14 'Gaza situation "extremely fragile", warns UN political chief', press release, United Nations, 22 January 2008, <www.un.org>.
15 Franco Frattini, 'From the outside, looking in: international perspectives on the Middle East', speech to Herzliya conference, 22 January 2008, <www.ec.europa.eu>.
16 Richard Owen, 'Mussolini follower Gianfranco Fini takes top job', *The Times*, 1 May 2008.
17 Meron Rapaport, 'Italian FM says Mughniyah killing in Damascus was act of "terror"', *Haaretz*, 22 February 2008.
18 'Sharon urges Jews to go to Israel', *BBC News*, 17 November 2003.
19 Barak Ravid, 'Lieberman's Italian job', *Haaretz*, 7 May 2009.
20 Soren Dosenrode and Anders Stubkjær, *The European Union and the Middle East*, London: Continuum, 2002, p. 65.
21 Stephen Sizer, 'The International Christian Embassy, Jerusalem: a case study in political Christian Zionism', in Prior, *Speaking the Truth*, p. 105.
22 Roni Sofer, 'Dutch FM calls on Hamas to cease Qassam fire', *Ynetnews*, 23 January 2009. <www.ynetnews.co.il>.
23 Guus Valk, 'After one Dutch minister visits Israel, another goes to Gaza', *NRC Handelsblad*, 30 June 2009.
24 Mark Kranenburg, 'Dutch get heated about Israel', *NRC Handelsblad*, 7 January 2009.
25 Petra de Koning, 'Brussels wants Dutch to chill out on human rights', *NRC Handelsblad*, 23 March 2009.
26 Greer Fay Cashman, 'Dutch FM to lobby for Israeli membership in EU', *Jerusalem Post*, 23 January 2008.
27 Khalidi, *Resurrecting Empire*, p. 198.
28 Mark Curtis, *Web of Deceit: Britain's Real Role in the World*, London: Vintage, 2003, p. 127.
29 Ricardo Gomez, *Negotiating the Euro-Mediterranean Partnership: Strategic Action in EU Foreign Policy?*, Farnham: Ashgate, 2003, p. 131.
30 Chris Patten, *Cousins and Strangers: America, Britain and Europe in a New Century*, New York: Owl, 2006, p. 128.
31 Nick Dearden, 'The end of their dreams', *ZNet*, 4 May 2004, <www.zmag.org>.
32 Curtis, *Web of Deceit*, p. 122.
33 Ben White, 'Israel's wall still deepening the divide', *Guardian*, 9 July 2009.
34 Mark Phythian, *The Labour Party, War and International Relations, 1945–2006*, Oxford: Routledge, 2007, p. 153.
35 Andy McSmith, 'Blair hit by Lebanon backlash as minister admits ceasefire "mistake"', *Independent*, 14 September 2006.
36 Curtis, *Web of Deceit*, p. 38.
37 Janis Mc Nair, 'Singing for peace: anti-war songs from Vietnam to Iraq', Glasgow Caledonian University Centre for Political Song, April 2003, <www.caledonian.ac.uk>.
38 Robert Fisk, 'Some lessons of sacrifice from Liverpool in two world wars', *Independent*, 18 July 2009.

39 'Peace mission or costly PR stunt? Just what has Tony Blair delivered as £400,000-a-year Middle East envoy?', *Daily Mail*, 17 May 2008.
40 'Blair wins $1m leadership prize', *BBC News*, 16 February 2009.
41 'A revealing visit', *Economist,* 24 July 2008.
42 'Britain, US refuse to call end to air strikes', *The Times*, 28 December 2008.
43 Noam Chomsky and Gilbert Achcar, *Perilous Power: The Middle East and US Foreign Policy*, Boulder: Paradigm, 2007, p. 94.
44 David Cronin, 'Liberators of "concentration camp Iraq" promise to preserve close links with US', *European Voice*, 11 September 2003.
45 David Cronin, 'On the sidelines', *European Voice,* 5 June 2003.
46 Michael Kimmelman, 'Poland searches its own soul', *New York Times*, 8 April 2009.
47 Gil Hoffman, 'Polish PM: EU inconsistent on Iran', *Jerusalem Post*, 10 April 2008.
48 Jacek Pawlicki, 'Tusk: no tolerance for anti-Semitism', *Gazeta Wyborcza*, 10 April 2008.
49 Alexander Vondra, 'Upgrading EU–Israel relationship', speech to conference, Berlin, 17 June 2008, <www.vlada.cz>.
50 Norman Berdichevsky, 'Who did what for Israel in 1948?', *New English Review*, December 2007.
51 Rob Cameron, 'Klaus: Czechs want "balanced" EU approach to Israeli–Palestinian conflict', Radio Prague, 15 September 2005, <www.radio.cz>.
52 'On Vaclav Havel speech', letter from Noam Chomsky to Alexander Cockburn, 1 March 1990, <www.chomsky.info>.
53 Andrew Osborn, 'Czech PM upbraided for comparing Arafat to Hitler', *Guardian*, 20 February 2002.
54 Zoltán Dujisin, 'Czech presidency promises controversy', Inter Press Service, 5 January 2009.
55 'Summit with Israel unlikely soon', *Jerusalem Post*, 31 March 2009.
56 Dinah Spritzer, 'Key European leader offers his take on Gaza', JTA, 12 January 2009.
57 Jan Richter, 'PM Fischer visits Israel', Radio Prague, 22 July 2009, <www.radio.cz>.
58 Jonathan Cook, 'Archaeology used to push out Silwan residents', *Electronic Intifada*, 26 September 2008.
59 Edward Herman, 'NATO: the imperial pitbull', *Z Magazine*, February 2009.
60 Noam Chomsky, 'A second Cold War with Russia? Not likely', *Counterpunch*, 15 September 2008.
61 'New figures on civilian deaths in Kosovo War', press release, Human Rights Watch, 6 February 2000, <www.hrw.org>.
62 Antonio Missiroli, *NATO and the EU: What a Difference a Decade Makes*, European Policy Centre, 17 July 2009, <www.epc.eu>.
63 Susan George, *We the Peoples of Europe,* London: Pluto, 2008, p. 74.
64 Ronald Asmus and Tod Tindberg (with a response by Robert Cooper),

Rue de la Loi: The Global Ambition of the European Project, Stanley Foundation, September 2008.

65 George, *We the Peoples of Europe,* p. 95.

66 'NATO ratifies ICP agreement with Israel', press release, Israeli Ministry of Foreign Affairs, 2 December 2008, <www.mfa.gov.il>.

67 Lawrence S. Kaplan, *NATO Divided, NATO United: The Evolution of an Alliance,* Santa Barbara, Calif.: Praeger, 2004, p. 70.

68 Mahdi Darius Nazemroaya, 'NATO and Israel: instruments of America's wars in the Middle East', *Global Research,* 29 January 2008, <www.globalresearch.ca>.

69 Ben Smith, 'Israel into NATO: Edwards, then Rudy', *Politico*, 20 September 2007. <www.politico.com>.

70 Rebecca R. Moore, *NATO's New Mission: Projecting Stability in a Post-Cold War World,* Santa Barbara, Calif.: Praeger Security International, 2007, p. 146.

71 Rupert Murdoch, 'Enlarging the Atlantic alliance', *Wall Street Journal,* 22 April 2008.

72 Moore, *NATO's New Mission*, p. 146.

73 Ronald D. Asmus, 'Contain Iran: admit Israel to NATO', *Washington Post,* 21 February 2006.

74 Ari Shavit, 'Power of deterrence', *Haaretz,* 10 July 2009.

75 'Israel has "150 or more" nuclear weapons, Carter says', Reuters, 27 May 2008.

76 Speech by Deputy Secretary-General, Ambassador Claudio Bisogniero, at the Second Annual NATO–Israel symposium, Herzliya, 23 October 2007, <www.nato.int>.

77 Amir Oren, '"This is a new NATO"', *Haaretz,* 16 March 2009.

78 Soren Dosenrode and Anders Stubkjær, *The European Union and the Middle East,* London: Continuum, 2002, p. 98.

79 Rosemary Hollis, 'Europe in the Middle East', in Louise Fawcett (ed.), *International Relations of the Middle East,* Oxford: Oxford University Press, 2005, p. 314.

80 Ricardo Gomez, *Negotiating the Euro-Mediterranean Partnership: Strategic Action in EU Foreign Policy?* Farnham: Ashgate, 2003, p. 123.

81 Nathalie Tocci, *What Went Wrong? The Impact of Western Policy Towards Hamas and Hizbollah*, paper from Centre for European Policy Studies, July 2007, <www.ceps.eu>.

82 'Middle East peace process', speech by Benita Ferrero-Waldner to European Parliament, 16 January 2006, <www.europarl.europa.eu>.

83 Jimmy Carter, *Palestine: Peace Not Apartheid,* updated edn, London: Simon & Schuster, 2007, p. 182.

84 'Statement of Preliminary Conclusions and Findings', European Union Election Observation Mission West Bank & Gaza, 26 January 2006, <www.domino.un.org>.

85 Eamonn McCann, 'How the West gives democracy a really good kick in the ballots', *Belfast Telegraph*, 3 July 2008.

86 David Rose, 'The Gaza bombshell', *Vanity Fair,* April 2008.

87 Ibid.
88 International Committee of the Red Cross, Bulletin for Gaza-West Bank, 15 June 2007, <www.alertnet.org>.
89 Cook, *Disappearing Palestine*, p. 114.
90 European Union, 'Council framework decision of 13 June 2002 on combating terrorism', *Official Journal of the European Communities*, 22 June 2002.
91 Gideon Levy, *Gaza: Articles pour* Haaretz, *2006–2009*, Paris: La Fabrique, 2009, p. 12.
92 'Palestinian families facing a $1 billion debt burden since aid embargo started, says Oxfam', press release, Oxfam, 12 June 2007, <www.oxfam.org>.
93 'UNCTAD report: Reviving the Palestinian economy requires alternate trade routes and more predictable public revenues', press release, United Nations Conference on Trade and Development, 30 August 2007, <www.unctad.org>.
94 Renata Goldirova, 'EU relaxes Palestine aid embargo', *EUobserver,* 12 June 2007, <www.euobserver.com>.
95 Virginia Tilley, 'Whose coup, exactly?', *Electronic Intifada*, 18 June 2007.
96 Kevin Peraino, 'Palestine's new perspective', *Newsweek*, 14 September 2009.
97 Council of the European Union, General Affairs and External Relations Council, press release, 18 June 2007, <www.consilium.europa.eu>.
98 Fidelius Schmid and Daniel Dombey, 'US, EU boycott of aid for PA to end', *Financial Times*, 19 June 2007.
99 Chris Patten, 'Time to judge Palestine on its results', *Financial Times*, 13 March 2007.
100 Steven Erlanger, 'France admits contacts with Hamas', *New York Times*, 20 May 2008.
101 David Cronin, 'The EU's Palestinian botch-up', *Guardian*, 22 November 2007.
102 Edward W. Said, *Peace and its Discontents: Essays on Palestine in the Middle East Peace Process*, New York: Vintage, 1996, p. 156.
103 Andrew Rettman, 'Europe should be talking to Hamas, says former EU advisor', *EUobserver*, 9 June 2009, <www.euobserver.com>.
104 David Cronin, 'Hamas against Zionist ideology, not Judaism', Inter Press Service, 14 May 2009.
105 Palestinian National Authority, *Building a Palestinian State: Towards Peace and Prosperity*, document prepared for Paris donors conference, 17 December 2007, <www.unispal.un.org>.
106 Julien Salingue, 'Palestine: the programmed failure of the "Silence for Food" programme"', *Z Magazine*, 20 June 2008.
107 Human Rights Watch, *Internal Fight: Palestinian Abuses in Gaza and the West Bank*, July 2008, p. 3, <www.hrw.org>.

CHAPTER 3

1 Nathalie Tocci, *The EU and Conflict Resolution: Promoting Peace in the Backyard*, Abingdon: Routledge, 2007, pp. 109–10.

2 Anton La Guardia, *Holy Land, Unholy War: Israelis and Palestinians*, 3rd edn, London: Penguin, 2007, p. 426.

3 Miller, 'Troubled neighbours' in Inbar, *Strategic Agenda*, p. 35.

4 'Summary of the remarks by Javier Solana, EU high representative for the CFSP, on Rafah', press release, Council of the European Union, 15 November 2005, www.consilium.europa.eu

5 'EU BAM still operational', factsheet, Council of the European Union, December 2007, <www.consilium.europa.eu>.

6 David Cronin, 'Call to halt EU trade with Israel', Inter Press Service, 1 September 2007.

7 'EU slams "collective punishment" in Gaza', *EUbusiness,* 21 January 2008, <www.eubusiness.com>.

8 Yaakov Lappin, 'EU monitors waiting to redeploy to Rafah', *Jerusalem Post,* 19 June 2008.

9 Gisha and Physicians for Human Rights – Israel, *Rafah Crossing: Who Holds the Keys?*, March 2009, pp. 65–115, <www.gisha.org>.

10 Palestinian NGOs Network, *Priorities and Needs of Health Sector in Gaza Governorates: Consequences of the Long Siege and the Last War on Gaza,* February 2009, <www.pngo.net>.

11 Conal Urquhart, 'Gaza on blink of implosion as aid cut-off starts to bite', *Observer,* 16 April 2006.

12 Jamal Dajani, 'No pasta for Palestinians', *Huffington Post*, 26 February 2009.

13 Rory McCarthy, 'Inside the Gaza tunnels', *Guardian*, 10 February 2009.

14 Laurence Boisson de Chazournes and Luigi Condorelli, *Common Article 1 of the Geneva Conventions Revisited: Protecting collective interests, International Review of the Red Cross*, No. 837, pp. 67–87, 31 March 2000.

15 'Gaza: humanitarian situation worst since 1967', press release, CARE International, 6 March 2008, <www.careinternational.org.uk>.

16 Toby Mendel, *Freedom of Information as an Internationally Protected Human Right,* paper for Article 19, 15 June 2000, <www.article19.org>.

17 David Shearer and Anuschka Meyer, 'The dilemma of aid under occupation', in Michael Keating, Anne Le More and Robert Lowe (eds), *Aid, Diplomacy and Facts on the Ground: The Case of Palestine,* London: Chatham House, 2005, pp. 165–76.

18 Regulations concerning the laws and customs of land, The Hague, 18 October 1907, <www.icrc.org>.

19 Cameron W. Barr, 'Aid gets political for Red Cross', *Christian Science Monitor,* 26 November 2003.

20 Miller, 'Troubled neighbours', in Inbar, *Strategic Agenda*, p. 30.

21 Hadar, *Sandstorm*, p. 125.

22 'Statement of the Rt. Hon. Chris Patten, commissioner for external

relations, on the situation in the Middle East at the plenary session of the European Parliament in Strasbourg', 9 April 2002, <www.eu-un.europa.eu>.

23 Alastair Crooke, *Resistance: The Essence of the Islamist Revolution*, London: Pluto, 2009, p. 210.

24 Edward W. Said, *The End of the Peace Process: Oslo and After,* 2nd edn, London: Granta, 2002, p. 25.

25 Said, *Peace and its Discontents,* p. 69.

26 Neve Gordon, *Israel's Occupation,* Berkeley, Calif.: University of California Press, 2008, p. 178.

27 Raja Shehadeh, *Palestinian Walks: Notes on a Vanishing Landscape*, 2nd edn, London: Profile, 2008, p. 109.

28 Mark LeVine, *Impossible Peace: Israel/Palestine Since 1989*, London: Zed, 2009, p. 9.

29 'Israel and the Occupied Territories: the issue of settlements must be addressed according to international law', Amnesty International, 8 September 2003, <www.amnesty.org>.

30 Reinhart, *Israel/Palestine*, pp. 236–7.

31 Anne LeMore, 'Is aid doing more harm than good? Fifteen years of diplomatic and aid policies in support of Israeli–Palestinian peacemaking', presentation to seminar organised by the Catholic anti-poverty group CIDSE, Brussels, 7 November 2008, <www.cidse.org>.

32 World Bank, *Twenty-Seven Months: Intifada, Closures and Palestinian Economic Crisis,* September 2003, p. 14, <www.worldbank.org>.

33 Anne LeMore, 'Killing with kindness: funding the demise of a Palestinian state', *International Affairs*, vol. 81, issue 5, 2005, pp. 981–99.

34 Sara Roy, 'Perspectives on Palestinian de-development', presentation to CIDSE seminar, 7 November 2008.

35 UNCTAD, *The Palestinian War-torn Economy: Aid, Development and State Formation*, 5 April 2006, p. 39, <www.unctad.org>.

36 Shir Hever, *Political Economy of Aid to Palestinians Under Occupation*, Alternative Information Centre, November 2008, p. 45, <www.alternativenews.org>.

37 'Israel letting some humanitarian aid into Gaza', *AsiaNews*, 24 November 2009.

38 David Cronin, 'EU paying for Gaza blockade', Inter Press Service, 20 February 2009.

39 Koen De Groof, *The EU's Aid to the Occupied Palestinian territory: The Deepening Crisis in Gaza*, CIDSE, June 2009, p. 3.

40 David Cronin, 'Israel set to escape claims over damage to EU sites', *European Voice*, 21 March 2002.

41 Wybe Th. Douma, 'Israel and the Palestinian Authority', in Steven Blockmans and Adam Lazowski (eds), *The European Union and its Neighbours: A Legal Appraisal of the EU's Policies of Stabilisation, Partnership and Integration,* The Hague: TMC Asser Press, 2006, p. 454.

42 Caroline Lucas, 'Gaza needs trust, not just aid', *Guardian*, 3 March 2009.

43 John J. Mearsheimer and Stephen M. Walt, *The Israel Lobby and US Foreign Policy,* London: Penguin, 2008, p.26.
44 Agnès Bertrand-Sanz, *The EU's Economic and Humanitarian Policy Towards the Palestinians: Building Blocks Against Roadblocks?*, as yet unpublished.
45 Pierre Avril, 'L'Europe lasse de financer le reconstruction palestinienne', *Le Figaro*, 16 January 2006.
46 Benita Ferrero-Waldner, 'European Union pledges support for reconstruction of Gaza', speech to Sharm el-Sheikh donors' conference, 2 March 2009, <www.ec.europa.eu>.
47 'Israel denies Gaza access to clean water', Press TV, 30 January 2009, <www.presstv.ir>.
48 'EU lambasts Israeli curbs on Gaza aid', *IslamOnline,* 5 February 2009, <www.islamonline.net>.
49 European Council, *A Secure Europe in a Better World: European Security Strategy*, 12 December 2003, p. 10, <www.consilium.europa.eu>.
50 Toby Vogel, 'The end of the road for EU sanctions?', *European Voice,* 13 November 2008.

CHAPTER 4

1 Dimi Reider, 'Israel's budding autocracy', *Guardian*, 30 April 2009.
2 Neve Gordon, 'How to sell "ethical warfare"', *Guardian*, 16 January 2009.
3 European Commission, *Security Research: Towards a More Secure Society and Increased Industrial Competitiveness,* May 2009, p. 3, <www.ec.europa.eu>.
4 Rivka Carmi, 'Neve Gordon's divisive Op-Ed', *Los Angeles Times*, 1 September 2009.
5 Arlene Getz, 'Targeting terrorism', *Newsweek*, 17 October 2001.
6 'About Athena GS3: Company Profile', <www.athenaiss.com>.
7 European Commission, *Security Research,* p. 80.
8 Michael Parks, 'Motorola sells subsidiary in South Africa – radio equipment unit supplied police, army', *Los Angeles Times*, 9 October 1985.
9 Israel Ministry of Defence, *Israel Defense Sales Directory 2009-10*, <www.sibat.mod.gov.il>.
10 'Motorola sells bomb fuse unit in Israel targeted by boycott', *Trading Markets,* 5 April 2009, <www.tradingmarkets.com>.
11 Human Rights Watch, *Precisely Wrong: Gaza Civilians Killed by Israeli Drone-Launched Missiles*, June 2009, p.12, <www.hrw.org>.
12 Israel Ministry of Defence, 'Israel at FIDAE 2008', document for Israeli firms taking part in the International Air and Space Fair (FIDAE), Santiago, Chile, <www.sibat.mod.gov.il>.
13 G. D. Bakshi, 'Israel–Hezbollah conflict', *Indian Defence Review*, Vol. 22, No. 1, 26 April 2007.

14 Israel Ministry of Defence, 'Israel at FIDAE 2008', <www.sibat.mod.gov.il>.
15 Yaakov Katz, 'Millions spent on "virtual fences"', *Jerusalem Post*, 8 September 2006.
16 European Commission, *Security Research*, p. 48.
17 Ben Hayes, *Israel's Participation in EU R&D Framework Programmes: Importing Homeland Security, Exporting R&D Subsidies?*, as yet unpublished.
18 'Seven major European aerospace manufactures sign LOI on a "Clean Sky" joint technology initiative', press release, Aerospace and Defence Industries Association of Europe, 19 July 2006, <www.cleansky.eu>.
19 Joe Charlaff, 'Israel's IAI tapped by EU to develop environmentally friendly air travel', *Israel21c*, 21 May 2007, <www.israel21c.org>.
20 Dan Ben-Ami, 'Négociations d'un mega-contrat de $1.5 milliard d'Israël en Inde', *Israel Valley*, 10 November 2008, <www.israelvalley.com>.
21 Stephen Gardner, 'How clean is Clean Sky?', *EUobserver*, 16 June 2009, <www.euobserver.com>.
22 Frank Slijper, *The Emerging EU Military-Industrial Complex: Arms Industry Lobbying in Brussels*, Transnational Institute, May 2005, p. 13, <www.tni.org>.
23 *Research for a Secure Europe: Report of the Group of Personalities in the field of Security Research*, European Commission, March 2004, p.14, <www.src09.se>.
24 Slijper, *The Emerging EU Military-Industrial Complex*, p. 18.
25 Hayes, *Israel's Participation in EU R&D Framework Programmes.*
26 European Security Research and Innovation Forum, *European Security Research and Innovation in Support of European Security Policies*, September 2008, pp.12–14, <www.esrif.eu>.
27 Israel Aerospace Industries, *The CAPECON Programme, Civil Applications and Economical Effectivity of Potential UAV Configurations*, paper to 'Unmanned Unlimited' conference, American Institute of Aeronautics and Astronautics, Chicago, 20–23 September 2004, <www.aiaa.org>.
28 Hayes, *Israel's Participation in EU R&D Framework Programmes.*
29 Christina Mackenzie, 'UAVs cruel as landmines, says senior British judge', *Aviation Week*, 8 July 2009.
30 Jimmy Johnson, 'Unmanned aerial vehicles and the warfare of inequality management', *Electronic Intifada*, 17 February 2009.
31 Tom Kington, 'EDA to manage UAVs' entry to civil airspace', *Defense-News*, 17 June 2009.
32 Brooks Tigner, 'Europe seeks stronger defence R&D', *Jane's Defence Weekly*, 27 May 2009.
33 Shimon Peres, 'This war has taught us that Israel must revise its military approach', *Guardian*, 4 September 2006.
34 'Israel developing bionic arsenal', *Sydney Morning Herald*, 18 November 2006.

35 'Israel looks at the next generation of warfare', *Spiegel Online International*, 17 November 2006, <www.spiegel.de>.
36 Judy Siegel and Greer Fay Cashman, 'Peres to present pope with nano-Bible', *Jerusalem Post,* 10 May 2009.
37 Yaffa Shir-Raz, 'The world salutes four Israeli scientists', *Ynetnews*, 5 May 2007, <www.ynet.co.il>.
38 'Touch but don't look: EU project to advance touch technology', *Cordis,* 14 February 2008, <www.cordis.europa.eu>.
39 'Boffins unveil SCRATCHbot, the robotic rat with special whiskers', *Playboy*, 1 July 2009.
40 Susan Rockwell and Charles Shamas, *A Human Rights Review on the EU and Israel: Relating Commitments to Actions, 2003–2004*, Euro-Mediterranean Human Rights Network, December 2004, p. 30, <www.euromedrights.org>.
41 Ben Hayes, *Arming Big Brother: The EU's Security Research Programme,* Statewatch and Transnational Institute, April 2006, p. 3, <www.statewatch.org>.
42 'EU and Israel reach agreement on Galileo', press release, European Commission, 17 March 2004.
43 Ora Coren, 'Israel joining Europe's Galileo space project', *Business Wire*, 9 June 2005, <www.businesswire.com>.
44 Richard North, *Galileo: The Military and Political Dimensions,* Bruges Group, undated, <www.brugesgroup.com>.
45 'How Israeli high-tech happened', *Globes*, 15 August 2000 (subsequently updated on the website <www.globes.co.il>).
46 'Military surveillance', European Commission's Research Information Centre, 15 February 2008, <www.ec.europa.eu/research>.
47 European Commission, *The European Dependence on US-GPS and the GALILEO Initiative*, 8 February 2002, <www.galileo.khem.gov.hu>.
48 Frank Slijper, *From Venus to Mars: The European Union's Steps Towards the Militarisation of Space*, Transnational Institute and Dutch Campaign Against the Arms Trade, November 2008, p. 18, <www.tni.org>.
49 'Galileo shows military face', *GPS World,* 24 October 2006, <www.gpsworld.com>.
50 Hayes, *Arming Big Brother,* p. 29.
51 Dan Bilefsky, 'Delays threaten Galileo project, EU warns', *New York Times*, 15 March 2007.
52 Peter B. de Selding, 'Half of Galileo PRS users expected to be military', *Space News*, 3 July 2008.
53 Laurence Frost, 'EU ready to switch off Galileo to aid US security', *European Voice*, 28 March 2002.
54 Slijper, *From Venus to Mars*, p. 41.
55 Timothy N. Barnes, 'Miscalculations of Galileo: Europe's answer to GPS is floundering', *Space Review,* 1 October 2007.
56 Ben Hayes, *NeoConOpticon: The EU Security-Industrial Complex*, Statewatch and Transnational Institute, September 2009, p. 53, <www.statewatch.org>.

57 Slijper, *From Venus to Mars,* p. 26.
58 'Vice-President of EU Commission visits Israel', press release, Israeli Ministry of Foreign Affairs, 26 January 2009, <www.mfa.gov.il>.
59 Dan Assayah, 'Israël-Europe spatiale – satisfaction après la signature de l'accord Galileo', *Israel Valley*, 25 April 2008.

CHAPTER 5

1 Liat Weingart, Valerie Heinonen and Mary Ann McGivern, 'Drawing Caterpillar out of its corporate cocoon: company should examine its role in Mideast violence', *Electronic Intifada*, 28 April 2004.
2 Stuart Littlewood, 'Church of England: dumping Caterpillar', *Palestine Chronicle*, 12 February 2009.
3 David Cronin, 'Commission shows its corporate hand', Inter Press Service, 28 October 2008.
4 'New strategy puts EU trade policy at service of European competitiveness and economic reform', press release, European Commission, 4 October 2006, <www.ec.europa.eu>.
5 'Norway divests from Israeli arms giant Elbit Systems Ltd.', Palestine News Network, 4 September 2009.
6 'Supplier of surveillance equipment for the separation barrier in the West Bank excluded from the Government Pension Fund – Global', press release, Norwegian Ministry of Finance, 3 September 2009, <www.regjeringen.no>.
7 'The Cellular Companies and the Occupation', newsletter, Coalition of Women for Peace, August 2009, <www.whoprofits.org>.
8 *Round Tables and Business Dialogues*, fact sheet, European Commission, 20 May 2009.
9 'EU to launch business dialogue with Israel', *Xinhua*, 31 October 2007.
10 Jennifer L. Schenker, 'Yossi Vardi: Israel's "Mr Tech"', *BusinessWeek,* 19 May 2008.
11 Roger Cohen, 'Her Jewish state', *New York Times*, 8 July 2007.
12 Julie Ball, 'Israel's booming hi-tech industry', BBC World Service (website), 6 October 2008.
13 Neve Gordon, *The Political Economy of Israel's Homeland Security/Surveillance Industry,* New Transparency Project, 28 April 2009, p. 3, <www.surveillanceproject.org>.
14 Naomi Klein, *The Shock Doctrine: The Rise of Disaster Capitalism,* London: Penguin, 2007, p. 435.
15 Sam-Perlo Freeman and Peter Stålenheim, 'The SIPRI top 100 arms-producing companies, 2007', <www.sipri.org>.
16 Naomi Klein, 'Gaza: not just a prison, a laboratory', *The Nation,* 15 June 2007.
17 'The government says it's perky', *Economist,* 9 July 2009.
18 Ramit Plushnick-Masti, 'Israel buys 2 nuclear-capable submarines', *Washington Post,* 25 August 2006.

19 'Israel gets two more German submarines', AFP, 30 September 2009.
20 Caroline Pailhe, 'Ventes d'armes à Israël: l'Union européene et son Code de conduite', in Patrice Bouveret, Pascal Fenaux, Caroline Pailhe and Cédric Poitevin, *Qui arme Israël et le Hamas?: La paix pass(é)e par les armes?* Brussels: Éditions GRIP, 2009, pp. 42–5.
21 Leïla Slimani, 'Arsenal sans frontières', *Jeune Afrique*, 8–14 March 2009.
22 Annick Cojean, 'Je ne serais pas arrivé là si...', *Le Monde Magazine*, 26 September 2009.
23 David Styan, *France and Iraq: Oil, Arms and French Policy Making in the Middle East*, London: IB Tauris, 2006, pp. 38–44.
24 Dosenrode and Stubkjær, *The European Union and the Middle East*, p. 60.
25 Barak Ravid, 'France implores Moscow to cancel sale of missiles to Iran', *Haaretz,* 11 September 2009.
26 Mandy Turner, *Arming the Occupation: Israel and the Arms Trade*, Campaign Against the Arms Trade, October 2002, <www.caat.org.uk>.
27 Patrice Bouveret, 'France/Israël: ventes d'armes et coopération militaire', in Bouveret et al., *Qui arme Israël et le Hamas?* pp. 57–8.
28 Nicole Krau, 'France and Germany stop arms sales to Israel', *Haaretz,* 17 December 2000.
29 David Cronin, 'Defying rules on arms sales to Israel', Inter Press Service, 29 May 2009.
30 Amnesty International, *Fuelling Conflict: Foreign Arms Supplies to Israel/Gaza*, February 2009, p. 15, <www.amnesty.org>.
31 Katherine Iliopoulos, *Israel's Attacks Against Hamas Police Officers in Gaza: A Case Study,* Crimes of War Project, 8 June 2009, <www.crimesofwar.org>.
32 Charles Levinson and Alistair MacDonald, 'Britain says Israel misused U.K. arms', *Wall Street Journal,* 14 July 2009.
33 House of Lords debates, 25 March 2009, <www.theyworkforyou.com>.
34 Curtis, *Web of Deceit*, pp. 127–30.
35 Mark Curtis, Helen Close, Vanessa Duffy and Roy Isbister, *The Good, the Bad and the Ugly: A Decade of Labour's Arms Exports*, Saferworld, May 2007, p.29, <www.saferworld.org.uk>.
36 Transcript of oral evidence, House of Commons Committee on Arms Exports Controls, 22 April 2009, <www.publications.parliament.uk>.
37 House of Commons, written ministerial statements, 21 April 2009, <www.publications.parliament.uk>.
38 Helen Close and Roy Isbister, *Good Conduct? Ten Years of the EU Code of Conduct on Arms Exports*, Saferworld, June 2008, p. 18, <www.saferworld.org.uk>.
39 *Arms to Israel,* Campaign Against the Arms Trade, 16 July 2009, <www.caat.org.uk>.
40 House of Commons, written answers, 7 May 2002, <www.publications.parliament.uk>.

41 Richard Norton-Taylor, 'MPs attack government for breaking its own guidelines on arms sales to Israel', *Guardian*, 3 August 2006.
42 *Stop Arming Israel*, factsheet,War on Want, undated, <www.stoparmingisrael.org>.
43 'Philips electronics corporation trading in violation of Dutch arms policy', *Electronic Intifada*, 1 April 2004.
44 Frank Slijper and Wendela de Vries, *Wapenhandel en militaire samenwerking met Israël,* Dutch Campaign Against the Arms Trade, October 2007, p. 29 (English summary), <www.stopwapenhandel.org>.
45 'Israel weapons ban', *The Bulletin*, 19 February 2009.
46 'Arms transfers to Israel fuel conflict', press release, Dutch Campaign Against the Arms Trade and Peace Action (Belgium), 14 January 2009, <www.vredesactie.be>.
47 Robert Fisk, *Pity The Nation: Lebanon At War*, 3rd edn, 2001, Oxford: Oxford University Press, p. 154.
48 Colin Murphy, 'State-funded company provides parts for Israeli war helicopters', *Village,* 10 August 2006.
49 Amnesty International (Irish section), *Claws of the Celtic Tiger: Irish Manufacture of Military and Security and 'Dual-Use' Components,* 2004, p. 7, <www.amnesty.ie>.
50 David Cronin, 'No conscription but another step on a military journey', *Village*, September–October 2009.
51 Tom McEnaney, 'US moved helicopters to Israel via Shannon', *Irish Independent,* 8 August 2006.
52 Amnesty International (Irish section), *Controlling a Deadly Trade: Recommendations for an Effective Law to Control the Trade in Military, Security and Police Goods in Ireland,* 2007, p. 1, <www.amnesty.ie>.
53 Andy Storey, 'Europe and Africa', *Indymedia Ireland,* 26 November 2008, <www.indymedia.ie>.
54 'The homesick UAV', 29 December 2008, *StrategyPage*, <www.strategypage.com>.
55 'Another shameful arms deal between Israel and Ireland', newsletter, Ireland Palestine Solidarity Campaign, 29 September 2009, <www.ipsc.ie>.
56 Don Lavery, 'Ireland risks backlash over defence deal with Israelis', *Sunday Independent,* 20 September 2009.
57 Barbara Opall-Rome, 'Elbit tightens grip on Israeli market', *DefenseNews,* 15 June 2009.
58 Eugene Kogan, *European Union Enlargement and its Consequences for Europe's Defence Industries and Markets*, Bonn International Center for Conversion, October 2004, p. 34, <www.bicc.de>.
59 Turner, *Arming the Occupation.*
60 'Israel, Romania seal F-16 sale deal', *Ynetnews,* 30 October 2005, <www.ynetnews.co.il>.
61 Kogan, *European Union Enlargement and its Consequences for Europe's Defence Industries and Markets,* p. 35.
62 Turner, *Arming the Occupation.*

63 'Remotely controlled weapons systems at the 2006 Eurosatory exhibition,' *Defense Update*, 24 July 2006, <www.defense-update.com>.
64 David Donald, 'Unmanned agility', 22 February 2009, <www.janes.com>.
65 'Elbit Systems awarded $55 million contracts in Europe', press release, Elbit Systems Ltd, 25 July 2007, <www.elbitsystems.com>.
66 Ido Efrati, 'Elbit Imaging to set up entertainment center in Romania', *Ynetnews*, 12 October 2006, <www.ynet.co.il>.
67 Nathan Sheva, 'Sir Bernard suing Elbit Medical over Romanian project', *Haaretz,* 26 January 2008.
68 Bruno Jäntti, 'Finnish–Israeli arms trade flouts EU regulations', *Electronic Intifada*, 27 May 2009.
69 Yossi Melman, 'Brothers in arms', *Haaretz*, 11 April 2008.
70 'Israel, Spain sign $400 million missile deal', *Defense Update,* 12 January 2007.
71 Turner, *Arming the Occupation.*
72 'Spike missiles for Spain', *Defense Industry Daily*, 28 January 2008, <www.defenseindustrydaily.com>.
73 'Israel joins EU competitiveness programme', press release, European Commission, 1 November 2007.
74 David Cronin, 'A law unto itself', *Guardian*, 18 November 2008.
75 'EIB Vice-President de Fontaine Vive in Israel: European Investment Bank (EIB) resumes its lending operations in Israel after 11 years', press release, EIB, 27 December 2006, <www.eib.europa.eu>.
76 Adri Nieuwhof, 'Israeli banks entrenched in settlement building', *Electronic Intifada*, 27 October 2009.
77 Manfred Gerstenfeld, 'European–Israeli relations: between confusion and change?' Jerusalem Center for Public Affairs, September 2007, <www.jcpa.org>.
78 Adri Nieuwhof, 'Belgian campaign targets bank financing Israeli settlements', *Electronic Intifada*, 1 April 2009.
79 Simone Korkus, 'Belgium's Dexia Bank asked to divest from Israeli settlement funding', *Fact International,* undated, <www.fact.jo>.
80 Scheherazade Daneshkhu and Ben Hall, 'Dexia receives €6.4 capital injection', *Financial Times*, 30 September 2008.
81 'Belgian campaign forces financial group to cancel settlement loans', *Electronic Intifada*, 15 June 2009.
82 'Dexia et les colonies israéliennes: nouvelles révélations', press release, Belgian campaign group Palestine Occupée – Dexia Impliquée, 16 September 2009, <www.intal.be>.
83 Sharon Wrobel, 'France has not done enough to become player in Israel's economy', *Jerusalem Post*, 25 June 2008.
84 'Action Alert: Ask Veolia advisors to take a stand for justice in Palestine!' International Solidarity Movement, 16 December 2006, <www.palsolidarity.org>.
85 'Connex "dumped" after 4 month boycott campaign', press release, Australians for Palestine, 25 June 2009, <www.australiansforpalestine.com>.
86 Adri Nieuwhof and Daniel Machover, 'Time to hold Veolia to account', *Electronic Intifada,* 10 February 2009.

87 'The writing on the wall of Galway City Council spells Veolia?' *Indymedia Ireland*, 21 April 2009, <www.indymedia.ie>.
88 'Stop Veolia running the London Cycle Hire Scheme', statement, Palestine Solidarity Campaign, 8 May 2009, <www.bigcampaign.org>.
89 Willy Jackson, 'Economic retaliation against Tel Aviv', *Le Monde Diplomatique* (English edn), September 2009.
90 'Jerusalem rail operator jumps ship, Tel Aviv group isn't even responding', *Haaretz*, 9 June 2009.
91 Jonathan Cook, 'Boycott derails Jerusalem's transit system – rail firm pays price for link to settlements', *Atlantic Free Press,* 22 September 2009.
92 Adri Nieuwhof, 'Veolia still intertwined with Israel's occupation', *Electronic Intifada*, 16 September 2009.
93 Ron Friedman, '10,000 urge boycott of Swedish companies', *Jerusalem Post,* 25 August 2009.
94 Jane Smith, 'House demolitions in the West Bank', International Women's Peace Service, 4 December 2006, <www.iwps-pal.org>.
95 'Volvo response to article about concerns on the use of Volvo vehicles in Israel and the Occupied Territories', Business and Human Rights Monitoring Centre, 6 July 2007, <www.business-humanrights.org>.
96 Per Martin Johansson, 'Strong order bookings for Volvo Buses in Israel', Volvo, 22 September 2009, <www.volvo.com>.
97 'Armored buses: ultimate protection, maximum comfort', Merkavim, undated, <www.merkavim.co.il>.
98 'Mars Prisoner Bus: for heavy-duty high-security transportation', Merkavim, undated, <www.merkavim.co.il>.
99 Adri Nieuwhof, 'Volvo providing armoured buses for Israeli settlements', *Electronic Intifada*, 7 October 2009.
100 Helen Close, *Profiting from the Occupation*, War on Want, July 2006, p.5, <www.waronwant.org>.
101 Kleeman, 'Les multinationales francaises au coeur de la colonisation israelienne', *Mediapart,* 17 May 2009, <www.mediapart.fr>.
102 *Dutch Economic Links in Support of the Israeli Occupation of Palestinian and/or Syrian Territories,* Profundo and United Civilians for Peace, September 2006, p. 37, <www.unitedcivilians.nl>.
103 *Companies Building the Apartheid Wall,* Palestinian Grassroots Anti-Apartheid Wall Campaign, undated, p. 6, <www.stopthewall.org>.
104 Erez Wollberg, 'Treasury opposes giant concrete merger', *Globes*, 3 December 2009, <www.globes.co.il>.
105 Adri Nieuwhof, 'HeidelbergCement tries to sell West Bank mines as legal, boycott pressure grows', *Electronic Intifada*, 13 July 2009.
106 Gomez, *Negotiating the Euro–Mediterranean Partnership,* p. 138.
107 Sharon Wrobel, 'Israel, EU agree on trade concessions', *Jerusalem Post,* 1 May 2008.
108 Peter Lagerquist, 'On settlement trade, Europe doesn't stand tall', *Middle East Report,* 8 April 2003, <www.merip.org>.
109 Ian Black and Andrew Osborn, 'EU gets tough on Israeli exports', *Guardian,* 13 November 2001.
110 Jan Willem van Gelder and Hassel Kroes, *UK Economic Links with*

Israeli Settlements in Occupied Palestinian Territory, School of Oriental and African Studies, University of London and Profundo, 10 February 2009, p. 10, <www.profundo.nl>.

111 Donald Macintyre, 'Britain to crack down on exports from Israeli settlements', *Independent*, 3 November 2008.

112 Barak Ravid and Anshel Pfeffer, 'Britain tells EU to clamp down on W. Bank imports', *Haaretz*, 4 November 2008.

113 Anshel Pfeffer, 'Britain confirms its anti-settlement push', *Jewish Chronicle*, 13 November 2008.

114 David Cronin, 'Made in Israeli settlements, but never mind', Inter Press Service, 3 April 2009.

115 European Court of Justice, Opinion of Advocate-General Bot, in Case C-386/08, Brita Gmbh v Hauptzollamt Hamburg-Hafen, 29 October 2009, <www.curia.europa.eu>.

116 'Lord Mandelson calls for more business with Israel', press release, UK Trade and Investment, 18 November 2008, <www.newsroom.uktrade invest.gov.uk>.

CHAPTER 6

1 Bernard Wasserstein, *Divided Jerusalem: The Struggle for the Holy City,* London: Profile, paperback edn, 2002, p. 247.

2 Lynn Sweet, 'Obama tells AIPAC Jerusalem must remain capital of Israel', *Chicago Sun-Times,* 4 June 2008.

3 Denis MacShane: *Globalising Hatred: The New Anti-Semitism*, London: Weidenfeld & Nicolson, 2008, p. 123.

4 Johnny Paul, 'European Friends of Israel inauguration attracts 100 parliamentarians, officials', *Jerusalem Post*, 19 September 2006.

5 Tim McGirk, 'U.N. says no Hamas fighters in bombed Gaza school', *Time*, 7 January 2009.

6 'Myth: 'Hamas behaved as any "resistance movement" would in reaction to Israel's Operation Cast Lead', statement by European Friends of Israel, January 2009, <www.efi-eu.org>.

7 Amnon Meranda, 'Sarkozy pledges France's support on Iran', *Ynetnews*, 7 November 2008. <www.ynet.co.il>.

8 Claude Moniquet and Dimitri Dombret, *Is Iranian Shiite Expansionism a Threat to the Arab Countries?* European Strategic Intelligence and Security Centre, 13 July 2009, p. 29, <www.esisc.org>.

9 Dan Fleshler, *Transforming America's Israel Lobby: The Limits of Power and the Potential for Change*, Dulles, Va.: Potomac, 2009, p. 78.

10 David Cronin, 'Defying rules on arms sales to Israel', Inter Press Service, 29 May 2009.

11 Erik Wesselius, *How successful is the Commission's Lobby Register?* Alliance for Lobbying Transparency and Ethics Regulation, 28 October 2009, <www.alter-eu.org>.

12 'Speech by Javier Solana, EU High Representative for the common

foreign and security policy, on the occasion of the opening of the Transatlantic Institute', 12 February 2004, <www.consilium.europa.eu>.

13 Alvin H. Rosenfeld, *'Progressive' Jewish Thought and the New Anti-Semitism*, American Jewish Committee, December 2006, foreword by David Harris, p.VII, <www.ajc.org>.

14 Hillel C. Neuer, 'The strange, enduring rage of Naomi Klein', *National Post,* 15 September 2009.

15 Fintan O'Toole, 'Israel must be held to account over Gaza action', *Irish Times*, 6 January 2009.

16 'Veteran Jewish MP compares Israelis in Gaza to Nazis', *Herald Scotland*, 15 January 2009.

17 Emanuele Ottolenghi, *Under a Mushroom Cloud: Europe, Iran and the Bomb,* London: Profile , 2009, pp. 71–148.

18 Belén Balanyá, Ann Doherty, Olivier Hoedeman, Adam Ma'anit and Erik Wesselius, *Europe Inc.: Regional & Global Restructuring and the Rise of Corporate Power,* London: Pluto, 2000, p. 17.

19 'ADL survey in seven European countries finds anti-semitic attitudes steady; 31 percent blame Jews for financial crisis', press release, Anti-Defamation League, 10 February 2009, <www.adl.org>.

20 European Union Agency for Fundamental Rights, *Anti-Semitism: Summary Overview of the Situation in the European Union 2001–2008*, February 2009, pp.20–1, <www.fra.europa.eu>.

21 European Monitoring Centre on Racism and Xenophobia, 'Working definition on anti-Semitism', 16 March 2005.

22 'European values in the new global governance', speech by José Manuel Barroso at opening of the Brussels office of the European Jewish Congress, 14 October 2009, <www.ec.europa.eu>.

23 'The European Jewish Congress acknowledges EU Parliament's Resolution on Gaza', press release, European Jewish Congress, 15 January 2009, <www.eurojewcong.org>.

24 Peter Beaumont, 'Israel outraged as EU poll names it a threat to peace', *Observer,* 2 November 2003.

25 'Racism and anti-Semitism have no place in the EU, nor elsewhere in the world', speech by Jacques Barrot to symposium organised by European Jewish Congress, 30 March 2009, <www.ec.europa.eu>.

26 Seumas Milne, 'What credibility is there in Geneva's all-white boycott?' *Guardian*, 23 April 2009.

27 'Questions à Paul-Éric Blanrue', *Science et Inexpliqué*, October 2009.

28 Paul-Éric Blanrue, *Sarkozy, Israël et les juifs*, Embourg: Oser Dire, 2009, pp. 50–158.

29 Gilles Paris, 'Un parc industriel franco-palestinien lancé à Bethléem', *Le Monde*, 4 September 2009.

30 Rory McCarthy, 'Israeli military occupation "severely compromises Bethlehem"', *Guardian*, 6 May 2009.

31 'BBC defends Gaza appeal decision', BBC News, 22 January 2009, <www.news.bbc.co.uk>.

32 Jeremy Bowen, 'Israel still bears a disastrous legacy', *Jewish Chronicle,* 31 May 2007.

33 Cook, *Disappearing Palestine*, p. 259.
34 Susannah Tarbush, 'Architects protest Brown's JNF patronage', *Electronic Intifada*, 10 September 2007.
35 White, *Israeli Apartheid*, pp. 19–35.
36 Tom Segev, 1967: *Israel, the War and the Year that Transformed the Middle East*, paperback edn, London: Abacus, 2008, p. 81.
37 'Profile: Lord Sainsbury', BBC News, 10 November 2006, <www.news.bbc.co.uk>.
38 Stuart Wavell, 'Lord Cashpoint's touch of money magic', *Sunday Times*, 19 March 2006.
39 Muhammad Idrees Ahmad, 'Labour Friends of Israel in the House', SpinWatch, 21 March 2005, <www.spinwatch.org>.
40 Rajeev Syal, 'How the pro-Israel lobby in Britain benefits from a generous London tycoon', *Observer*, 4 January 2009.
41 James Jones and Peter Oborne, *The Pro-Israel Lobby in Britain*, pamphlet accompanying a Channel 4 documentary broadcast 16 November 2009, p. 31, <www.channel4.com>.
42 Lorna Fitzsimons, 'The UCU is wasting time and money', *Independent*, 5 June 2008.
43 Andrew Pierce, 'Cameron faces revolt over Israel', *The Times*, 3 August 2006.
44 'Speech by Conservative Party Leader David Cameron to the Conservative Friends of Israel Annual Lunch', 18 June 2009, <www.cfoi.co.uk>.
45 Christopher Dickey, 'Mohammed El Baradei: "They are not fanatics"', *Newsweek*, 1 June 2009.
46 Noam Chomsky, 'War, peace and Obama's Nobel', *In These Times*, 5 November 2009, <www.inthesetimes.com>.
47 Anica Pommeray, 'JCall, "the European J Street" to be launched in Brussels', *Jerusalem Post*, 30 April 2010.
48 Emanuele Ottolenghi, 'As mainstream as they come', *Haaretz*, 7 May 2010.
49 Cnaan Liphshiz, 'Watchdog: British anti-Semitism doubled after Gaza war', *Haaretz*, 24 July 2009.
50 Jean Bricmont, 'French echoes of the Israeli–Palestine conflict', *Counterpunch*, 12 February 2009, <www.counterpunch.org>.

CONCLUSION

1 Isabel Kershner, 'Netanyahu backs Palestinian state, with caveats', *New York Times*, 14 June 2009.
2 Barak Ravid and Assaf Uni, 'Israel blasts "dangerous" EU call for deadline on Palestinian state', *Haaretz*, 12 July 2009.
3 Hasan Abunimah, 'Using the UN to undermine Palestinian rights', *Electronic Intifada*, 29 July 2009.
4 David Bar-Illan, 'Palestinian self-rule, Israeli security – an interview', *Palestine-Israel Journal of Politics, Economics and Culture*, Vol. 3, Nos. 3&4, 1996, <www.pij.org>.

5 Ben White, 'Fragmenting Palestinian land', *Guardian*, 12 November 2009.
6 Jeff Halper, 'Dismantling the matrix of control', *Middle East Report Online*, 11 September 2001, <www.merip.org>.
7 Ali Abunimah, 'Israeli Jews and the one-state solution', *Electronic Intifada,* 10 November 2009.
8 Amira Hass, 'Acceptance speech, International Women's Media Foundation, Lifetime Achievement Award 2009', October 2009, <www.iwmf.org>.
9 Michael Neumann, 'Criticism of Israel: a wonderful hiding place', *Counterpunch*, 29 October 2009, <www.counterpunch.org>.
10 Tobias Buck, 'Israel shrugs off boycott effort', *Financial Times*, 19 November 2009.

USEFUL CONTACTS

The following organisations campaign for Europe to pay greater heed to human rights in its relations with Israel:

Euro-Mediterranean Human Rights Network
17 rue de Londres, 1050 Brussels.
Phone: +32-2-5408647 www.euromedrights.net

Palestinian Centre for Human Rights
29 Omar El Mukhtar Street, Gaza City.
Phone: +972-8-2824776/2825893. www.pchrgaza.org

Alternative Information Centre
PO Box 31417, Jerusalem.
Phone: +972-2-6241159 www.alternativenews.org

Al Haq
PO Box 1413, Ramallah, West Bank.
Phone: +972-2-2954646/2954647/2954649. www.alhaq.org

CIDSE (alliance of Catholic anti-poverty groups)
16 rue Stévin, 1000 Brussels.
Phone: +32-2-2307722 www.cidse.org

War on Want
Development House, 56-64 Leonard Street, London EC2A 4LT.
Phone: +44-20-75490555. www.waronwant.org

Oxfam International
Suite 20, 226 Banbury Road, Oxford OX2 7DL.
Phone: +44-1865-339100. www.oxfam.org

United Civilians for Peace
PO Box 8190, 3503 RD Utrecht.
Phone: +31-30-8801534. www.unitedcivilians.nl

Palestine Solidarity Campaign
Box BM PSA, London WC1N 3XX.
Phone: +44-20-77006192. www.palestinecampaign.org

Amnesty International
1 Easton Street, London WC1X 0DW.
Phone: +44-20-74135500. www.amnesty.org

INDEX

A
Abbas, Mahmoud, 59, 61–2, 65–6
Abu Kabir, 1
Abunimah, Ali, 161
Adams, Gerry, 64
Aeronautics Defense Systems, 91, 119
Aerostar, 121
Afghanistan, 36, 52, 56, 65, 73, 96–8, 119, 123
Africa, 29, 65
African National Congress, 31
Aftonbladet, 1, 128–9
van Agt, Dries, 41
Ahmadinejad, Mahmoud, 37, 48, 149
aid
EU aid to Palestinian Authority, 5, 11, 41, 43, 60–1, 66, 72–85
humanitarian aid to Gaza, 41, 51, 83–4
US aid to Israel, 82–3
Al-Aish, Ezzedine Abu, 19
Ajax (football club), 40
Albania, 112
D'Alema, Massimo, 40
Ali, Tariq, 45
Alleanza Nazionale, 39–40
Alstom, 127
Alternative Information Centre, 163
American Colony (hotel), 46
American Israel Public Affairs Committee (AIPAC), 137–9
American Jewish Committee, 142–5, 147–8, 150–1
American Jewish Congress, 151
Ammunition Hill, 127
Amnesty International, 9, 114, 154
Amsterdam, 40, 116
Annapolis 'peace conference', 26–8
Anti-Defamation League (ADL), 146–8, 150
anti-Semitism, 2, 38–40, 48, 64, 137–8, 142–4, 146–8, 150, 155–8, 164
AOL, 108
Apache helicopters, 117–19, 154
apartheid, 29–33, 77, 90–1, 107, 149, 153, 162–4
Apartheid Museum, 164
Aprodev, 83
Arab Association for Human Rights, 32
Arab League, 60
Arabs for Israel, 140–1
Arad, Uzi, 55–6
Arafat, Yasser, 50, 62, 74, 118, 131
Arbour, Louise, 27
archaeology, 8–9, 51
Ariel, 68, 100, 108, 125
Arlosoroff, Chaim, 30
Aron, Raymond, 150
Arrow missiles, 102
art, Israeli, 7
Ashkelon, 64, 69, 87–8
Ashkenazi, Gabi, 53
Asmus, Ronald, 54–5
ASN (bank), 128
association agreement, 33, 101, 131–4, 162, 165
Athena SG3, 90
Auschwitz, 48
Australia, 54
aviation, 91–4, 97
Avione Craoia, 121
Avital, Colette, 141–2
Aznar, José-María, 54

B
B'nai B'rith, 51, 145–8
BAE Systems, 95, 116
Balfour, Arthur James, 42
Balkans, 42
Balkenende, Jan Peter, 41
Bank Hapaolim, 124
Bank of Israel, 31
Bank Leumi, 108, 124
Bantustans, 77
Bar-Ilan University, 159
Bar-Illan, David, 159–60
El Baradei, Mohammed, 156
Barak, Ehud, 27, 154
Barak, Rafi, 23
Barghouti, Mustafa, 28, 81
Barkan, 124
Barroso, José Manuel, 148
Barrot, Jacques, 103, 149
Basic Law (in occupied Palestinian territories), 62

Baunton, Michael, 106–7
Beckett, Margaret, 45
Begin, Menachem, 57
Belarus, 85
Belfast, 64
Belgium, 24, 53, 111–12, 118, 125–7, 150
Ben-Gurion, David, 22, 38, 49, 153
Ben Gurion University of the Negev, 89–90
Berlusconi, Silvio, 21, 38–40
Bertrand-Sanz, Agnès, 83
Bethlehem, 26, 75–6, 151
Beyond Chutzpah, 32
Bezeq, 107–8
Bierset Airport, 118
Bildt, Carl, 1–2
Blair, Tony, 27, 42–6, 62, 115, 135, 153–4
Bingham, Thomas, 96–7
Bisogniero, Claudio, 56
Blanrue, Paul-Éric, 150–1
Boeing, 114
Bologna, 143
border assistance mission (BAM), 68–72
  see also Rafah
Bosnia, 112
Boström, Donald, 1
Bouveret, Patrice, 113
Bowen, Jeremy, 152
boycott
  Arab boycott of Israel, 109
  campaign for boycott of Israel, 155, 163–5
  EU boycott of Hamas, 61–5
  Israeli consumer boycott of Sweden, 1, 128–9
Bradshaw, Ben, 44, 154
Brazil, 120
Breaking of Nations, The, 27
  see also Cooper, Robert
Bricmont, Jean, 157–8
Al Brij refugee camp, 15
Brita, 133–4
Britain
  arms industry, 110, 112, 114–17, 120, 154
  historical role in Middle East, 42, 57, 153
  influence of pro-Israel lobby, 150, 152–6
  passport forgeries, 11
  position on Gaza war, 3, 19, 144
  position on settlements, 101, 132–5
  relations with NATO, 55
  relations with US, 103–4
  upgrade in EU-Israel relations, 24, 38, 42–6
British Broadcasting Corporation (BBC), 42, 109, 152
British Israel Communication and Research Centre (BICOM), 154–5
Brok, Elmar, 139–40
Brown, Gordon, 11, 42, 46, 152–3
Brussels, 7, 16, 21, 24, 29, 54–5, 57, 80–1, 87–8, 97, 106, 123, 126–7, 133, 136–46
Bucharest, 121–2
Burg, Avraham, 5
Bush, George W, 16, 26, 34–5, 43–5, 90, 103
BusinessEurope, 106–7
Busquin, Philippe, 94–5
Buzek, Jerzy, 148

C
Cameron, David, 153, 156
Canada, 8, 33, 143
Carmi, Rivka, 89–90
Carter, Jimmy, 17–18, 56, 58
Caterpillar, 106–7, 129
Cato Institute, 23
Ceausescu, Nicolae, 120–2
Cement-Roadstone Holdings (CRH), 130–1
Central Intelligence Agency (CIA), 36
Centre for European Policy Studies (CEPS), 57
Centurion tanks, 115
Chad, 119
Charles University, 49–50
Chavez, Hugo, 121
checkpoints in West Bank, 25, 28, 30–1, 80, 90
Chicago, 48
childhood mortality, 32
Chile, 91–2
China, 20, 84, 102, 104
Chirac, Jacques, 35–6, 74, 101, 103, 113, 127, 150
Chomsky, Noam, 47, 156
Christian Democrats (Netherlands), 40–1
Church of England, 106
Church of Scotland, 46
Cibrian-Uzal, Ramiro, 20
Cimoszewicz, Wlodzimierz, 48
City of David Park, 8, 51
City Pass consortium, 124, 128
Clean Sky, 91–4
climate change, 91–4, 104, 162
Clinton, Bill, 34, 54
CNN, 141
Coalition of Women for Peace, 107–8
Cohn Bendit, Daniel, 157
Cold War, 34, 49, 52
collective punishment, 3, 32, 44, 68–72, 80, 144, 164
Colombia, 54
Committee for Accuracy in Middle East Reporting in America (CAMERA), 152
Congo, Democratic Republic of, 152

Connex, 128
 see also Veolia
Conservative Friends of Israel, 155–6
Conservative Party, 115, 139, 153, 155–6
Cook, Jonathan, 28–9
Cook, Robin, 43
Cooper, Robert, 27, 52–53
Cordis, 100
Cork, 118–19
Corrie, Rachel, 106
Counter Terrorism Board (Israel), 96
Crooke, Alistair, 64, 75
Crusades, 45
curfews, 27
Curiel, Ran, 23, 124
Cyprus, 3, 22, 24, 52
Czech Republic, 3, 16–19, 21, 48–51, 56, 84, 112, 123
Czechoslovakia, 57, 49–50

D
Daily Telegraph, 11–12, 140
Dan (transport firm), 128
Dana International, 22
Darwish, Nona, 140–1
Dassault, 93, 112
Data Device Corporation, 118–19
data protection, 10
David, Dan, 46
Dead Sea, 7–8
Dead Sea Scrolls, 8
Deane, Raymond, 37
Déby, Idriss, 119
de-development, 78–9
 see also economic development
Defense News, 95
Dehaene, Jean-Luc, 125–6
demolition of Palestinian homes, 3, 25, 32, 51, 83, 106–7, 129
democracy
 in occupied Palestinian territories, 57–9
 in Israel, 55, 88, 162
Democratic Party, 54
Denmark, 3
Dermer, Ron, 159
Devedjian, Patrick, 151
Dexia, 125
Disappearing Palestine, 28–9
 see also Cook, Jonathan
Diskin, Yuval, 139
Dolphin helicopters, 113
Dolphin submarines, 111
Dombret, Dimitri, 138, 140, 142
Dor Alon, 80
Dubai, 11
Dublin, 118–20, 131
Durban II conference, 149

E
EADS, 93, 95
ECHO (European Commission humanitarian aid department), 84
economic development
 in Israel, 109
 in the occupied Palestinian territories, 75–80, 151
Economist, 110–11
education, 70, 73, 104
Edwards, John, 54
Egged (company), 128, 130
Egypt, 4, 17, 25, 41, 57, 63, 68, 70, 83, 110, 140–1
El Al, 118
Elbit Imaging, 121–2
Elbit Systems, 94, 96, 107, 119–23
Electronic Intifada, 161
Elkana, 125
Elta Systems, 109
energy, 80, 124
Enterprise Europe Network, 123
environmental policy, 77, 92–4, 106–7, 124, 162
Eran, Oded, 102, 124–5
Erekat, Saeb, 27
Ericsson, 95
Ethiopia, 77
Euro-Mediterranean Human Rights Network, 100-1
Eurobarometer, 148–9
Euromed Heritage, 8
European Bank for Reconstruction and Development (EBRD), 125
European Commission, 8, 19–21, 25–6, 29, 36, 38–9, 43, 50, 58, 63, 80–5, 87–105, 106–11, 123–4, 132–4, 139–40, 142, 145, 148
European Court of Justice (ECJ), 124, 133–4
European Defence Agency (EDA), 97
European Economic Community (EEC), 21–2, 56–7
European Friends of Israel (EFI), 138–42
European Investment Bank (EIB), 124–5
European Jewish Congress (EJC), 147–9
European Monitoring Centre on Racism and Xenophobia (EUMC), 147–8
 see also Fundamental Rights Agency
European Neighbourhood Policy, 25–33
European Parliament, 16, 20, 28, 34, 39, 58, 82, 94, 104, 125, 138–40, 143, 148, 165
European Policy Centre, 52
European Security Research and Innovation Forum (ESRIF), 96
European Space Agency (ESA), 104
European Strategic Intelligence and Security Centre (ESISC), 140
European Union–Israel business dialogue, 107–11

Europol, 9–10
Eurovision Song Contest, 22

F
F16 warplanes, 14, 93, 115, 117, 121, 154
Falk, Richard, 16
Fatah, 3, 58–9, 66
Fatchett, Derek, 42–3
Fayyad, Salam, 28, 61–2, 65–6
Ferrero-Waldner, Benita, 25–6, 58, 82–4, 139–40
Fini, Gianfranco, 39–40
Finkelstein, Norman, 32
Finland, 3, 112, 122
Finmeccanica, 95–6
Fischer, Jan, 51
Fisk, Robert, 45, 118
Fitzsimons, Lorna, 154–5
de Fontaine Vive, Philippe, 124
Forbes, 107
FoxNews, 141
Framework Programme for Research, 84–105, 165
  see also scientific research
France
  arms industry, 97, 109, 112–14, 120
  business links with Israel, 104–5, 125–8
  colonial history, 119
  historical position on Middle East, 40, 57
  influence of pro-Israel lobby, 150–1, 157
  migration to Israeli settlements, 77
  passport forgeries, 11
  position on Gaza war, 3, 17
  referendum on EU constitution, 104
  relations with USA, 35–6, 47, 55
  space policy, 102–3
  upgrade in EU–Israel relations, 24, 36–8
France–Israel Association, 151
Frattini, Franco, 38–40
freedom of expression, 88
Fundamental Rights Agency (FRA), 146–8
Al Funduq, 129

G
Gal, Yossi, 23
Galileo, 101–4
  see also satellite navigation
Galway City Council, 128
de Gaulle, Charles, 36, 47, 109, 112–13, 150
Gaza
  administration by Hamas, 59, 62, 64, 66
  airport, 43
  blockade, 3, 17, 28, 38, 46, 64, 72, 77, 80, 84, 141, 160, 164
  civilian casualties, 3, 19–20, 83, 114
  demolition of homes, 106
  'disengagement', 68–72
  malnutrition, 17, 38, 71
  poverty, 61, 72–3, 108
  settlements in, 18, 56, 67–8,160
  war of 2008–9, 2–4, 14–21, 41–2, 46, 50–1, 81, 84, 88, 91, 111, 113, 116, 119, 139, 141, 144, 146, 148, 152, 154, 157, 160
Gaza Community Mental Health Programme, 15–16
Geneva, 143, 149
Geneva Convention, 32, 69, 71–3, 114
genocide, 28–9, 33, 45
George, Susan, 52
Georgia, 4, 49, 52
German Marshall Fund of the United States, 54–5
Germany
  arms industry, 97, 111–13, 120
  export on goods from Israeli settlements, 132–4
  passport forgeries, 11
  position on Gaza war, 3, 18–19
  relations with USA, 35–6, 47
  role in Second World War, 144, 164
  upgrade in EU–Israel relations, 36–8, 42
Gilo, 124
Ging, John, 41
Gisha, 69–70
Giuliani, Rudy, 54
Giv'at Zeev, 125
Global Europe, 107
  see also trade
Global Monitoring for Environment and Security, 104
  see also satellite navigation
Global Positioning System, 102
  see also satellite navigation
Globalising Hatred, 138
  see also MacShane, Denis
Globes, 102
Goasguen, Claude, 151
Godfrey Goldstein, Angela, 77
Goebbels, Joseph, 143, 164
Golan Heights, 100, 107, 124
Goldberg, Moshe, 99
Goldstone, Richard, 3, 111
Gorbachev, Mikhail, 52
Gordon, Neve, 76
Gothenburg, 129–30

Green Party (Germany), 111
Group of Eight (G8), 44
Guerin, Orla, 152
Gush Etzion, 68

H
Haaretz, 132–3
Hadar, Leon, 22–3
Hafez, Mustafa, 140
Hague Regulations, 73
Hague, William, 155
Hague, The, 40, 42
Haick, Hossam, 100
Hain, Peter, 101
Halberstadt, Jerzy, 48
Halper, Jeff, 119, 160
Halvorsen, Kristin, 107
Hamas
  arms smuggling, 84
  freeze in EU relations with, 58–65, 161–2
  popular support, 75, 141
  rocket attacks on southern Israel, 3, 17–18, 38, 41, 46, 51, 64, 80, 139, 148
  suicide bombings, 63–4, 136
  victory in 2006 election, 58–60
Hamburg, 133
Hamid, Tawfik, 141
HaMoked, 160
Haniyeh, Ismail, 61, 63
Hanson Israel, 131
Al Haq, 76, 117
Har Hebron, 125
Har Homa, 26, 43
Harris, David, 143
Harvard University, 78
Hass, Amira, 162
Havel, Vaclav, 50
healthcare, 70–1, 73, 104
Hebrew University, 22
Hellfire Systems, 114, 117
Herman, Edward, 52
Herzl, Theodor, 22
Herzliya, 38, 54, 56
Hezbollah, 40, 44, 98
Hiss, Yehuda, 1
hitkansut (convergence), 67–8
Hitler, Adolf, 4–5, 50, 57, 144
Hnizdo, Borivoj, 49
Hoffenberg, Valérie, 151
Hogan, Barbara, 31
Holocaust, 4–5, 29, 37–40, 48, 144, 146–7, 149
de Hoop Scheffer, Jaap, 56, 117
House of Commons, 144, 153
House of Lords, 114–15, 154–5
Howells, Kim, 45
Howitt, Richard, 20
Human Rights Watch, 10, 44, 52, 91
Hungary, 3, 122
Hussein, Saddam, 32

I
IAR (Romania), 121
ICQ (company), 108
Ilan Ramon international space conference, 21
Independent, 132, 155
India, 20, 102, 104, 108, 156
Inside Jihad, 141
  see also Hamid, Tawfik
Insta DefSec, 122
Intel, 110–11, 119
Inter-American Development Bank, 125
International Atomic Energy Agency (IAEA), 5, 156
International Court of Justice (ICJ), 40, 44, 107, 130
international law, 8, 32, 33, 38, 40, 44, 55–56, 69–74, 78–9, 84, 101, 107, 110, 114, 129–30, 152
International Monetary Fund (IMF), 62, 65
International Women's Peace Service, 129
intifada, 1, 39, 70, 73, 78, 81, 113, 115, 160
Iran, 6, 18, 32, 37, 48, 55–6, 85, 111, 113, 140, 144–5, 156
Iraq, 32, 35–6, 43, 46, 48, 63, 102, 119, 156
Ireland, Republic of, 3, 11, 24, 37, 63, 118–20
Islamic Jihad, 63
Israel Aerospace Industries (IAI), 91–4, 96
Israel Antiquities Authority (IAA), 8–9
Israel Defence Forces (IDF), 44, 68, 75, 88, 93, 107, 113
Israel Electric Company, 31
Israel–Europe R&D Directorate for the EU Framework Programme (ISERD), 87
Israel Lobby and US Foreign Policy, The, 137
Israel Military Industries (IMI), 91
Israel National Nanotechnology Initiative (INNI), 98–9
Israel Science Foundation, 84
Israel21c, 93
Israel Valley, 104–5
Israeli Air Force (IAF), 91, 94, 112
Israeli Committee Against House Demolitions (ICAHD), 77
Israeli Municipality Treasury Bank, 125
Istanbul, 140
Italy
  arms industry, 97, 112, 123
  historical position on Middle East, 40
  position on Gaza war, 3, 18–19
  upgrade in EU–Israel relations, 38–40
Itzik, Dalia, 140
Izbet Abo Rabo, 14

J
J Street (organisation), 157
Jabarin, Shawan, 117
Jane's Defence Weekly, 97
Japan, 54, 84, 108
JCall, 157
Jemaah Islamiyyah, 141
Jenin, 44, 76, 106
Jericho, 75
Jerusalem
 East Jerusalem, 8, 25–6, 28, 41, 43, 46, 51, 58, 60, 68, 81, 90, 101, 124, 126–8
 status of city, 19, 21–2, 24, 36–7, 41, 46, 56–7, 101, 126–7, 137, 156
Jerusalem Post, 22, 35–6, 69, 92, 154
Jewish Chronicle, 133, 152
Jewish National Fund (JNF), 152–3
Johannesburg, 164
Johnson, Boris, 128, 156
Jordan, 8, 25, 41, 63
Jordan Valley, 100, 127
Judenstaat, Der, 22
 see also, Herzl, Theodor

K
Kadima, 16, 24, 67, 141
Kalms, Stanley, 155
Kapah, David, 125
Karadzic, Radovan, 42
Karni, 71
Kashmir, 156
Kasrils, Ronnie, 31
Kassir, Samir, 4
Kaufman, Gerald, 144
Kedumim, 125
Kerem Shalom (Karim Abu Salam), 68–9
Khalidi, Rashid, 34
Kielce pogrom, 48
Kissinger, Henry, 45, 57
Klein, Naomi, 109–10, 143
Knesset, 5, 32, 37–8, 41, 46, 125, 140–1, 153
Koenders, Bert, 41
Kopernikus, 104
 see also satellite navigation
Koran, 64
Kosovo, 45, 46, 73
Kouchner, Bernard, 24, 140, 151

L
Labour Friends of Israel, 153–5
Labour Party
 British Labour Party, 12, 20, 42–6, 115–16, 137–8, 153–5
 Israeli Labour Party, 141
Labuda, Barbara, 48
bin Laden, Osama, 65
Land Rover, 154
Landaburu, Eneko, 124
Lebanon, 6, 25, 32, 44–6, 74, 91, 97–8, 111–12, 115–18, 152, 155
Lemkin, Raphael, 29
LeMore, Anne, 78
Lenihan, Brian, 118
Lévy, Bernard-Henri, 157
Levy, Gideon, 61
Levy, Michael, 154
Liberal Democrats, 155
Libya, 25
Lieberman, Avigdor, 40, 53–4, 114
Liège, 118, 126–7
Likud, 24, 67, 110, 141
Lisbon strategy, 84
Lisbon Treaty, 52–3, 104
Livnat, Israel, 109
Livni, Tzipi, 11–12, 20–8, 53–4, 56, 62, 84
Loach, Ken, 45
lobby
 influence of corporate lobby, 106–8, 142
 influence of pro-Israel lobby, 11, 34, 38–9, 136–58
Lockheed Martin, 114, 116
London, 43, 128, 140, 152–6
Luxembourg, 103, 124–5, 133–4

M
M'aale Adumim, 67, 76–7, 108, 127, 133, 155
Al-Mabhouh, Mahmoud, 11
Machlis, Butzi, 121
MacShane, Denis, 137–8
Madrid, 95
Mallah, Beniko, 36
Malloch-Brown, Mark, 114–15
Malta, 3, 24
Mandela, Nelson, 30–1
Mandelson, Peter, 135
Manitou, 130
Manufacturers Association of Israel (MAI), 123
Mapai, 30
Marker, The, 126
Matimop, 90, 123
Mattin Group, 80, 134
Mayer Cars and Trucks, 130
McMillan Scott, Edward, 58
Mearsheimer, John, 137
Meggitt Avionics, 117
Mein Kampf, 57
 see also Hitler, Adolf
Mekel, Arye, 7
Melbourne, 128
Mer Group, 90
Merkava tanks, 14, 154
Merkavim, 130
Merkel, Angela, 18, 36–8, 47
de la Messuzière, Yves Aubin, 63
Meyer, Anuschka, 73
Michel, Louis, 83
Miliband, David, 11, 46, 115–16
Millon, Alain, 113
Milverton, Nigel, 69

Mishor Adumim, 124
Mitterrand, François, 37
Mladic, Ratko, 42
Modi'in Illit, 26–7
Monde, Le, 7
Moniquet, Claude, 140
Moratinos, Miguel Angel, 74
Morocco, 25, 40
Mossad, 11, 90
Motorola Israel, 90–2
Mugniyah, Imad, 40
Mullin, Chris, 45
Murdoch, Rupert, 54
Murray, Eoin, 69
Musameh, Sayed Abu, 64–5
Muslim Brotherhood, 63
Mussolini, Benito, 39

N
Nablus, 75
Nakbah, 4, 38, 49
nanotechnology, 97–100
National Assembly (France), 151
National Centre for Space Studies (France), 103
National Rifle Association (NRA), 137
natural resources, exploitation of, 3, 77–8
Nazis, 4, 29, 48, 143–4, 147, 149
neoconservatives, influence on US policy, 34–5, 47, 103–4
neoliberal economics, 62, 65, 84, 101, 106–11, 118
Netanyahu, Binyamin, 19, 24, 34–5, 43, 51, 55, 91, 159–60
Netherlands, the, 3, 38, 40–2, 104, 112, 117–18, 123, 132
Neuer, Hillel, 143
Neumann, Franz Leopold, 164
Neumann, Michael, 164
New Profile, 88
New York, 1, 35, 90–1, 140–1, 145–6, 151
New York Times, 108
Newsweek, 27, 99–100
Nielson, Poul, 83
Nigeria, 29
Nixon, Richard, 34
Nobel Peace Prize, 45, 98
Non-Proliferation Treaty (NPT), 6, 56, 111
  see also nuclear weapons
North Atlantic Treaty Organization (NATO), 35–6, 51–6, 97, 117, 120–1
North Korea, 85, 149
Northern Ireland, 46, 63–4, 161
Norway, 107
El Nounou, Husam, 16
nuclear weapons
  Israel's nuclear capability, 4, 36, 56, 111–13, 140, 145, 149
  Iran's nuclear programme, 6, 55–6, 140, 144–5, 149, 156
Nuit Blanche (festival), 7

O
Obama, Barack, 6, 16, 137, 156
Observer, 154–5
Ofeq (satellite), 102
Olmert, Ehud, 19, 24–7, 31–2, 108
Operation Cast Lead, 3, 14, 16–18, 20, 41, 46, 50–1, 84, 88, 91, 113, 148, 160
  see also Gaza
Operation Grapes of Wrath, 74
Operation Rainbow, 83
Organisation for Economic Cooperation and Development (OECD), 12
Oser Dire, 150
Oslo Accords, 74–9, 141, 160
Otte, Marc, 18
Ottolenghi, Emanuele, 143–5, 157
Oxfam, 61
Oxfam-Novib, 82

P
Page Aerospace, 117
Pailhe, Caroline, 111–12
Pakistan, 97, 156
Palestine Liberation Organisation (PLO), 50, 56, 60, 63, 118
Palestinian Authority (PA), 3, 44, 59–62, 65–6, 75–7, 81, 84, 134
Palestinian Legislative Council (PLC), 36, 57, 62, 64, 160
Panther helicopters, 113
Pape, Ilan, 142–3
Paris, 7, 112, 140, 148, 151, 157
Pascoe, Lynn, 38
Patten, Chris, 43, 63, 74–5, 81
Paz Oil, 108
Peace Now, 26–7
Pelephone, 107
Pentagon, 9, 34–5, 102, 109
Peres, Shimon, 48, 51, 98–9, 112, 135, 155
Perle, Richard, 35
Philips, 117
Physicians for Human Rights, 69–70
Pisgat Ze'ev, 108, 124
Playboy, 100
Poland, 3, 29, 47–9, 112, 122–3, 148
police cooperation, 9–10
Pope Benedict XVI, 99
Portugal, 3, 110
Potocnik, Janez, 87–8
Potuznik, Jiri, 17
Prague, 49–51
Prodi, Romano, 39–40, 95
propaganda, 5, 19–20, 32, 37, 39, 88, 136–43

Protocols of the Elders of Zion, 2
Public Committee Against Torture in Israel (PCATI), 10

Q
al Qaeda, 43, 95, 98, 109, 141
Qalqilya, 75
Qana, massacre in, 44–5, 91
Quartet, 6, 45, 60
Qassam rockets, 38

R
Rabin, Yitzhak, 19, 74
Rabintex Industries, 119
Rafael (company), 91, 99, 122–3
Rafah, 68
Ramallah, 59, 75, 80, 117
Rammell, Bill, 115
Ramstein, 35
Reagan, Ronald, 52, 102
Red Cross, International Committee of, 18, 73
refugees, 24, 41, 44, 70, 106
Reinhart, Tanya, 77
Republican Party, 110
Research for a Secure Europe, 95
  see also security research
Rice, Condoleezza, 58–9, 62
right to information, 72
Riwal, 130
Rockefeller Museum, 8
Romania, 18, 112, 120–3, 141
Rome, 40
Rome, Treaty of, 22
Roy, Sara, 78–9
Royal Ontario Museum, 8
Rumsfeld, Donald, 35
Russia, 4, 6, 44–5, 49, 52, 108, 110, 113, 137
Rwanda, 152

S
Saab, 93
Saban Capital Group, 107–8
Saban, Haim, 107–8
Sadat, Anwar, 4
Saferworld, 115
Safran, 93
Said, Edward, 63–4
Sainsbury, David, 153–4
Salama, Majed Abu, 15
Salfeet, 129
Sandwell Borough Council, 128
Sarkozy, Nicolas, 6, 17–18, 36–8, 47, 63, 113, 127, 140, 150–1
satellite navigation, 101–5
Saudi Arabia, 60
Schiphol Airport, 117–18
Schreier, Bernard, 122
Schröder, Gerhard, 35–6
Schwarzenberg, Karel, 21, 51
scientific research, 11, 84–105, 108, 165
Scud missiles, 102
Sderot, 41, 64
Seal, Gail, 152–3
security research, 87–97
Serbia, 42, 45, 52, 112
settlements, 23–8, 43, 56, 67–8, 75–7, 80, 90–2, 100–1, 107–8, 124–35, 151, 155
Shaer, Nasser, 59
Shalgi, Giora, 99
Shalit, Gilad, 69
Shalom, Silvan, 22–3
Shamas, Charles, 80, 134
Shamir, Yair, 93–4
Shamir, Yitzhak, 93–4
Shannon Airport, 119
Sharm El-Sheikh, donors' conference, 83–4
Sharon, Ariel, 22–3, 41, 43–4, 67–70, 109, 127, 149
Shavit, Shabtai, 90
Shawa, Amjad, 14–15
Shearer, David, 72–3
Shehadeh, Raja, 76
Shek, Marie, 6
Shifa Hospital, 139
Shock Doctrine, The, 109–10
  see also Klein, Naomi
Silicon Valley, 104, 108
Silwan, 8, 51
Simon Wiesenthal Centre, 148–9
Sinn Féin, 63–4
Slovakia, 3, 112
Slovenia, 3
Smith, Jane, 129
Smiths Industries, 117
Smuts, Jan, 30
Social Democrats (Germany), 39
Soda Club, 133
Solana, Javier, 2, 28, 52, 64, 67–9, 142, 159
Soltam, 155
South Africa, 3, 29–33, 77, 90–1, 149, 161, 163–4
South Korea, 120
Soviet Union, 34, 47–8, 50, 120
space, 21, 87, 101–5
Spain, 3, 19, 54, 67, 74, 97, 112, 123
Spike missiles, 122–3
SpinWatch, 154
SPS Aerostructures, 117
Sri Lanka, 4
Statewatch, 101
Steimatsky, 108
Steinitz, Yuval, 12, 110–11
Steinmeier, Frank-Walter, 25
Stockholm Community Council, 128
Stockholm International Peace Research Institute (SIPRI), 110
Stork Special Products, 117
Straw, Jack, 43–4, 116
Sudetenland, 57
Suez Canal, 57
Sunday Times, 155
SuperPharm, 108
surveillance, 69, 90–2, 96, 109–10
Svoboda, Ludvik, 49

Sweden, 1–3, 97, 128–30
Syria, 18, 25, 32, 41

T
Tadiran, 94
Tajani, Antonio, 21
Tamil Tigers, 4
Tannock, Charles, 139
Technion (Israel Institute of Technology), 94, 99–100
Tel Aviv, 1, 20–1, 38, 41, 87, 100, 102, 159
Tel Aviv University, 77, 90, 96
Temporary International Mechanism (TIM), 61
terror, war on, 35, 43, 51, 89–90, 100, 109–10, 120, 139
terrorism, EU definition of, 53, 59–60, 63
Thales, 93, 95
Thatcher, Margaret, 50, 153
think tanks, 52, 57, 140, 145
Third Way (political party), 62
Thompson, Mark, 152
Topolanek, Mirek, 50–1
torture, 3, 9–10, 36, 66, 130, 144
Tovias, Alfred, 22
trade
    EU–Israel trade, 11, 106–35, 162, 165
    tariffs on imports to occupied territories, 75, 79
    underground trade in Gaza, 71, 84
Transatlantic Institute, 142–5
Trócaire, 69
Tunisia, 25
Turkey, 35, 47, 52
Tusk, Donald, 48, 122
Tutu, Desmond, 30
Twersky, David, 151
Twin Towers, 9, 109

U
Ukraine, 25, 52
Under a Mushroom Cloud, 144
    see also Ottolenghi, Emanuele
unemployment
    in Israel, 109
    in occupied Palestinian territories 70, 77–8
Union of European Football Associations (UEFA), 22
United Nations
    agency for Palestinian refugees (UNRWA), 41, 139
    aid to Palestine, 73
    conference on racism, 149
    Conference on Trade and Development (UNCTAD), 61, 79
    Convention Against Torture, 9
    General Assembly, 17, 30, 44, 72
    Genocide Convention, 29
    guidelines on business and human rights, 130–1
    investigations into Gaza war, 3, 111
    Millennium Development Goals, 115
    Office for the Coordination of Humanitarian Affairs (OCHA), 72–3, 151
    peace-keeping in Lebanon, 118
    position on blockade of Gaza, 38
    relations with USA, 52
    role in foundation of Israel, 72
    role in 'Quartet', 6, 45
    Security Council, 43, 159
UN Watch, 143
    see also American Jewish Committee
United States, 1, 5, 11, 16, 20, 27–9, 34–65, 68, 74, 77, 82–3, 84–5, 90, 96–9, 102–4, 106–10, 112–13, 116, 118–22, 129, 137–8, 140–4, 146, 150–1, 156–7, 161, 165
    US Air Force, 35
universal jurisdiction, 11–12
University and College Union (UCU), 155
University of Texas, 62
unmanned air vehicles, 93, 96–7, 104, 107, 110–11, 119
upgrade
    in EU–Israel relations, 20–33, 50–1, 53
    in NATO–Israel relations, 53–6

V
Vardi, Yossi, 108–9
'Velvet Revolution', 50
Venezuela, 121
Venice declaration, 56
Veolia, 127–8
Verhagen, Maxime, 40–2
Verheugen, Günter, 108
Verwoerd, Henrik, 29–30
Vienna, 146
Vietnam, 34
Vilenski, Dan, 99
Volvo, 1, 128–31
Vondra, Alexander, 49

W
wall, in West Bank, 25, 31, 40, 44, 107, 119, 130, 151
Wall Street, 110
Wall Street Journal, 54, 141
Walt, Stephen, 137
War on Want, 130–1
Warsaw Ghetto, 48, 144
Washington, 23, 27, 34–5
water, 75, 77, 84
weapons, 3, 11, 14, 38,

87–105, 109–24, 129, 154–5, 165
Weisglass, Dov, 68, 71
Weitz, Joseph, 153
Weizmann, Chaim, 38
West Bank, 3, 6, 25–8, 40, 43–4, 58–61, 63, 66–8, 70, 73–7, 80, 82, 92, 100, 107–8, 119, 124–7, 129–30, 132–5, 151–2, 155, 159–60
Western Wall, 51
White House, 16, 74
Wikforss, Mårten, 129
Wilson, Woodrow, 47–8
Wolfowitz, Paul, 103–4
World Bank, 62, 65, 78, 124
World Food Programme, 82
World Health Organization, 71
World War, Second, 2, 35, 40, 48, 72–3, 144

Y
Yediot Ahronot, 100
Ynet, 100
Yom Kippur War, 54
Yugoslavia, 42

Z
Zabludowicz, Paju, 154–5
Zabludowicz, Shlomo, 155
Zahar, Mahmoud, 63
al-Zawahiri, Ayman, 141
Zeman, Milos, 50
Zimbabwe, 85
Zionism, 22, 29–30, 38, 42, 46, 49–50, 55, 64, 89–90, 143, 145, 151–4
Zionist Federation of Great Britain and Ireland, 152
Zisser, Motti, 121–2
Zwolle, 117